2001: an Energy Odyssey
The Fürigen Papers

A god who wills it can bring anyone safely home, however far away he may be.
– Pallas Athene in Homer, Odyssey, 3, 230f.

2001: an Energy Odyssey
The Fürigen Papers

Willem Lammers and Beate Kircher (Eds.)

ias institute
for the application of
the social sciences

Copyright ©2001 by Willem Lammers and the authors
Published by IAS, CH-7304 Maienfeld
ISBN 3-8311-2094-3
Printed by Books on Demands (Schweiz) GmbH

All rights reserved. No part of this book may be reproduced in any matter whatsoever without written permission except in the case of brief quotations embedded in critical articles and reviews. For Information, address IAS Publications, Bahnhofstrasse 2, 7304 Maienfeld, Switzerland, info@iasag.ch.

Preface

Maienfeld, Ruggell, in May 2001

This book has been a very inspiring joint project. In the editing proces, the concept of the Odyssey got an entirely new meaning for both of us. In the beginning the title of the book was just a name, unmistakeably inspired from Kubrick's 1967 movie. In the course of months, a new, metaphorical quality of the Odyssey as a Way for all of us manifested. The chapters of the individual authors represent different views on the development of the amazing field of energy psychology We have learned a lot on our way, and we wish you a similar learning pleasure.

Willem Lammers and Beate Kircher

Contents

ALPHA:	THE WAY HOME	1
	WILLEM LAMMERS	
BETA:	CREATING	5
	BEATE KIRCHER	
1.	RADIANT CIRCUITS: THE ENERGIES OF JOY	7
	DONNA EDEN AND DAVID FEINSTEIN	
2.	ACCESSING CREATIVITY THROUGH THE HUMAN VIBRATIONAL MATRIX	19
	DOROTHEA HOVER-KRAMER	
3.	ENERGY THERAPY, EDGE-FIGURES AND THE PHASES OF THE CREATIVE PROCESS	31
	JOAN HITLIN	
GAMMA:	HEALING	39
	WILLEM LAMMERS	
4.	ENERGY-BASED HEALING: FOUNDATIONS AND APPLICATIONS	41
	MARTIN F. LUTHKE AND LINDA STEIN-LUTHKE	
5.	INTEGRATIVE HEALING: AN ENERGY AND SPIRITUAL APPROACH	51
	PHIL FRIEDMAN	
6.	THE MONOPOLY THEORY OF THE UNIVERSE AND THE THREE STEPS OF HEALING	65
	ALAN HANDELSMAN	
7.	QIGONG AND ENERGY PSYCHOTHERAPY: FOUNDATIONS OF ENERGY PSYCHOTHERAPY HEALING	71
	LARRY STOLER	
DELTA:	WHAT MOVES US	79
	WILLEM LAMMERS	
8.	AN INTRODUCTION TO THOUGHT ENERGY	81
	GREG NICOSIA	

9.	At Play in the Fields of the Mind: Personal Myths as Fields of Information	89
	David Feinstein	
10.	The Phenomena of Psychokinesis	101
	Marla Brucker	

Epsilon	The Art of Healing	109
	Willem Lammers	
11.	Getting on the Same Page: How all the Different Energy Psychology Approaches Fit Together	113
	David Grudermeyer	
12.	Confessions from the Heart of Ethics	117
	Pati Beaudoin	
13.	Energy Medicine for the Emotional Body	127
	Sharon Cass Toole	
14.	Four Stages of Trauma Treatment	133
	Mary Sise	
15.	Energy Meridian Tapping and EMDR	141
	Jim Lane	
16.	Self-Healing: Meridian-based Therapies and EMDR	149
	Dan Benor	
17.	Relationship-Oriented Meridian-based Psychotherapy and Counseling	155
	Thomas Weil	

Zeta	Mastery	167
	Willem Lammers	
18.	Touch And Breathe	169
	John Diepold	
19.	The Power of Using Affirmations with Energy Therapy	179
	Pat Carrington	

Contents

20.	Freedom from Fear Forever: The Acu-Power Way	189
	Jim Durlacher	
21.	Conscious Healing and Repatterning Therapy: CHART	201
	Paula Shaw	
22.	Energy Psychology Treatment of Allergy-like Reactions	215
	Sandi Radomski	
23.	Treating ADHD through Allergy Elimination	223
	Sherry Tenpenny	
24.	Evaluating the Effects of Energy Psychology Using prognos Analysis	231
	Tom Narvaez	
Eta:	Home	239
	Homer	

Appendix

A:	Author Biographies	241
B:	Energy Psychology Abbreviations	249
C:	Energy Psychology Ressources	251

x

α

The Way Home

Willem Lammers

Whoever undertakes to set himself up as judge in the field of truth and knowledge is shipwrecked by the laughter of the gods.
– Albert Einstein

This book celebrates the occasion of the First European Conference on Energy Psychology named *2001: An Energy Odyssey*. Homer's Odyssey is the story of a man finding his way home.

After a ten-year long siege, the proud city of Troy was finally conquered by the Greeks, with the help of an ingenuous stratagem. They built an enormous, wooden horse and put it near the city walls. Then word was spread it was a gift from the gods. The Trojans believed the lie, and took the horse into the city. The gift proved to be a curse: The horse was a hiding place for Greek soldiers. In the night they left the wooden structure and opened the city gates to let their army in. The war was over, and Troy was destroyed. The creative man who designed the horse was Odysseus, the sharp-minded king of Ithaca.

Odysseus, or *Ulysses* by his Latin name, left the sacked city with his companions. On the way they insulted the mighty Poseidon, the lord of the seas. He took revenge, and it took Odysseus ten years to get home, to his wife Penelope and his son Telemachos. The story of his return to Ithaca was recounted by Homer in the eighth century before Christ, in the second work of Western literature, the Odyssey. The book is, according to Peter Jones (1991) "rich in character, adventure and incident, reconciling reality with fantasy, the heroic with the humble, the intimate with the divine".

In Western culture, the word "odyssey" has received two different meanings. One is the long journey through adverse circumstances, in which an individual shows amazing resistance to the challenges of the environment. We've seen this in Stanley Kubrick's film from which we borrowed the title of the First European Conference on Energy Psychology. The second meaning of the word is far less spectacular compared to the demons, witches, giants and plagues of the first, but very interesting in an age in which people were seen as no more than toys of the gods. It's the way home, and for the first time in the history of literature the home becomes the center of the world.

Our own odyssey offers both options. In the world of energy psychology we have started a trip, of which we don't know when, where and how it will end, and which already showed us a strange world. What we know is that in the end this trip will lead us home, a home within ourselves, within this world and within the universe.

Human searching is often described as a way. In the Bible, the children of Israel followed the way out of slavery, through the deserts of experience, to the Promised Land. Islam regards the pilgrimage to Mecca as one f the five pillars of faith. Chinese spirituality expresses the paradox of the journey in the Tao. The Buddhists seek the Way to Enlightenment, the first Christians were known as the People of the Way, and Jesus identified himself as the Way (Silf, 2001).

The Odyssey shows us first signs of a Western process of individuation, as Zeus complains to his god-colleagues: "What a lamentable thing it is that men should blame the gods and regard *us* as the source of their troubles, when it is their own transgressions which bring them suffering that was not their destiny." (Homer, 1991, I, 33–35).

Odysseus' journey challenged him in many ways, and his journey is a metaphor for the human condition. Odysseus is in us, in each of us on our way through existence. Although, in our culture, the physical dangers have ceased for most of us, the challenge remains. As Joan Hitlin puts it in Chapter 3, "at each edge, you can expect to find edge-figures – subpersonalities, shadows, demons, gremlins, introjects, inner children, archetypes – who are invested, for better or for worse, in keeping you from going past your edges". We are kept from our way home the way Odysseus was, and we have to find the way again and again, each of us in our own way.

We all aboarded an odyssey for ourselves. We're on our way to our spiritual home and that way surprises us with ever new adventures. The challenges requires the utmost of our creativity, our flexibility and our endurance.

References

Homer(1991). *The Odyssey*. Translated by E.V. Rieu. London: Penguin Classics.
Jones, P. (1990). Introduction. In: Homer(1991). *The Odyssey*. Translated by E.V. Rieu. London: Penguin Classics.
Silf, M. (2001). *Sacred Spaces. Stations on a Celtic Way*. Oxford: Lion Publishing.

β
Creating

Beate Kircher

Since we have established the frame of Homer`s Odyssey to hold all the articles together, there is much space for individuality.
– Email to the authors of this book, on April 16, 2001

When I look at this book it is also a record of the creative joy of editing it. Somehow, 24 original articles have joined to resonate with Homer`s perennial "winged words" and I am delighted with this concert. Individual sounds have become one tune that accompanies Odysseus on his way home, to the place of his belonging. He is listening, and so are we.

Embedding 24 contributions on energy psychology in the wider context of Homer's great epic has somehow changed their meaning – it was like laying out bait for the "radiant energies" (Eden and Feinstein), finding the keyword that invited them to help weave the fabric of this book. Creating meant appreciating their presence and allowing them to work, by observing what would manifest rather than interfering with it.

Calling upon an old myth invited its power into the creation process which became an odyssey of its own – Scylla demanded the sacrifice of texts and spring days that could have been spent outside in exchange for a save passage. Charybdis appeared disguised as linear time, threatening us with the promise she would swallow the whole project if we spent too much time on details. All that is no longer there is also part of this odyssey.

When I was attempting to write something "significant" on creativity, the authors` voices all of a sudden transformed into Sirens' songs. I could no longer hear my own voice, an experience within a creating process that Joan Hitlin might term the "Tooting Your Own Trunk Phase". In Dorothea Hover Kramer`s words, I had to "heal into my true self by reclaiming my innate human inventiveness for personal creativity". Tracing my joy in the whole project brought me back on track. At some point, Poseidon's winds stirred the seas against our computers and files were shipwrecked. However, Penelope kept on instilling into the project: her patience in weaving her shroud, and her trust in Odysseus' arrival back home.

Homer's wonderful imagery and vivid, rhythmic language helped to structure the book in chapters and taught us to listen to the tone of each article. And some good gods appeared with precious gifts: one line or a whole passage by Homer that would contain a hint on how to proceed, that would contribute to a deeper understanding of issues. They connected the rhythms of energy psychology tapping to the rhythms of Greek hexameter verse in the insight that both help the bard remember his lines.

On looking back, I see the floor of my living room covered with papers – all the articles arranged to form one circle. This is the more "real" image of their order – within this book this order had to be converted into something sequential. To me, the circle is still there. Originated by the Muse, the Guardian of Creativity. We honor her presence by asking her to speak first.

The book starts with the alpha and finishes with the 7th Greek letter eta – a long way still from omega, with much space to be filled individually. And it closes with Homer – with the lines that are believed to be the final lines of the original Odyssey.

Enjoy them!

1

Radiant Circuits: The Energies of Joy[1]

Donna Eden and David Feinstein

Wherever the radiant energies move, they bring strength and resilience, joy and vitality. These energies are a precious resource, and it is the body's design that they jump to wherever they are most needed. Beyond doing repair work, these are also primary energies in exhilaration, falling in love, orgasm, hope, gratitude, rapture, and spiritual ecstasy. Called the "strange flows", "collector meridians" or "extraordinary vessels" in Traditional Chinese Medicine (Gallo, 2000), they are not exactly flows, meridians, or vessels. More like hyperlinks on the web, they jump instantly to wherever they are about to travel, which is one reason the Chinese found them to be both strange and extraordinary. Through them all of the body's energy systems are linked and energetic deficiencies and excesses regulated. Because they are associated with the awakening of psychic abilities and the capacity to channel healing energies into the body, they were also sometimes called the "psychic channels" (Teeguarden, 1978).

Looking for a more accurate and broadly descriptive name for these critically important yet largely misunderstood and under-appreciated energies, we chose the term "radiant" because people who see energy experience this force as carrying a radiant glow, and we chose the term "circuits" because one of their most important functions is to create instant circuits that distribute energies throughout the body. They bring a radiant charge as they connect all the energies and energy systems of the body, and they connect us with vital energies in the universe (Blofeld, 1973). Just as they literally have a radiant appearance to people who are able to see energies, they bring a radiant, joyful, uplifting quality to all they touch.

The radiant energies were first described in ancient Chinese texts dating back some 4500 years (Matsumoto & Birch, 1986), and their use continues to be reported within the clinical literatures of acupuncture (O'Conner and Bensky, 1981), acupressure (Teeguarden, 1978), Jin Shin Do (Teeguarden, 1978), Qigong (Johnson, 2000), and shiatsu (Blanchard, 2000). A study reportedly conducted in China and subsequently suppressed found that treatments which focused on the radiant energies were "far more effective than those of the traditional Chinese protocols" (Johnson, 2000, p. 157). While the radiant energies have not to our knowledge been verified via scientific measures, other subtle energies, including the meridians, chakras, and aura have been (see Collinge, 1998; Gerber 1996; Hunt, 1995). And we have repeatedly seen in our classes that the hands of a sensitive person can readily detect the radiant circuits. The descriptions of radiant energy found in this chapter are based on the first author's clairvoyant ability to literally see these energies and on her experiences working with them over the past 24 years within a clinical practice in energy medicine.

We believe the electromagnetic dimension of the radiant circuits will be measured relatively soon, but that they share properties with more subtle energies as well. One of the most striking qualities of subtle energies is that, like prayer and visualization, as well as quantum matter, they can influence events from a distance (Feinstein, 1998; –> Brucker, Feinstein). The radiant circuits not only connect the energies within our body, they attract us to, and attract to us, uplifting circumstances and events in the outer world. Their involvement in psychic phenomena is another reason the Chinese physicians applied the word "extraordinary" to them. Developing the radiant energy system is a path toward developing greater intuition and psychic ability.

The radiant circuits appear to predate the meridians, and they are the first energy circuit to appear in the developing fetus (Johnson, 2000). We believe, in fact, that a meridian is a pathway that was once, in the course of evolution, a radiant circuit. Both meridians and radiant circuits can be seen by the first author (who sees eight human energy systems in varying colors, intensities, and geometric patterns; Eden, 1998) in humans and in animals, but she cannot see meridians in simpler organisms, only the radiant energies. As creatures became more complex, radiant energies that moved along the same lines day after day, generation after generation, plausibly formed the meridians. Meridians are the energy equivalent of riverbeds, habits of energy movement that have become entrenched in the body's energy system. A meridian is highly efficient for specific, repetitive tasks. Radiant energy, on the other hand, spontaneously jumps to wherever it is needed. It appears capable of intelligent choice. Meridians accomplish more narrowly defined tasks. They appear capable of doing these tasks with intelligence and efficiency, but their creative problem-solving abilities are limited to their own pathways.

Radiant Circuits: The Energies of Joy

The radiant circuits, serving as "inner wells of joy," support a vibrancy and a harmony throughout the entire body-energy system. Working with the radiant circuits can change a person's future, orienting the psyche toward ecstasy rather than despair. They can be marshaled for overcoming self-sabotage and negative thinking. They bring us in contact with our core self, showing us how healthy functioning felt before life's inevitable woundings (Porter, 1996). By countering the Triple Stimulator[2] system's lock on habitual thought and behavioral patterns, they can help people trapped in dysfunctional habits to change them. And to the degree we can cause our radiant energies to be activated more consistently, the greater our inner peace and enjoyment of life.

The Radiant Circuits and Psychological Health

The way that some of the radiant energy of early organisms historically began to move along fixed pathways and become habitual also takes place in the evolution of individual lives. When you were an infant, your energies were less programmed and were available for the surprises of the moment. As you learned routines and patterned responses to life, certain meridians or chakras or rhythms became habitually more highly charged than others. Freely flowing energies became fixed within established patterns. We literally become set in our ways.

These fixed constellations of energy, personally-generated and unique to each of us, both serve us and trap us. They make us more efficient, providing automated sequences of thought and behavior in repetitive situations. They also make it difficult to change those patterns and to marshal our energies in new directions. They become so deeply assimilated in the body-energy system that they operate like instincts. They not only become embedded in the aura, chakras, meridians, and other energies, they are reflected in our unquestioned behaviors and our core beliefs. These core beliefs or guiding myths (Feinstein & Krippner, 1997) become your body's truth and seem like your soul's knowing. They have helped you survive, and you will not alter them lightly (–> Shaw, Sise, Weil).

Even guiding myths that have become outdated or otherwise dysfunctional do not easily lend themselves to change. Activating the radiant circuits is a uniquely powerful way of bringing about a change in your psychological foundation. They impart a sense of safety and well-being. The psyche relaxes its grip on old survival strategies. Engaging the radiant circuits also gives the psyche a burst of positive energy that brings benefits similar to those that psychologists have identified in studies of "learned optimism" (Seligman, 1990), such as greater confidence, increased effectiveness, and more robust health.

The dance between the radiant circuits and dysfunctional patterns of belief and behavior is worth understanding. The radiant energies are the most direct influence for balancing the excesses of Triple Stimulator, which is the keeper of energetic habits and holds the authority of a commander-in-chief during wartime (Eden, 1998, Chapter 8).

Triple Stimulator is concerned with your survival, not your evolution or happiness, and it regards your core beliefs as assets that have helped you survive. True or false, functional or destructive, it will fiercely protect your deepest myths. Fight-or-flight trumps constructive change. Triple Stimulator carries a pervasive, insistent energy that leaves people trapped in their negative patterns. Activating the radiant energies, particularly in times of stress, relaxes Triple Stimulator, radiating a sense of safety and facilitating an opening for new guiding myths and coping strategies.

Reasons to Focus the Treatment on the Radiant Energies

Your emotions, thoughts, and beliefs are not just ethereal events; they exist in your energy system and they permeate your cells (–> Luthke, Nicosia). Some become so deeply embedded that they seem to carry the weight and structure of absolute truth, settling into your deepest perspectives about life. Initiating shifts in these deep habits and states of mind, even if they are clearly dysfunctional, can be deceptively difficult. The radiant energies can be directed to impact them perhaps more profoundly than any of the other energy systems. Consider activating the radiant energies:

- *If Negativity is a Persistent Theme in a Person's Life.* Because the radiant circuits are a distinctly "positive" energy, they erode negativity and leave a positive, optimistic, hopeful psychological imprint.

- *To Overcome Resistant Habits.* Energy habits are part of the body's survival strategy, a primal value system that operates far beneath the conscious mind. Radiant circuits have better access for causing shifts in this value scheme than any of the other energy systems. They are also able to permeate the cells and thus spread new information as cells replicate.

- *When Caught in the Past.* Even if a person's energy system is holding onto a habit, a belief, or a dream that is no longer viable, hooking up the radiant circuits as the person thinks about the issues forges a fresh pathway that allows a new truth to become embedded.

- *When Other Corrections Won't Hold.* When energy treatments result in improvements, but the improvements are short-lived, older energy habits

(–> Carrington) may be winning the battle. Activating the radiant circuits can weave the corrections into the larger energy system.

- *When Stress Cancels Improvements.* If an energy correction holds, or if self-defeating patterns have been overcome, but these improvements do not have much resilience when stressful situations are encountered, the radiant energies can be a powerful ally. If you can make them a more pervasive force in an ongoing and consistent manner, you will be less vulnerable to the way that stress tends to engage old habits or activate past fears and trauma.

- *When Energies Won't Stay in Balance.* Top-bottom, left-right, and front-back splits in people's energies (all the meridians or chakras above the waist are strong and below the waist are weak, etc.) are common, costly, and the radiant circuits are the great balancers within the body's energy system.

Another time to work with the radiant circuits is at the end of a good treatment session. When the body is open, receptive, and in harmony, hooking up the radiant energies reinforces this state while instilling further openness, receptivity, and harmony.

Three Easy Turn-Ons
Working with the radiant circuits can set off waves of energy that feel good. At the same time, they connect the meridian lines, make the chakras spin, and engage all of the other energies. But they do not lend themselves easily to formulas. The "formula" is to model oneself after the radiant energy itself, which is to be absolutely spontaneous. Think a surge of excitement, falling in love, becoming enchanted. The radiant circuits are the polarity of "staying on track."

Many things we do naturally and spontaneously activate the radiant circuits. Joy begets joy. When you smile from a deep natural space, it sends joy all the way down to your soul and up again. A deep smile is not an ornament or a mask. It engages your radiant energies. So does listening to music you love, being overtaken by beauty, reveling in nature, laughing uncontrollably, abandoning yourself in play, love, or dance. As does anything that moves out negative thoughts, painful emotions, or stagnant energies, including exercise, laughter, or energy techniques such as "Expelling the Venom" (Eden, 1998, p. 219). But it is also the case that "if you don't use it", you really do lose it. The radiant energies can become stagnant and unable to easily move to where they are needed. This is the plight of many of us today where work, computer screens, and passive entertainment have taken precedence over deeper pleasures. The more the radiant energies are exercised, the more available they are to you.

Three simple ways of turning on the radiant energies (requiring less than 3 minutes each) are:

Blow Out and Zip Up. When you are feeling tight, depressed, or overwhelmed—as if you have become a collector of stress, anger, or disappointment—stand with your hands on your thighs, fingers spread, and take a deep breath in and out. With your next deep inhalation, make fists and swing your arms up and around until they are high above your head. Then turn your hands so your knuckles are facing toward you. Bring your fisted hands down swiftly, opening them as you blow out the accumulated stress with force. Repeat, and then on the third repetition, move your arms down slowly and deliberately on the exhale. Next, with a slow deep in-breath, open your hands, move them in front of your thighs, "zip" up the front of your body, to your chin, and on the out-breath, drop your hands back to your thighs. Zip up again. On the third zip-up, continue your hands straight up through your face, reach high, look up and stretch to the heavens. Connect with the radiant energies of the universe.

Dancing to the Eights. Like the double helix of DNA, the figure eight is one of nature's most basic patterns. Weaving your energies in figure eight curves activates the radiant energies and brings the body into greater health and vitality. Put on music and move your hips to a figure eight; then your arms. Flow freely, moving your entire body and creating as many small and large figure eight patterns as feels good to you.

Butt in the Air. On its own, or after you have blown out your stress and zipped up and weaved your radiant energies, this exercise is a peaceful, relaxing way of further cultivating a more radiant presence. Kneel down on all fours, with your knees on the floor, push back so your butt is resting on your heels, and bring your hands by your sides as you gently lower your head to the ground. If, and only if, it is comfortable to move your body and your head forward and lay your face to one side so your butt can go higher, do so, resting like a baby. Hold this position for about two or three minutes. Use the time to meditate, contemplate on a positive thought or image, or just let your mind go.

The Individual Radiant Circuits

Why do we need to know about the specific radiant circuits when we can just stick our butts in the air and activate all of them? You can bolster the overall radiant system by strengthening its weakest links. In addition, individual radiant circuits have, over evolutionary time, taken on specific roles and they serve different functions. So you can bring about changes in habits that are entrenched not only in the psyche but also in the body by focusing on and strengthening the action of specific radiant circuits [sections describing the individual radiant circuits, and how to check and correct the energy flow of each can be found in the full paper referenced].

Additional Techniques for Turning on The Radiant Energies

The radiant energies may be activated by anything that helps make space in the body, such as stretching or yoga; anything that crosses the energies from one side to the other, such as walking or swimming; anything that engages your spirit, such as a beautiful sunrise or an inspiring story; and anything that improves your environment, even as simple an act as walking outdoors to get more air and space around you. Why then learn special exercises for them? It is something like taking vitamins. Ideally, the food you eat would provide all the vitamins you need. Ideally, the activities in your life would keep your radiant energies flourishing. For most of us, neither is the case. We can stay healthier by taking vitamin supplements and we can stay happier by attending to our radiant energies. The following six techniques, like those already presented, are immediate, direct, and always available, nature's Prozac. Some methods will feel better to you than others, and the ones that feel better work better. It is worth keeping a couple of these techniques in your back pocket for daily doses as well as those moments in the psyche's weather patterns when your spirit begins to darken.

Crown Pull. Energy naturally accumulates at the top of your head, and if it doesn't circulate freely, it becomes stale or congested. The crown pull creates more space in your head for that energy to move, and it literally releases stagnant energies from your skull (through the crown chakra), making way for radiant energies to enter. The crown chakra is your gateway to the higher energies of the cosmos, and the crown pull also helps the intellect surrender to transcendent sources of information. Place your thumbs at your temples, on the side of the head. Rest your fingertips at the center of your forehead. Slowly and with some pressure, push in and then pull your fingers apart so you stretch the skin to the sides. Bring your fingertips back to the center of your forehead and repeat the stretch. Then bring your fingertips to your hairline and repeat again. Continue this pattern of pushing in and pulling apart as you move up and over your head, ending at the back of your neck.

Ab Stretch. Just as the head becomes clogged with residue that prevents the radiant energies from linking freely to the mind, energetic residue also tends to accumulate at the midline of your body. The ab stretch clears this residue, allowing the radiant circuits to flow between the top and bottom halves of the body. Standing at the back of a chair with your body straight and your hands wrapped over the chair, lift one leg backwards on an inhalation, stretching the abdomen. Release and then lift the other leg. Repeat several times.

Toweling Off. You can trace your meridians and activate your radiant energies every day when you bathe or shower, or when you towel off afterward. Beginning with the bottom of one foot, rub the towel or washcloth up the inside of your leg, over the front of your body, up over your shoulder, down the inside of your arm, and off your fingertips. Repeat on the other side. Then starting at the back of either hand, travel up the fingers, up the outside of your arms to your shoulders. Repeat on the other side. Then with both hands, reach up as high on your back as you can and rub down the entire length of your back, down the outsides of your legs, and off the top of your feet. Finish by toweling your face downwards, continuing to the bottom of the neck. Then curl your fingers over the back of your shoulders at the neck and drag them forward and off your body.

Triple-Stimulator/Spleen Hook-Up. Balancing the polar energies of Triple Stimulator and spleen helps with a range of problems, including addictions, overwhelm, overweight, compulsive behaviors, cravings, and blood-sugar mood swings. Place your left hand above your elbow, in the indent that is in line with your ring finger. Place your right hand under your left breast, over the area of your pancreas and spleen. Stay in this position for up to two minutes. Repeat on other side. If you wish to get more for your money, activate your radiant imagination.

The Radiant Imagination

Recall the glow you feel when you see someone you find attractive. This is how quickly your radiant energies can spring into action. Your internal images can also give a sudden boost to your radiant energies. At any given moment, you may become peaceful or anxious, happy or sad, based on what is playing in the theatre of your mind (–> Nicosia). By focusing your imagination, you can make that program not only enjoyable but a force that boosts your radiant energies. Use any of the following or write your own script: Imagine that someone who makes you feel alive and happy has just greeted you. Bring to mind a color you love. Imagine the energy of this color flowing through and infusing every cell of your body. Bring to mind something in your life about which you can feel thankful. Gratitude is among the most profound spiritual healers and the mascot of the radiant energies (–> Handelsman). Send this feeling of gratitude through your body. Say thank you to your heart, your lungs, your kidneys, all your organs. Thank your legs for walking you. Thank your environment, your loved ones, and your creator for supporting you. A great time to use the mind to focus color, healing rays of light, other healing uses of the imagination, gratitude, or prayer is when you are lying down while someone else is giving you a radiant energy treatment.

Heaven Rushing In. When you are hungering for more meaning in your life or feeling despair and isolation, step outside under the sky and stand tall. Ground yourself by focusing on where your feet meet the earth. Take a deep breath in. Exhale fully. Spread your fingers on your thighs. With your next inhalation, circle your arms out to the sides and then over your head until your hands touch. On the exhalation, bring your hands slowly down over your face, coming to rest at your chest, hands now in a prayer position. With another deep breath, open your arms wide, lifting them slightly, and look to the heavens. Sense the vastness above you and stay alert as a larger energy comes in through your hands and chest and breath. You are not alone. You may first feel this larger energy as a tingling. Allow your arms to accumulate this energy and scoop it into your chest, placing your hands over the center of your chest, the vortex called "Heaven Rushing In." Receive the energies of the heavens and allow your mind to open to a larger story.

Habits and the Radiant Energies

Habits run deep. Beneath your habits of thought and behavior are habits in your body and its energy system. Just as you may habitually avoid people who treat you with disrespect, your body may habitually cascade chemicals into your bloodstream that create feelings of aversion when you encounter someone who has harmed you. Just as it is not necessary to figure out how to turn up the thermostat in your house whenever you feel chilled, the body does not have to figure out anew how to maintain its internal 98.6° temperature every time the weather turns cold. But habits of both energy and behavior trade the possibility of creative response for the efficiency of practiced routine. They conserve energy and allow the precious resource of your attention to be focused upon new challenges. This economy often generalizes, however, to circumstances for which it does not serve you. If the person who harmed you had a mustache and you are stricken with feelings of revulsion every time you encounter someone with a mustache, economy has made way for folly. As go your energies, so you go.

Habitual responses that have become conditioned to stimuli that are perceived to be threatening cause us the greatest emotional distress. The prototype of this psychological syndrome is a physical allergy (–> Radomski, Tenpenny). The substance in a grape that causes someone to break out with a rash was not in itself toxic, but the immune system treats it as if it were. A woman we know was eating red grapes at the moment she learned her mother had just died in a car crash, and she has been violently allergic to red grapes ever since. The perceived threat is not necessarily a real threat, but the response of the energy system is no less vehement. Triple Stimulator governs our habituated responses to perceived threat. Because the body is saturated in conditions that evolution did not anticipate (such as our overloads of information, expectation, speed, stress, stimulation, unnatural foods, and electromagnetic and other pollutants), Triple Stimulator treats much of normal life as being foreign and thus as a primal threat.

Triple Stimulator and the rest of the radiant energy system differ markedly from one another in the kinds of habits they form. Not only does each system operate according to a different "morality" or logic for determining what is desirable, each system uses different strategies to bring about the inner conditions it considers favorable. Triple Stimulator's habits are oriented toward your physical and emotional safety. The habits of the radiant energy system are oriented toward spontaneity, love, and joy. While the original impulse of the habits maintained by Triple Stimulator was to insure your physical survival, harmful side effects may reverberate throughout the years. Like the broom of the Sorcerer's Apprentice, a useful routine may escalate into a compulsion that overwhelms the spirit. Able to pull rank over the other radiant energies, its strategies, and then its habits, become deeply embedded, while the habits that support spontaneity, love, and joy are eclipsed.

To live with greater love and joy in your heart, and to live free of antiquated dysfunctional habits, this Triple Stimulator/radiant energy imbalance needs to be overcome. First you can strengthen the overall radiant system using methods such as those described above. You can also re-condition your habituated responses to stressful situations that elicit Triple Stimulator's threat response. Your responses to troublesome images, feelings, and thoughts, as well as to physical situations, may also be changed in this way. Many of the developments in energy psychology involve reconditioning the meridian system's response to a disturbing stimulus (e.g., Gallo, 2000). Triple Stimulator recruits energy from the other meridians for the fight-or-flight response when a threat is perceived. If you are able to identify which meridians become drained when emotional stress or a bogus threat is present and use tapping and other techniques to keep those meridians in balance, the habituated response to the threat is interrupted.

Another approach to counter the grip of the conditioned threat responses sustained by Triple Stimulator is to enlist the radiant circuits. When Triple Stimulator is activated, the radiant circuits step down. It is as if there is no time for joy, love, or happiness when there is an immediate threat to survival. With Triple Stimulator over-activated so much of the time in most people, the radiant energy system becomes chronically depressed. It is not able to balance Triple Stimulator's actions and certain meridians may be taxed without protection, ultimately leading to breakdown or illness. To alter this pattern:

- Regularly stimulate the radiant energy system with positive experiences, or if they aren't happening, use the energy techniques presented above.
- Energy check to identify the radiant circuits that are the weakest link in your system and keep them strong.
- Recondition the radiant energy system by activating vulnerable circuits while a troubling situation is occurring or being imagined vividly.

Any of the techniques presented above can be applied toward this end. One of the most powerful, once you know through energy checking which circuit or circuits go out when the stressful situation is imagined, is to use the "Anchor and Wander" technique on yourself while imagining the situation. If you can get the radiant circuits to stay strong under stressful conditions, they will tend to take care of chronically weak meridians. Their job is to connect and balance the energies throughout the body, and they do it with a joyful touch.

This paper has presented general techniques for strengthening the radiant energy system, techniques for working with specific radiant circuits, and a strategy for changing habits by reconditioning the body's energy response to stressful situations, thoughts, and images. While the numerous techniques presented may begin to seem like just a bunch of formulas and a bit overwhelming when offered all at once, they are actually easier to do than to read about, they do not take much time, and they will bring more joy into your life.

NOTES
1   Excerpted from a substantially longer chapter scheduled for publication in Energy Psychology in Psychotherapy (edited by Fred P. Gallo, New York: W. W. Norton, in press). The complete citation material for references in this excerpt can be found there.
2   We use the term Triple Stimulator instead of the more traditional Triple Warmer or Triple Heater to emphasize its vital role in stimulating the immune system, the fight-or-flight response, and the body's habits.

References

Blanchard, B. (2000, May/June). What is acupressure shiatsu? *Spirit of Change*, 13, 29 – 30.
Blitzer, L. E., Atchison-Nevel, D .J., Kenny, M. C., & McGee-Brown, M. J. (1999). An examination of the use of acupuncture's extraordinary vessels on major depression: A pilot investigation [abstract]. *Alternative Therapies in Health and Medicine*, 5(2), 93-94.
Blofeld, J. (1973). *The secret and the sublime: Taoist mysteries and magic.* New York: Dutton.
Collinge, W. (1998). *Subtle energy.* New York: Warner Books.
Diamond, J. (1988). *Life-energy analysis.* Valley Cottage, NY: Archaeus.
Eden, D. (with Feinstein, D.) (1998). *Energy medicine.* New York: Tarcher/Penguin Putnam.
Feinstein, D. (1998). At play in the fields of the mind: Personal myths as fields of information. *Journal of Humanistic Psychology*, 38(3), 71-109.
Gerber, R. (1996). *Vibrational medicine* (Rev. Ed.). Santa Fe, NM: Bear & Co.
Gallo, F. P. (2000). *Energy diagnostic and treatment methods.* New York: Norton.
Hunt, V. (1995). Infinite mind: *The science of human vibrations.* Malibu, CA: Malibu.
Johnson, J. A. (2000). *Chinese medical quigong therapy: A comprehensive clinical text.* Pacific Grove, CA: The International Institute of Medical Qigong.
Matsumoto, K., & Birch, S. (1986). *Extraordinary vessels.* Brookline, MA: Paradigm
O'Connor, J., & Bensky, D. (1981). *Acupuncture: A comprhensive text.* Seattle: Eastland Press.
Porter, A. (1996). Recipes for magic. In I. M. Teeguarden (Ed.), *A complete guide to acupressure* (pp. 122 – 129). Tokyo/NY: Japan Publications.
Teeguarden, I. M. (1978). *Acupressure way of health: Jin shin do.* Tokyo/NY: Japan Publications.

2

Accessing Creativity Through the Human Vibrational Matrix

Dorothea Hover-Kramer

Survival no longer depends on biological equipment alone but on the social and cultural tools we choose to use. The inventions of the great civilizations – the arts, religions, political systems, sciences and technologies – signal the main stages along the path of cultural evolution. To be human means to be creative.
— *Michael Csikszentmihalyi, 1996, p. 318.*

About Creativity

Creativity, or bringing something new into being, is the most decisive and distinguishing characteristic of mankind. For over one million and a half years, since our ancestors found ways to split rocks to make tools, we have been creating new forms, thoughts, ideas, and resources. Creativity brings a sense of fulfilment and deeper enjoyment to our lives. It is indeed the most human of our traits.

All of us share in the potential to create something original and innovative. In his book, *Creativity*, author M. Csikszentmihalyi (1996) distinguishes the Creativity, (with a capital "C") of those few individuals who are actually recognized as changing the world, from what he calls "personal creativity." Personal creativity may be accessed in simple ways to enhance our daily lives and by exploring a knowledge domain. Some examples of knowledge domains are gardening, musical performance, writing, counseling, or business management. Exploring a domain in depth eventually may bring about recognition by other contributors and serve to benefit the world community. For example, Einstein's work became more widely known following the support and recognition of the experts in his field and the greater scientific community.

But, for most of us, our ability to put things together in new ways and living creatively is simply a better way of finding personal fulfilment and meaning. Personal creativity has value whether or not we master a domain or ever achieve the recognition of a wider field.

While this personal creativity may be an inherent potential for each of us, many people lead lack luster day to day lives, letting vague, random, disorganized thoughts dominate. If we are to heal and develop ourselves, we must reclaim our potential for personal creativity, reconnecting with our innate human capacity for innovation. Beyond recovery from life's challenges through effective psychotherapy, we need to access higher levels of actualization through expressions of personal vitality and creativity.

A good place to start accessing principles of creativity is to watch how young children open to the world around them: almost anything new is fascinating and attracts their curiosity. As they explore, they may play, ask, move, shove, and put things together in new ways. They seem to derive pleasure and satisfaction from building something, tearing it down, then building something even grander. They are in a flow, just doing something for its intrinsic pleasure and satisfaction. There is no thought about the future; they are totally in the moment.

Few adults maintain this sense of flow, simply enjoying an activity for its own worth with the possibility for new discovery and invention. We may rightly ask ourselves how we can recover the spontaneity we once knew as children. How does a playful, productive, explorative, imaginative youngster become a somewhat burdened, colorless adult, who often may even dislike his chosen career?

From a psychological point of view, we may point to early life traumas, not only loss or violation but also lack of recognition or validation, as major factors in influencing core beliefs about ourselves. Thus, a young person may come to think of herself as stupid, incapable, or unworthy. In addition, we also note that many limiting beliefs are held and repeated in our social environments about innovation and creativity. These beliefs and patterns – such as, "I never could sing," "I can't draw," I'm too awkward to dance" – become internalized so that we are hardly conscious of their presence. They are powerful influences, nonetheless, and may require intensive, committed work to reprogram (–> Shaw, Weil). Fortunately, through the psychoenergetic resources that we will explore here, there are significant ways to release limiting beliefs and access more functional, empowering thought patterns to nurture our creative zest and innate abilities (–> Eden & Feinstein).

Qualities of Personal Creativity and Self-Inventory

To explore personal creativity and give us a sense of direction, let us consider some qualities that support originality and generativity. The hallmark of highly creative people, according to Csikszentmihalyi's research, is their willingness to think outside of established, accepted parameters. Rather than being oddballs or outsiders, though, creative people seem to be those individuals who go deeper, venture further than the ordinary person. Most importantly, they seem to be on a lifelong quest for learning and growing. They are able to direct and focus their energies toward their interests in an enthusiastic search for knowledge and excitement. These same qualities can be cultivated in each of us as we learn to note our strengths and deficits, as we contact limiting beliefs and open to more desirable possibilities.

As your review the list of characteristics for personal creativity given here, you may wish to note which areas you have already incorporated into your lifestyle, and which areas need further development. You may ask yourself which limiting beliefs prevent you from fully exercising this specific aspect of your personal creativity, which is your human birthright.

Some of the personal qualities that are essential to developing your own creativity are as follows:

- Be curious about something everyday. Enjoy surprises.
- Explore what is mysterious to you.
- Maintain a sense of openness and wonder.
- Consider the many domains that attract you.
- Find at least one domain to explore in depth. Master as much available information about it as possible.
- Be persistent in learning the rules of the domain and in increasing your skills and level of complexity.
- Apply problem solving skills to a specific issue regarding the domain (i.e., identify a problem, generate possible solutions, implement solutions, evaluate, re-identify, regenerate solutions, etc.)
- Be willing to learn from everything, even what may appear to be a mistake or a wrong turn.
- Actively engage in divergent thinking – produce as many ideas as possible, make them as different as possible, consider the unlikely or opposite to your usual way of thinking.
- Be flexible. Pay attention to feedback so that you can correct your course as you go.

- Organize the mundane aspects of daily life (like knowing where your car keys and glasses are) so your train of thought is not continuously interrupted by looking for things.
- Take charge of your schedule.
- Cultivate a sense of flow. Take time to reflect. When something sparks your interest, follow it.
- Develop the aspects of your personality that are lacking. If you are predominantly rational, put conscious energy into developing your intuitive knowing.
- Know what you like and don't like
- Enjoy who you are.

To continue with this self-exploratory exercise, select the item(s) that seems the most difficult to you. For example, taking charge of your schedule to have time for reflection and inner quiet may trigger several limiting beliefs: "I am at the mercy of others' schedules," "There is never enough time for my needs," I don't deserve to run my schedule for me," "I am incapable of controlling my time." As a divergent thinking exercise, now generate four totally opposite thoughts that can form the basis of your focus on a desired, more creative belief. Examples might be as follows: "Others' schedules affect me only as I choose," "I now make time for my needs," "I decide & take charge of my schedule," "I am capable & effective in controlling my time." As you can see, each of these new, desired beliefs generates a host of related possibilities and decisions that may also require intentional work and redirection.

Redirecting a limiting pattern toward a more effective behavioral style can often be surprisingly easy if we allow a psychoenergetic approach to assist. Working with the chakras, the biofield, and the meridian acupoints—all major aspects of the human vibrational matrix—gives delightful resources for self-care as well as for assisting others. We will explore some of these resources here and give ample references for you to continue further exploration at your own pace.

Psychoenergetic Principles for Treating Systemic Imbalance, Reversals, and Limiting Beliefs

Energy psychology is emerging as an extension of the many mind/body psychologies, permitting us to address mental and emotional patterns of distress by working with the human vibrational matrix. This matrix, which is just beginning to be measured with current scientific technology (Becker, 1990; Motoyama, 1998; Cho et al. 1998) is a complex of electromagnetic flows and vortices that are an information delivery strategy, that appears to be parallel to the human nervous system Becker, 1990, p. 80). A large and growing literature supports the effects of working with the human subtle energies for physical relief from discomfort and pain (Eden, 1998; Hover-Kramer, 2001; Krieger, 1994) as well as release from psychological tension and anxiety (Gallo, 1999, 2000a; Lambrou & Pratt, 2000; Quinn, Heidt, 1999, etc.). Some authors focus on balancing the human biofield as the major source of healing, others address energy vortices (chakras) and biofield together. Most of the current energy psychology literature focuses on work with the meridian acupoints, while integrative movements that combine all aspects of the human vibrational system into a comprehensive energy psychology are also developing (Eden, 1999; D. & R. Grudermeyer and Hover-Kramer, 2000).

The theory base of these approaches may differ but the underlying principles are very similar. For one, the whole energy system, either of yours or a client's, must be in balance for other more specific interventions to be effective. Thus, direct ways of rebalancing the entire biofield and its energetic components on a daily basis are essential. In the extensive Therapeutic Touch literature and research of the last thirty years, "centering" as a means of focusing and balancing the energetic system is required prior to any healing efforts, whether on oneself or with others. Below are samples of some ways of centering that could be used prior to therapeutic work or creative enterprise.

Centering Exercises

Exercise #1. *Brush Down*
While thinking of a recent stressful event, set your intent to release its effects in your biofield. Allow yourself to take a deep breath and let it go fully. Again, breathe and let go of tension especially out through your hands and your feet. Bringing your hands above your head on the next in-breath, breathe out fully while gently brushing downward head to toe. Allow a sigh or groan to help release the tension fully as the hands touch the floor. Continue brushing down with each out-breath, down the front of the body, from under each arm, the upper and lower back, and the groin area.

Explore how far away from the body your hands can be while still feeling the releasing sensation. Notice how you feel after 3-5 minutes of this exercise.

Exercise #2. *The Energy Spin*
A powerful psychoenergetic effect comes with purposeful movement. This one combines awareness of the biofield and chakras which moves upward from the base of the spine to help bring more Qi into the system.

Set your intent for balancing of the entire psychoenergetic system while feeling your connection to the earth through your feet. While standing tall allow your hips to spin to the right as if spinning a hula hoop. Allow yourself to feel the joy of your aliveness at the base of the spine while spinning in big circles.

After a while, you may shift attentional focus to the sacral center, and its meaning while continuing the spinning. Then, move upward to the solar plexus, the heart center, the throat area, the brow and crown centers while continuing the spins.

Notice how your body wants to spin less in certain areas. Explore the sensation of spins to the left, or try moving hips and arms in a "figure 8" motion. As you end, integrate right and left hemispheres by bringing all the fingertips together and hold for a few minutes. Note any changes in your body/mind.

Exercise #3. *The Central Alignment*
This is one of many centering practices that allows a sense of inner focus to develop and can be used frequently throughout the working day.

Standing or sitting comfortably, visualize a vibrant line of energy that flows through the center of your body in relation to your head and spine. See the connection from the base of the spine and through the feet to the very core of the earth. Place your hands on the gravitational center of the body, which is just below the navel. You will always move balanced ways when your focus is on this hara area, which is a yoga point for focusing. Visualize the connection between the hara and the earth's core.

With one hand, let your awareness shift to the mid-upper chest, while keeping the other hand on the hara. The upper mid-chest is considered the "soul seat," the area where we begin to manifest our sense of purpose and meaning. Allow the connection between the two hands to strengthen while breathing fully. Continue to feel the grounding to the earth.

While keeping the hand on the hara, allow the other hand to go to the crown of the head and to stretch upward to your favorite celestial star. Sense the alignment between all parts of your unique energy line, the hara, the soul seat, your star, and the connection to the earth. Allow any sense of color or sound to assist your image of this central line. Some people enjoy vibrant images of the spiral double helix that is also present in every cell as the DNA structure.

Applications for Treating Psychoenergetic Reversals

Another major stumbling block to accessing our full potentials lies in the arena of psychological reversals. In the language of Dr. Roger Callahan, a psychological reversal is the time when "...your actions are contrary to what you say you want to do... You are sabotaging your own efforts, your feel helpless and you don't know why" (Callahan & Perry, 1991, p. 40–41). Because these reversals seem to emanate from underlying limiting beliefs that affect the entire psychoenergetic informational network, I prefer the term "psychoenergetic reversal." It is certainly not in the person's conscious intent to sabotage present cognitive decisions; neither are these subconscious patterns purely psychological in nature for they do indeed hold a pattern that can be sensed in the client's vibrational matrix. Reversals do however constitute significant objections to treatment or to accessing creativity.

In the biofield, reversals may be sensed with the hands as areas of density or congestion, heat or coolness, over a particular area of the body. In the chakras, they are sensed either as a depletion or overabundance of Qi, too much or too little energy, with either constituting a form of imbalance. While balanced, open chakras spin in a clockwise direction, a chakra impacted by a limiting belief pattern or reversal, will literally be reversed – spinning counterclockwise or having no movement at all.

Some of the patterns that become established in the client's informational network are highly complex as one limiting core belief can determine other patterns throughout a whole lifetime. Treatment of psychoenergetic reversals in meridian therapies is effected by checking muscle strength in relation to intent, deserving, safety, and other statements of what is true or untrue for the client. In chakra/biofield therapies, we might simply ask the client to state a limiting belief that he or the therapist have identified and ask where, in relation to the physical body, the client experiences the impact of that belief the most intensely. This usually gives a strong indication of the most impacted chakra, as most people have a sense of energy blockage in relation to their bodies. they may sense "weakness" or a "sinking feeling" in specific parts of the body.

For example, a client stated her limiting beliefs about her ability to finish her doctoral dissertation. After writing down as many of these patterns as possible, I asked her where in relation to the physical body she most felt the impact of each belief. She pointed to a "weak" sensation in the sacral area. As she held her hands over the area, a whole flood of memories seemed to release. The most damaging belief pattern occurred when a fourth grade teacher doubted her integrity. The child had written an unusually deep poem about friendship and read it to the class. So great was the trauma over the teacher's accusations of plagiarism before a classroom of children, that this client resolved never to write again for any teacher. This would definitely be a limiting belief if one seeks a doctorate. When asked where she felt the most intensity in the body about this incident and its consequent decisions, she continued to hold the sacral center, the focusing area for feelings, making choices and releasing. With several counterclockwise spins over the sacral chakra, she released the traumatic event, sending the teacher to the light to get more training in working with creative kids. The client's field was then ready to bring in new, more effective beliefs about her writing and to repattern the incomplete or diminished structure of the chakra.

The following exercises give examples of ways you might address psychoenergetic reversals in yourself or in clients to help return the vibrational matrix to optimum functioning.

Exercise #1. *Reversals as Imbalance in the Biofield*
After centering or grounding with the exercises in the previous section, allow yourself to scan the body/mind intuitively for areas of congestion, blockage or depletion. Scanning head to toe, notice areas that are pink and lively, notice areas that seem gray or sluggish. Make a note of what you see or sense.

Another option is to scan to biofield with the hands, moving the hands 2–5 inches above the body, and noting differences – where does the field seem cooler, denser, warmer, more sticky, or open and flowing? Make a note of these perceptions and ask yourself, or the client, if this has any personal meaning. Even if there is no immediate recognition of relevance, repeated scanning over several times usually leads to some awareness that points to a reversal in the psychoenergetic system.

Exercise #2. *Reversals as Imbalance in a Specific Chakra*
After centering, set your intent to learn from your chakras. Think of a limiting belief that you currently hold and want to release. Allow yourself to notice where this pattern most impacts the physical body. Notice all the ramifications of this pattern as you move the hands over this area of the body. Note any other energy centers that hold different aspects of the same issue.

While thinking of the psychoenergetic reversal, clear, smooth or "unruffle" the congested area in the biofield. If it is held in the emotional body for example, the pattern and its heaviness will clear with quick downward movements. You might wish to add the image of releasing this constriction to the universe to be healed and transformed, so that it no longer needs to burden you or anyone else.

Exercise #3. *Release of a Reversal in the Chakra(s)*
Since healthy, open energy centers spin in a clockwise direction, the release of any disturbed or limiting pattern would most easily be effected with a counterclockwise spin over the specific chakra(s). While thinking of the pattern of which you wish to let go, move both hands over the most impacted chakra first in a counterclockwise direction, while literally spinning out and releasing the belief and all its many antecedents.

As sometimes nearly all chakras are impacted by a limiting core belief, you can also spin out over each center, thereby informing the related dimension of the biofield as well. Letting go and clearing work is generally more effective working downward, from the crown toward the root chakra, or from the most impacted chakra downward.

The psychological quality of each center can help you in designing a helpful mantra, or repeated phrase, to attune to the issue at hand. For instance, "I am talking to my survival and safety consciousness (root chakra)... I want you to hear me and make sure all parts are in agreement. . . I am releasing (with several counterclockwise hand spins) my old belief that there is not enough love for me...I release all parts that made this old agreement in the past from responsibility for holding this belief... I ask the universe and those parts that know how to do this work to revise and update this pattern that is no longer helpful to me."

Installing Desired Beliefs

After pervasive psychoenergetic disturbances and reversals have been cleared, the vibrational matrix is ready to install new, more functional thoughts patterns about personal creativity. While meridian work proceeds with eliciting an algorithm via muscle checking or intuition, chakra/biofield work proceeds with direct interventions to the affected aspect of the informational network.

For each limiting, or negatively phrased belief, new and positively phrased patterns can be installed (–> Carrington). This is usually most effective moving upward through the chakra sequence, from the most basic parts of ourselves to the most forgiving and spiritually aware aspects. Holding focus over each chakra in the sequence while recognizing the new pattern, tapping the area, or spinning clockwise help to strengthen the intervention. For example, a limiting pattern around, say, public speaking may have a message for each chakra via a new pattern that the client selects. A new desired belief, such as, "I own my birthright to speak effectively and to be heard," has relevance not only for the throat center of self-expression but for all of the energy centers. Beginning with conscious intent and focused hands held over the root, the client might say, "I inform my basic survival and vitality and all related parts that I now speak effectively with a full voice." As images of insecurity or fear related to the issue arise, they can be readily released with the clearing of reversals mentioned in the previous section. Then, we can proceed to the sacral center with the same message but this time with awareness of feelings and the need to discriminate between appropriate and inappropriate settings for self-expression. Thus, we can assist each chakra to release and let go of its reversed, limiting patterns, so that the desired belief can be installed and felt throughout the energy system.

Conclusion

Because most trauma to our self-esteem and creativity occurred in the preverbal stage of life, the psychoenergetic resources of meridian, chakra and biofield work can be more effective than cognitive therapies with selected clients. With the tools and concepts described here, we have a variety of additional, complementary approaches that widen our creativity as therapists. In addition, we are empowered to access our resources for personal inventiveness and original thinking.

References

Csikszentmihalyi, M. (1996). *Creativity: Flow and the psychology of discovery and invention.* New York: HarperCollins.
Becker, R. (1990). *Cross currents.* New York: Tarcher/Putnam.
Motoyama, H. (1997). *Treatment principles of Oriental medicine from an electrophysiological viewpoint.* Tokyo: Human Sciences Press.
Cho, Z.H., Chung, S.C., Jones, J.P., Park, M.B., Park, J.J., Lee, H.J., Wong E.K., & Minn, N.I., (1998). New findings of the correlation between acupoints and corresponding brain cortices using functional MRI. *Science,* Vol 95. p. 2670-2673.
Davidson,R.J., Marshall, J.R., Tomarken, A.J., & Henriquest, J.B. (2000). While a phobic waits; Regional brain electrical and autonomic activity in social phobics during anticipation of public speaking. *Biological Psychiatry,* Vol. 47, p. 85-95.
Eden, D. & Feinstein, D. (1998). *Enegy medicine.* New York: Tarcher/Putnam.
Grudermeyer, D., Grudermeyer, R. and Hover-Kramer, D. (2000). *Comprehensive energy psychology manual—Level 2.* Del Mar, Ca: Willingness Works.
Hover-Kramer D. (2001). *Healing Touch.* Albany, NY: Delmar International.
Krieger, D. (1994). *Accepting your power to heal.* Santa Fe, NM: Bear & Co.
Gallo, F. (1998). *Energy psychology.* Boca Raton, FL: CRC Press.
Gallo, F. (2000a). *Energy diagnostic and treatment methods.* New York: W.W. Norton Co.

Lambrou, P. & Pratt, G. (2000). *Instant emotional healing*. New York: Broadway Books.
Quinn, J. F. (1989). Therapeutic touch as energy exchange: *Replication and extension. Nursing Science Quarterly*, 2:2, p. 79-87.
Heidt, P. (1991). Helping patients to rest: Clinical studies in therapeutic touch. *Holistic Nursing Practice*, 5:4, p. 57-66.
Callahan, R. & Perry, (1991). *Why do I eat when I'm not hungry?* New York: Doubleday.

3

Energy Therapy, Edge-Figures and the Phases of the Creative Process

Joan Hitlin

The process of bringing something into being has many acts and scenes, many stages and phases. At every phase, there are blocks and stoppers that are intimately linked to that particular time in the creative timeline of your project. It is almost as if each phase comes with a genie in the bottle: you have to rub the bottle to manifest the creativity, but – horrors – rubbing the bottle also outs the fearful gremlins.

There is another way of expressing this: at every phase in your creative process you can expect to come face to face with one of your edges. (An edge being a psychological barrier that you cannot go beyond.) And at each edge, you can expect to find edge-figures – subpersonalities, shadows, demons, gremlins, introjects, Inner Children, archetypes – who are invested, for better or for worse, in keeping you from going past your edges. Think of them as temple guardians. From an energy therapy perspective, we might say that the edge-figure is the metaphoric manifestation of the disruption in your energy system. Before the new energy therapies came along edge-figures were often able to sabotage the entire creative process, keeping us from going beyond our edges and manifesting our genius – that's the other side of the genie in the bottle. Now, using the wonderful new energy therapies we can integrate our edge-figures, and smooth a path through our edges.

Just as children go through phases as they develop, creative projects go through phases too, and each phase may be said to have an edge-figure lurking around. If you are experiencing creative blockage, it will help to notice which creative phase you are in, and which edge-figures are present. For each phase, I will suggest some EFT, or TAT statements and I will also name some potential edge-figures who may be lurking nearby. It is always appropriate for you to use your instant BSFF cue-word and to use other energy therapies that you are familiar with. The following are some of the phases in the life cycle of a creative process and some of the edge-figures that may be lurking nearby. You may discover other phases, and other edge-figures as you explore your own creative process.

The Butterpillar Phase

The caterpillar goes into the cocoon, incubates, and comes out a butterfly. While it is still in the cocoon it is neither here nor there. It is a butterpillar. To incubate, or "to butterpillar," is to generate ideas, to select the idea, and to let the idea percolate until it is ready bubble up. If you try to pull the butterfly out of the cocoon prematurely, you will find a butterpillar that can neither crawl nor fly. An important phase, which cannot be bypassed, this incubation phase can look like wasting time, but it is an essential aspect of creativity. If you are feeling like a butterpillar, you might be in the presence of an edge-figure who is "the impatient one" or "the one who doesn't trust the process."

EFT: Even though I am impatient...
Even though nothing seems to be happening...
TAT: Nothing is happening.
I trust that this process is unfolding exactly as it is supposed to.

The Procrastination Phase

Perhaps you are sleeping late, or talking on the phone for hours, or you might be cleaning out the closets, baking cookies, or making deals on the Internet. You are doing everything except what you think you should be doing. Procrastination can take the appearance of laziness or busy-ness, it may be a sign of blocks and stoppers such as post traumatic stress, negative beliefs or fears. What's more, procrastination may be signaling that you are on the wrong track.

If you are putting off working, you might be in the presence of an edge-figure who is "the pessimistic one" or "the one who got punished for expressing herself."

EFT: Even though I don't know why I am procrastinating...
Even though I can't make myself get started...
TAT: I am resisting this project.
I am not resisting this project.

The Crunching Phase

Sooner or later there will come a time when you feel as if you just have to barrel through. You are wanting to take control of the outcome, and you want to make the project succumb to your will. I call this doing Creative Crunches. Creative juices dry up when they are squeezed too hard. What is needed here is what the Taoists call *wu wei*. Wu wei means "not blocking, not making, not forcing, not interfering." Wu wei is going with the grain, rolling with the punch, swimming with the current. At its best, when you practice wu wei, you almost feel as if you are channeling your project from a higher source.

When you feel as if you are doing Creative Crunches, you might be in the presence of an edge-figure who is "the pushy one" or "the one who needs to be in control."

EFT: Even though I'm trying to force myself to continue...
      Even though I can't just go with the flow...
TAT: I have to push myself.
      I can swim with the current.

The I Can't Get Into the Studio Phase

One of my art teachers, Fletcher Benton, a well known Californian sculptor, used to say that no matter what else was going on, no matter how he felt, he came to the studio every da. Sometimes all he did was clean up, or rearrange the furniture, or stare at his work. This is how he put it: "I go to the studio everyday, no matter what. And I stay there all day. Because, I know that if anything is gonna happen, it's gonna happen in the studio, and I don't want to miss it." Showing up may not be a sufficient condition for creativity... but it is a necessary condition.

If you can't get yourself into the studio, you might be in the presence of an edge-figure who is "the reluctant one" or "the one who thinks it will happen by magic."

EFT: Even though I can't get my butt over to my desk...
      Even though I'd rather be watching TV...
TAT: I can't get myself to the studio.
      I can get myself to the studio.

The Blankpageitis Phase

Imagine that you are sitting at your desk, staring at a piece of very white paper. Minutes go by, hours go by; the paper is still blank. Perhaps you have started to write, struggled to get something down. And then you read it back, rolled your eyes, and tore up the page. So this blank piece of paper may be far from the first blank piece of paper that you have been staring at. I call this phase blankpageitis.

If you are in the blankpageitis phase, you might be in the presence of an edge-figure who is "the critical one" or "the one who has trouble starting things."

EFT: Even though I can't bear looking at this blank page...
      Even though I will never have a good idea again...
TAT: I will never think of anything to say.
      I have a lot to say.

The Antsy Stage

It is hard to sit still when you can't tolerate the anxiety of the blank page, the emotional content of the material that you are dealing with, your inability to make progress, or even your excitement about your last breakthrough. Your inability to stay put represents your inability to tolerate your own experience. Energy therapies can now help you to develop sitzfleisch (or sticktoitiveness) as you deal with issues, problems, muse abandonment or over-excitement.

If you are in the antsy phase, you might be in the presence of an edge-figure who is "the running away one" or "the one who can't tell anxiety from excitement."

EFT: Even though I need to get up every 2 minutes...
      Even though I can't stand being this excited...
TAT: I can't sit still.
      I can sit still.

The Zoning Phase

Can you remember being so deeply absorbed in what you were doing that time fell away – you weren't aware of what was going on around you – you forgot about problems and concerns that had been on your mind hours, or even minutes, earlier? We call this "being in the zone." Some of us need a ritual for getting into the zone quickly. Others go on artistic binges: once they get into the zone they will work until they drop. With energy therapies, we can now get into the zone more quickly and dependably.

If you are having trouble getting into the zone, you might be in the presence of an edge-figure who is "the linear one" or "the one who is afraid to lose herself."

EFT: Even though I can't seem to get into the zone...
Even though I keep thinking about X, not my work...
TAT: I don't want to get lost in my work.
I want to get lost in my work.

The Intrusions Phase

Most of us feel lucky to get a free day now and then, and even so, there are many intrusions that can invade our trance. Disturbances, sooner or later, will happen. Even without an outside intrusion, intrusive thoughts will creep into the studio, willy nilly. So it is important to develop the ability to recover from the disturbance, reenter the zone, and temporarily forget that anything ever happened. For those of you who are familiar with iBSFF (instant BSFF), this is the perfect time to use your cue word.

If you feel like you never have a moment that is totally your own, you might be in the presence of an edge-figure who is "the responsible one" or "the one who has to keep it all going."

EFT: Even though my client is in crisis...
Even though my bank account is overdrawn...
TAT: I can't tolerate interruptions.
I can deal with interruptions.

The Getting Past Mistakes Phase

Mistakes happen. Sometimes they are pure catastrophes. (In the age of computers a most common mistake is to forget to save your work, and then to lose it irretrievably.) Energy therapy can help you to speed up the grieving process, and to move on fast, before you have time to become hopelessly depressed over the loss. If you are crying over spilt milk, you might be in the presence of an edge-figure who is "the clumsy one" or "the one who screws up."

EFT: Even though I blew it...
Even though all my hard work just went down the drain...
TAT: I can't recover from this loss.
I will recover from this loss.

The Serendipity Phase

John Cage, the composer and painter, relied largely on chance to create his pieces. He depended upon the throw of the dice to decide which kind of sound to allow into his composition, and which kind of mark to put on the paper. His music and his paintings have a fresh, unforced, natural quality.

Ideas and materials can come to us in the strangest ways, from the most unexpected sources. If we think that we have to plan everything out, and be totally in control, we actually reject these unexpected gifts or seeming mistakes. It pays to sit back and look at what is happening with a clear eye and an open mind. Today's messes can turn out to be tomorrow's innovations – the fresh, inventive, original input that you were needing.

If you are in the serendipity phase, you might be in the presence of an edge-figure who is the one who thinks outside the box or the one bearing gifts.

EFT: Even though I can't see any good in this...
         Even though I liked it the way it was...
TAT: I blew it.
         I created new possibilities.

The Muse Abandonment Phase

There will always come a time when you are in the middle of a project and you can't remember what you were doing the day before, or what you need to do now. Or, you know what needs fixing, but you can't figure out how to fix it. The fire has gone cold. Energy therapy can be used to rekindle the glow.

If you feel as if your muse has abandoned you, you might be in the presence of an edge-figure who is "the dried up one" or "the one who had no talent to begin with."

EFT: Even though I lost my train of thought...
         Even though I'm all dried up...
TAT: I'm stuck and I don't know what to do.
         I can incubate this.

The Committing and Completing Phase

Finishing a painting, an aria or an article can be the most painful thing. You need to commit to the piece as it is, not as it might become, or as it might have been. You have to say goodbye to a relationship that may have become the mainstay of your life for quite a long time. Finishing a piece or a project also brings up many questions: is the piece good enough to show? How will it be received? Am I any good? What will I do next?

If you find yourself unable to complete your project, you might be in the presence of an edge-figure who is "the option loving one" or "the one who is afraid to take a stand."

EFT: Even though I am afraid to finish (commit, complete)...
Even though I won't know what to do with myself once this project is done...
TAT: I can't finish this.
I can finish this.

The Show & Tell Phase

Some of us love being in the " doing" phases of creativity, but suddenly become all tied up when it comes time to put our work out in the world. It may be that the work was really a creative meditation all along – never intended for public scrutiny. You might want to muscle test, and check out whether your work is an artistic diary, or if it is meant to be seen, heard and shared with an audience. If it is meant to be shared, you might want to think about who your intended audience might be.

If you are feeling shy & secretive about your work, you might be in the presence of an edge-figure who is "the hidden one" or "the one who should be seen and not heard."

EFT: Even though I have stage fright...
Even though I'm not supposed to stand out...
TAT: I don't want to show my work.
I want to show my work

The Tooting Your Own Trunk Phase

Once upon a time, I participated in a shamanic power animal retrieval ceremony, and the power animal I retrieved was an elephant. I asked my elephant what power she was bringing me, and she said, "I'm here to teach you to toot your own trunk!" This didn't make much sense to me until much later, when it became obvious that I had a block against "tooting my own trunk." I saw it as a form of bragging, or worse still, a symptom of OPD (Obnoxious Personality Disorder). After doing energy work to heal this limiting belief, I came to see that "tooting my own trunk" meant sharing my excitement, getting the word out, being a part of, rather than apart from, the universe.

If you have a block against tooting your own trunk, you might be in the presence of an edge-figure who is "the humble one" or "the one who thinks it's dangerous to outshine anyone else."

EFT: Even though I'm supposed to be modest...
  Even though I was scolded for bragging...
TAT: It's safe to talk lovingly about my work.
  It's dangerous to talk lovingly about my work.

Dealing with Fear and Doubt

Fear and doubt are the alpha and the omega of the creative process. I've never met an artist, writer or musician who wasn't scared at least some of the time. Joseph Conrad said: "My fate is in my own hands, and my hands are weak." Although this is probably the all-purpose, universal fear, there are as many fears and doubts as there are potentially creative people poised on the edge of the creative brink. At any phase, if you are blocked, you are probably in the presence of an edge-figure who is "the frightened one" or "the one who is full of doubt."

EFT: Even though I am afraid to...
  Even though I doubt that I can...
TAT: I can't handle this.
  I can handle this.

Conclusion

In every phase of your artistic process you are likely to come up against the after-effects of past trauma, and the lingering effects of early decisions made in response both to trauma and to perceptions about the world around you (–> Feinstein, Hover-Kramer, Shaw, Weil). Identity reversals, negative self-talk, negative beliefs and societal injunctions can prevent the creative process from flowing smoothly. Edge-figures in the guise of the introjected parent (with her beliefs and criticisms) and edge-figures in the guise of the introjected child (with her fears, fantasies and world views), as well as other dissociated parts and sub-personalities will need to be treated (–> Shaw, Weil). Self-punishment, judgementalism, high expectations, perfectionism, fastidiousness and the talent-myth are also likely to get in the way. I deal with these issues in more detail in my energy therapy manual: *Tapping Into Creativity*.

γ
Healing

Willem Lammers

All experiences are available to the One Mind, and the One Mind is all of us or any of us at the highest level of expansion.
– Thaddeus Golas

In the Odyssey, goddesses and gods guide our hero in daily life, and seldom they choose another option than this guidance. There was a good reason for obeying: If you didn't follow the gods' directions, they might turn against you and as a ordinary mortal, you were no match: Poseidon, the mighty god of the seas, has been insulted by Odysseus early on his journey home, and has decided to punish him. When he learns that the other gods have freed Odysseus in his absence, "...he marshalled the clouds and, seizing his trident in his hands, stirred up the sea. He roused the stormy blasts of every wind that blows, and covered land and water alike with a canopy of cloud. Darkness sooped down from the sky." (5, 292).

Resources come from the gods: "And then some god was pitied by my forlorn condition. For when I had almost reached the ship, he sent a great antlered stag right across my path." That means dinner for the starving crew.

Good ideas come from the gods: "...a tremendous wave swept him forward to the rugged shore, where his skin would have been torn off him and all his bones broken, had not the bright-eyed goddess Athena put into his head to grab hold of a rock with both hands as he was swept in." In our days, we attribute such reactions to the fight-flight mechanisms of the brain's limbic system, the quick-and-dirty way of information processing.

Healing is also done by the gods. It can have simple forms, like when Odysseus finally stranded at the island of the Phaeacians, the goddess Athena "filled his eyes with sleep and sealed their lids – sleep to soothe his pain and utter weariness." It can also have the character of total regeneration, as happened to Odysseus' father, the former king Laertes, of whom Odysseus had noticed that "old age has hit him very hard":

> ... The Sicilian maid-servant bathed the great-hearted Laertes in his room and rubbed him with oil and put a cloak around him. Athene came and filled out the limbs of this shepherd of his people, making him seem taller and sturdier than before, so that as he stepped out of the bath his own son was amazed to see him looking like an immortal god (24, 363).

For a long time in Western civilization, we have taken the divine out of the healing, reducing the body to a machine-like organism, the brain to a molecular biological computer, and the subtle and spiritual dimension to the "wet mind" (Kosslyn & Koenig, 1992). Physics has lost all the security it had after the discoveries of the nineteenth century, and openly admits uncertainty as the base of its system, although even concepts like the speed of light seem to have lost their everlasting certainty (–> Nicosia). Neurobiology, however, still confines itself to the checks and balances of dopamine and serotonine, to the narrow boundaries of DNA-directed molecules. Our emotional household is similar to those of reptiles, managed by the limbic system in the brain. How different is the view of humans as energy beings!

References

Golas, T. (1971). The lazy mans' guide to enlightenment. Toronto: Bantam.
Kosslyn, S.M. & Koenig, O. (1992). *Wet mind. The new cognitive neuroscience*. New York. The Free Press.

4

Energy-based Healing: Foundations and Applications[1]

Martin Luthke and Linda Stein-Luthke

Foundations

The new, energy-based paradigm that is the foundation of energy psychology is not so new, after all. Many Eastern philosophers, mystics, and scientists have long espoused an understanding of creation as a sea of energies in motion, existing on many different levels of frequency. While leading-edge physicists may embrace a compatible view of reality, the predominant mind-set of our times is still based on an understanding of reality more closely related to the physics of the 19th century rather than the 21st. Although tempted, we will not launch into a dissertation on this complex subject. You may wish to refer to writers such as David Bohm, Michael Talbot, and Fred Alan Wolf[2] who have built a convincing case tracing the lines of thought – and demonstrating the convergence – of ancient Eastern and modern Western views of reality (–> Nicosia).

Review of Basic Premises

To lay a foundation of understanding for our purposes, a condensed review of some of the basic premises of metaphysical teachings is in order. Let us begin with a simple definition: What is metaphysics? The American Heritage Dictionary has the following to offer: "The branch of philosophy that systematically investigates the nature of first principles and problems of ultimate reality. Metaphysics includes the study of being (ontology) and, often, the study of the structure of the universe (cosmology)". For our purposes, we would add that we are not interested in metaphysics as a mental exercise motivated by a desire to fill books or gain tenure. We call our work "applied metaphysics": We strive to truly understand, apply and live the principles we espouse. The ultimate test of a philosophy is not its logical consistency and irrefutability, but a very simple question: Does it work?

As we have come to understand, there are a limited number of universal laws that are rather simple. (This is not to say that they are readily understood by the human mind). Here are some of the truths as we comprehend them:

1. There is order in the Universe. The infinite number of forms and appearances are but variations of an underlying theme. There is uniformity in diversity.
2. All of creation is vibration or patterned energy that can be perceived and described as light, sound, or a sensation of vibration.
3. There is an infinite number of frequencies that comprise the totality of creation.
4. The material world is just one level of reality. Just as the visible colors or audible tones are only segments of the full spectrum of light or sound, so is the material world only a segment of the totality of creation.
5. All of creation originates on the subtle planes. Material creation is a manifestation of subtle vibrations originating on the higher planes and then transformed into denser material vibrations (–> Eden & Feinstein, Nicosia). A good metaphor for this manifestation process is the transformation of H_2O from humidity to vapor to water to ice, a condensation or crystallization process.
6. "As above, so below" – as in heaven, so on earth. Macrocosm and microcosm are analogous to one another in their essential constitution, evolution and mode of operation. Again, there is uniformity in diversity.
7. Time and space are not what they seem to be. Our perception of time and space is bound to the human level of awareness. Once we transcend this level of awareness, the limits of time and space that appear so real to the human mind dissolve. (This is a vast and complicated topic, which we will set aside for the time being.)
8. All is connected to everything, and all is affected by everything. There is oneness, despite the illusion of separation (–> Handelsman).
9. Change is the order of the Universe. We are constantly changing and evolving, and that is true both for the macrocosm and the microcosm.

It is Time for a New Paradigm

We are living in a time of radical change. A characteristic of our times is the significant increase in higher-vibrational energies permeating our universe with ever-increasing intensity[3]. The influx of higher vibrations accelerates the frequencies prevalent on the earth plane. Consequently, the gap between material and non-material levels of vibration is diminishing. The veil that used to separate the two domains is thinning and becoming increasingly more permeable. Thus, more and more human beings are becoming aware of the multidimensional nature of reality. Concepts such as energy fields, auras, spirit communication, intuitive perception, healing energies, etc., are gradually entering mainstream consciousness.

A new view of reality demands changes on many levels, including the way we approach physical and emotional healing. When medicine discovered the microscopic levels of reality, such as the cell, genes, microbes, and bacteria, the practice of medicine had to change drastically. We are now at a similar juncture in the practice of the healing arts. We can no longer ignore the many dimensions of our being that transcend earth-plane thinking and perception. It is time to recognize that we are more than what, for a long time, we thought we were, specifically in the Western world (–> Handelsman). It is time to remember and honor the fact that we are multidimensional beings of Light having a human experience.

Toward a New Paradigm of Healing

Our work is about healing, and it is time to examine and define what this means from a metaphysical perspective. Healing simply means to shift the balance of energies within an energy field (human or otherwise) toward harmony and higher vibrations, or, conversely, to reduce the prevalence of disharmony and lower vibrations. As there are no "empty spaces" in an energy field, one shift goes hand in hand with the other. Having given this fundamental definition, we can move on to some basic points about healing:

1. All illness and dis-ease, be it mental, emotional or physical, is an expression of an energetic imbalance or disharmony (–> Stoler). As all manifestation steps down from the subtle to the denser levels of vibration, the presence of a disease indicates an imbalance on the subtle levels.
2. Healing is a manifestation of increased balance and harmony; as with all manifestations, it, too, originates on the subtle planes. There is no essential difference between physical, emotional, mental, or spiritual healing.
3. Higher levels of vibration are more harmonious and thus more healing than lower levels. Higher vibrations can be experienced as love, joy, peace, happiness, forgiveness, gratitude, bliss, etc. Lower vibrations are associated with the experience of anger, depression, fear, guilt, shame, greed, etc. The highest levels of vibration are customarily called the spiritual levels.

4. Effective healing occurs when a more harmonious energy field interacts with a less harmonious frequency, resulting in a transmutation from lower to higher frequency.
5. An effective healer is someone who channels or emits more harmonious energies and facilitates the transmutation process. Likewise, an effective healing agent is something that emanates more harmonious energies (such as an undisturbed natural environment), something we charge with thoughts of healing (such as a medication or a placebo), or something that contributes to a greater degree of balance (on the physical, emotional, mental, or spiritual level). Effective treatment aims to transform the barriers that were put in place between lower-vibrational energies (for instance, fears) and higher-vibrational energies such as trust or peace, so that the latter can transform the former.
6. Not all treatment is healing, and not all healing results from treatment. All we need to do to achieve healing is to allow the perfection that already exists on the highest levels of our being to "percolate" down to the level that holds the imbalance. Ultimately, all healing is self-healing.
7. All healing is possible. If we think of the physical, emotional, and mental bodies as clouds of "patterned" energies, there is virtually no limit to the creation of harmony. In other words, nothing is "written in stone," as all is in flux and constantly changing, similar to clouds in the sky.
8. We distinguish between healing and a "cure," i.e., the disappearance of pathological symptoms. Whether healing leads to a cure depends on many factors, such as a person's karmic agenda, that may be beyond comprehension for the human mind.
9. Healing may take many forms; it is unique for each individual and situation. The healing process occurs on many levels simultaneously. Although we often have preconceived ideas about the desirable outcome, our human minds are not equipped to accurately judge the outcome of a healing process as "success" or "failure."
10. Healing is an ongoing process. Just as our physical cells are continuously breaking down and continuously being repaired, so is energetic healing a never-ending process. The notion that you are either healthy (i.e., health defined as the absence of any diagnosable disease), or sick (defined as the presence of a diagnosable disease) is simplistic and mistaken. Emotional, physical, or energetic health is a matter of degree, not an either-or dichotomy.
11. Given humanity's level of evolution at this point in history, all of us carry a certain degree of imbalance and disharmony, reflected in a disturbance of the flow of subtle energies throughout the human energy field. Thus, all of us could benefit from healing, on one level or another.

As we stated earlier, our universe and all that is within it are moving toward a higher level of vibration, which makes higher-vibrational frequencies ever more readily accessible. Future advances in the healing arts will be achieved most effectively by using those energies in a systematic manner that hold the greatest healing power, such as love, joy, peace, forgiveness, gratitude, bliss, and other spiritual frequencies (–> Eden & Feinstein, Friedman, Handelsman, Hover-Kramer).

We predict that during this period of transition, we will be observing more and more illnesses and dis-eases that will not respond well to treatment limited to gross material frequencies, such as the prescription of pharmaceuticals. As the health care establishment will find itself increasingly overwhelmed and impotent, practitioners who use higher-vibrational approaches to healing will be increasingly in demand.

Applications

In the foregoing paragraphs we outlined our understanding of the nature of reality as essentially energetic. However, we are not interested in metaphysics as a mere intellectual exercise; as the saying goes, "nothing is as practical as a good theory". If metaphysical principles contain some truth, they should also bear fruit in practical applications. One such application is Psychoenergetic Healing, an energy-based healing method we will describe briefly in the subsequent paragraphs.

Psychoenergetic Healing: A Brief Introduction

Searching for Better Ways: Can you imagine the practice of medicine before the invention of X-ray machines or microscopes? Would you want to refer someone to a doctor who refuses to consider anything that is not visible to the naked eye? The field of psychotherapy, as it is taught in graduate school today, can be likened to the practice of medicine based on a 19th-century view of the world. While there are many fine, traditionally trained psychotherapists out there, psychotherapy is still very much a "hit or miss" endeavor.

We propose that the practice of psychotherapy (and healing in general) cannot advance significantly without a shift in paradigm, i.e., a fundamental reorientation. Within the established paradigm there is no convincing explanation for phenomena such as the placebo effect, "spontaneous" remissions, psychosomatic illnesses, miracle cures, healing through prayer or touch, etc. As long as the premises of the healing arts are based on a material or mental – rather than energetic – understanding of reality, their efforts resemble attempts to assemble a million-piece puzzle without an idea of the larger picture. In the final analysis, scientific "progress" based on a misunderstanding is like getting better at "barking up the wrong tree."

Psychoenergetic Healing is based on a "new" paradigm that is compatible with ancient wisdom teachings as well as modern sciences. Leading-edge physicists have now come to insights similar to those of ancient mystics: All there is, all matter and all of Creation, is patterned energy, vibrating to specific frequencies that distinguish one manifestation of energy from another (–> Nicosia).

What is Psychoenergetic Healing?

All psychological manifestations, such as thoughts, feelings, and behavior patterns, are also patterned energy. Effective psychological healing, regardless of the method or technique, occurs when there is a change in the basic energies that charge our feelings, thoughts, memories and habits (–> Eden & Feinstein, Hover-Kramer). While all psychotherapeutic methods are intended to produce such healing, most do not target the energetic level directly.

Psychoenergetic Healing takes into account the fact that human beings are not only physical, emotional, and mental beings, but also, and most essentially, spiritual beings. This truth is not a mere statement of faith; it can be experienced in a direct, tangible manner. No matter what names or interpretations we prefer, a spiritual, healing energy, or Light, can be accessed by all human beings regardless of our belief systems and can be utilized effectively for healing on all levels.

The practitioner of Psychoenergetic Healing uses a variety of techniques that affect the mental and emotional energies on a fundamental level, thus going directly to the source of the individual's discomfort. While going to the core of the matter may be a frightening thought to many, it is actually a very healing, safe, efficient, and effective method that does not require the unbuffered reliving of traumatic memories or painful feelings.

What Happens in a Typical Session?

What happens in a session is very much guided by the individual's issues and needs, making each session a unique experience. Most sessions include elements of traditional "talking therapy," expanded upon with work performed in an altered state of consciousness we call "Inner Space"4 where the client can experience the richness of his or her multidimensional nature. Facilitated by the therapist, the client achieves a heightened state of consciousness in which he or she may become aware of colors, images, thoughts, memories, feelings, or physical sensations, such as pain, heat, weight, etc. The range of experiences in Inner Space is virtually unlimited and may include an awareness of past lives, other dimensions, the presence of beings of Light, and more.

While each client has a different experience, all are able to perceive the flow of energies within. These inner perceptions then guide the course of the healing work. Using what could be called a "psychological X-ray technique," the client can become aware of the core issue and then observe the process of healing on an energetic level as it is occurring. Although getting in touch with painful feelings or experiences may cause some temporary discomfort, an energetic shift and tangible relief can often be felt within minutes. Because the client has control over his or her Inner Space and all therapeutic interventions are guided by the client's inner perceptions, this approach to healing is experienced as empowering and safe.

Who Can Benefit From Psychoenergetic Healing?

Clients of all ages, including children and adolescents, have benefited greatly from Psychoenergetic Healing, regardless of their belief systems or prior experience with energy-based healing. Psychoenergetic Healing can be an effective approach regardless of the presenting problem, as all thoughts, memories, feelings, and habits exist as "patterned" energies and can be treated as such. Psychoenergetic Healing has been successfully applied to a wide variety of psychological issues, including anger, fear, depression, addictions, sexual issues, co-dependency, low self-esteem, traumatic experiences, grieving and loss, relationship problems, etc.

Since working in Inner Space transcends the limits of time and space, the healing that can be accomplished in such a manner extends far beyond the domain of classical psychotherapy. For instance, we frequently work through reverberations of past-life trauma and their effect on a client's current life situation. In addition, the same methods of energy-based healing can be successfully used for the healing of psychosomatic illnesses, pain, and a wide array of physical complaints.

Synopsis

"The times they are a'changing..." At this point in the evolution of consciousness more and more people in the Western world embrace age-old (and very modern) views that can be summarized most simply in a few fundamental insights: "All of creation is vibration" and "all manifestation originates on the subtle planes." Applied to the area of healing, it follows that all illness – and all healing – originate on the subtle planes. Psychoenergetic Healing is one method of accessing the higher planes for healing purposes in a systematic and effective manner. As we shift our collective consciousness away from the limitations of the gross-material plane and open our minds to the realization that we are multi-dimensional beings of Light, the healing arts are bound to change accordingly.

Notes

1. ©2001 Institute of Psychoenergetic Healing; P.O. Box 516, Chagrin Falls, OH 44022, USA; expansion@u-r-light.com; www.u-r-light.com; phone/fax: USA-440-338-3370.
2. For details, see our reading suggestions at the end of this article.
3. Scientific evidence for this statement is discussed in Gregg Braden's book Awakening to Zero Point.
4. A more complete definition and explanation of the term "Inner Space" can be found in Beyond Psychotherapy: Introduction to Psychoenergetic Healing by Martin F. Luthke, Ph.D. & Linda Stein-Luthke.

References

Bohm, D., & Hiley, B.J. (1993). *The undivided universe: An ontological interpretation of quantum theory.* London; New York: Routledge.
Braden, G. (1997). *Awakening to zero point.* Bellevue, WA: Radio Bookstore Press.
Hunt, V. (1996). *Infinite mind: Science of the human vibrations of consciousness.* Malibu, CA: Malibu Publishing.
Liderbach, D. (1989). *The numinous universe.* New York: Paulist Press.
Luthke, M., & Stein-Luthke, L. (2001). Beyond psychotherapy: *Introduction to Psychoenergetic Healing.* Chagrin Falls, OH: Expansion Publishing.
Mindell, A. (2000). *Quantum mind: The edge between physics and psychology.* Portland, OR: Lao Tse Press.
Talbot, M. (1991). *The holographic universe.* New York: HarperCollins.
– (1992). *Mysticism and the new physics.* London: Arkana.
Wolf, F. A. (1991). *The eagle's quest: A physicist's search for truth in the heart of the shamanic world.* New York: Summit Books.

Wolf, F.A. (1994). *The dreaming universe: A mind-expanding journey into the realm where psyche and physics meet.* New York: Simon & Schuster.

Wolf, F.A. (1999). *The spiritual universe: one physicist's vision of spirit, soul, matter, and self.* Portsmouth, NH: Moment Point.

– (2001). *Mind into matter: A new alchemy of science and spirit.* Portsmouth, NH: Moment Point.

5

Integrative Healing: An Energy and Spiritual Approach[1]

Phil Friedman

Integrative healing from an energy and spiritual perspective (IHES) is an approach I developed that integrates a wide variety of theories, tools, and techniques in the energy and spiritual arena. Using intuition and assessment tools, I select from these approaches and employ whatever tools work best for a particular client. Integrative healing from an energy and spiritual perspective (IHES) is an expansion and refinement of ideas published in a series of articles on Integrative psychotherapy (IT); Integrative marital and family therapy (IMFT) and Integrative assessment (IA) dating back 20 years (Friedman, 1980a, 1980b, 1981, 1982a, 1982b, 1982c). In addition the integrative psychospiritual (IPS) approach described in Creating Well-Being: The Healing Path to Love, Peace, Self-esteem, and Happiness (Friedman, 1989), the Coaching Workbook for Creating, Understanding and Enhancing Well-Being (Friedman, 1999) and an article on integrative healing and the psychological acupressure techniques (Friedman, 2000) have added additional creative ideas to this therapeutic approach.

Integrative Meta-Model

The way in which various schools of healing in general, and energy and spiritual therapy in particular, select different concepts, techniques and roles is somewhat like the story of the 10 blind men and the elephant who each touch different parts of the elephant. Each theorist/therapist perceives the elephant through his/her own selective and particular lens. Each "sees" a different part of the elephant and no one sees or reports on the nature of the whole elephant. In order to see the whole elephant, I developed a meta-model.

PHIL FRIEDMAN

The earlier set of articles on Integrative healing and therapy was based on a three dimensional meta-model, emphasizing structure, focus and category. The focus dimension was divided into intrapersonal, interpersonal and transpersonal; the structure dimension was divided into concept, technique, and role, and the category dimension was divided into humanities, economic, political-legal-judicial, social-educational, philosophical-ethical, spiritual-religious, pure science, applied science and recreation-nature. I also referred to the three dimensional meta-model as a three dimensional "matrix of metaphors" because it organizes the major metaphors in the field of healing and psychotherapy into a 3x3x9 matrix (Diagram 1). The point of view presented in those earlier papers is that the meta-model or matrix of concepts, techniques and roles can be used to guide the Integrative healer in his/her transactions with clients.

Integrative Psychotherapy

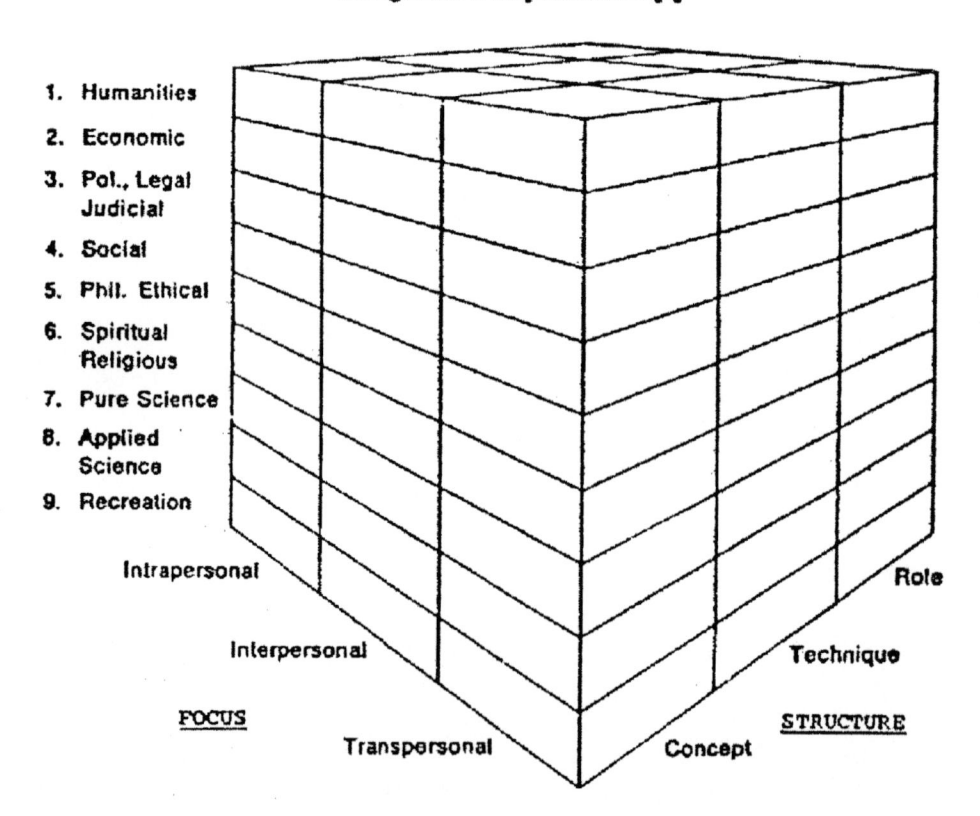

1. Humanities
2. Economic
3. Pol., Legal Judicial
4. Social
5. Phil. Ethical
6. Spiritual Religious
7. Pure Science
8. Applied Science
9. Recreation

Intrapersonal
Interpersonal
Transpersonal

FOCUS

Concept
Technique
Role

STRUCTURE

An attempt to see the intrapersonal dimension of the whole meta-model in the energy and spiritual healing and therapy field is seen in Table 1. A comprehensive and integrated view of the energy and spiritual healing field encompasses all these metaphors. By being aware of the entire map of the territory (matrix of metaphors), an energy and spiritual theorist/therapist/healer can more wisely choose the ones that will benefit his/her approach.

Table 1. Intrapersonal dimensions of the meta-model
(Examples of the matrix of metaphors for energy and spiritual healing and therapies)

CATEGORY	CONCEPT
1. Humanities	Scripts, (body) language, imagining inner dialoguing, journaling, drama, play, bibliotherapy beliefs/attitudes, affects/feelings
2. Economic	Contracts, rules, solutions bargaining, negotiating
3. Political-Legal-Judicial	Sabotage, struggle, battle, fight, conflict, destroy, resolve in prison (or free from), power (ful), weak, triggers, destructive-constructive
4. Social and Educational	Boundaries, learnings (priority) blocks, communicating, restructuring, teaching, educating, releasing, holding conscious, subconscious, unconscious memory
5. Philosophical-Ethical	Opposites/polarities (integration of) positive/negative, yin-yang, light-dark, higher-lower, purpose vision, mission
6. Spiritual-Religious	Forgiveness, miracles, healing, grace, spirit, soul, gratitude,

divine, blessings, unconditional love, acceptance, prayer
Self, Atman, God, One, essence center, inner guidance/intuition
unity, wholeness, interconnected
reunion, meditation, peace, intention, grievances, judgments, levels of consciousness, faith, service, superconscious, faithful servant, aura, meridians, chakras, subtle energy

7. Pure Science
(mathematics, physics, biology, archeology)

Algorithms, templates, grids
thought & energy fields, perturbations, energy/bioenergy,
cellular, polarity reversals, charge, neuroprints
implicate/explicate order, matrix
inertial, levels, core-deep-surface
toxins, holons, forces, catalyst
coherence, resonance, bilateral
balance, imbalance, codes
structure, function, dysfunction
respiration (breath),

8. Applied Science
(medicine, ecology, geography, computers)

Cure, healing, growth, development, wounds, fracture, trauma, boundaries, programs, barometer, experimental, diagnostic, assessment, percussing/tapping acupoints, SUDS, voice technology, tonify, sedate

9. Recreation and Nature

River, flow(s), dam, damming
switching, zip (up and down),
coaching, path, journey

Assessment Tools

One of the key aspects of my earlier work was an emphasis on using assessment tools to track changes over time and also to assess outcome. (Friedman, 1982a, 1982b) Each of the scales I use has to be relatively short and easy to score, understand and record so that the results can be immediately given to the client. I have developed five assessment tools of my own, the Friedman Well-Being Scale, Friedman Belief Scale, Friedman Quality of Life Scale, Friedman Affect Scale and the Friedman Personal/Spiritual Growth Scale (Friedman, 1992, 1994, 1996, 1997, 1998, 2001). These scales are used regularly along with others such as a modified version of the SCL-90 (Derogatis et.al, 1976) and the Bradburn Well-Being Scale (Bradburn, 1969) to track change more easily over time. In addition I frequently use the PAI (Morey, 1991) and NEO-PIR (Costa and McCrae, 1978) clinical and personality inventories, to track change from the beginning of the healing process to later in the healing process.

Balance: Cognitive, Affective and Energy Dimensions

One of the major findings of extensive research with these assessment scales is that measures of cognitive-affective balance correlate highly with measures of well-being, self-esteem, and life satisfaction. Cognitive-affective balance probably correlates with energy balance as well but there are currently few empirical measures to assess energy balance (–> Narvaez). It is highly likely that changes in energy balance effected by energy and spiritual healing and therapies simultaneously effect changes in cognitive-affective balance.

Psychospiritual Frame of Reference
Grievances and Forgiveness

In *Creating Well-Being: The Healing Path to Love, Peace, Self-esteem, and Happiness* (1989), I discuss 12 core principles of well-being from a psychospiritual perspective that is heavily influenced by an extensive study of *A Course in Miracles* (1975) and yoga. The key concept in ACIM is forgiveness and two key lessons among the 365 lessons summarize its application: first, that "forgiveness is the key to happiness" (Workbook, page 214), and second, that underneath all problems is one key problem which is a grievance held against oneself or someone else, and one key solution which is forgiveness. "Unforgiveness", is a grievance or judgment that separates us from our true Self (–> Handelsman). In *A Course in Miracles* this Self is seen as synonymous with God, i.e., the God within. Separation from the Self, in turn, generates fear. Forgiveness allows us to release our grievances or judgments and returns us to our true essence, which is love. Anger, guilt, sadness, resentment, shame, and hurt all cover up fear which is a call for help or love. Fear, separateness, and grievances all represent the state of consciousness called the "ego". Thus the path of healing is clear: fear (the ego), is calling for a return to love (the Self).

However, we learn in *A Course in Miracles* that this shift in perspective from fear to love, grievances to forgiveness, the ego to Self cannot be accomplished alone. It is only under the guidance of the Higher Self or Inner Voice that this shift in consciousness can take place. The role of the healer and therapist is to continuously listen within to his or her own Higher Self/Inner Voice for inner guidance, when working with a client (–> Feinstein).

Positive Psychology and Inner Worth

From yoga I learned two basic teachings: "God dwells within you as you" , and "See God in each other." Translated into energy/spiritual healing language, this means that the inner core of each person is divine, holy, blessed, light, love, strong, balanced, well and worthy and that we can learn to see these qualities in each other. Healing can be seen as a shift in consciousness from darkness to light, from grievances to forgiveness and from fear to love. In energy terms this means there is shift from imbalance to balance. However, it is also clear that the true nature of a human being is light, love, holiness, divinity, strength, worthiness, balance, blessedness and well-being (–> Luthke). This is in alignment with the recent emphasis in positive psychology by Mihaly Csikszentmihalyi and Martin Seligman (2000), Ed Diener (2001) and others that focuses on peoples stengths, joy, love, resourcefulness, happiness and well-being.

The Two Paths

Early in therapy I clarify a concept which I call the 2 paths: i.e., the path of love and the path of fear; the path of harmony and the path of conflict; the path of forgiveness and the path of unforgiveness; the path of positive attitudes/beliefs and the path of negative attitudes/beliefs; the path of peace and the path of anxiety; the path of choice and the path of emotional reactivity; the path of self-empowerment and the path of self-disempowerment; the path of energy flowing smoothly and in balance and the path of energy disruption/ blockage and imbalance; the path of the Self and the path of the ego. In my office there are two diagrams that visually demonstrate these paths, so that clients can readily grasp the idea. Clients are then introduced to the idea that they can choose between these two paths. I explain that each path has different consequences.

Integrative Healing: An Energy and Spiritual Approach

Current Issues in Meridian-based Healing and Therapy

<u>Twenty Key Questions</u>
Differences among the meridian approaches can be identified by the answers to the following 20 key questions:

1. How many meridians have to be tapped or touched?
2. How important is the sequence of the points tapped or touched?
3. How important is it to diagnose the sequence of points used rather than using one all encompassing tapping/touching sequence?
4. How important is it to tap the meridian points rather than touch the points?
5. How important are the affirmations used while tapping/touching meridian points?
6. Does this importance increase or decrease depending on the specific wording of these affirmations such as the use of releasing vs. enhancing affirmations and phrases?
7. How important is muscle testing in the approach?
8. How important is the use of breathing techniques?
9. How important is the role of forgiveness in particular?
10. How important is the role of spirituality in general?
11. How important is the therapist's intention while using these three approaches?
12. How important is the client's receptivity to the approach?
13. How important is it to use psychological reversal techniques?
14. How important is the role of the subconscious, unconscious and or superconscious mind?
15. How important are belief structures in using the technique?
16. How important are cues, anchors, phrases, and instant/rapid triggers?
17. How important is it to tap one or both of the bilateral meridians?
18. How beneficial is it to cross over from one side of the bilateral meridian to the other?
19. How important are the particular metaphors used to explain these approaches/techniques?
20. How important is the use of the meridians themselves?

<u>Techniques in Integrative Energy and Spiritual Healing</u>
I draw upon many techniques in an Integrative Energy and Spiritual Healing approach. They can be classified into 6 categories:

A. Meridian Energy Tapping/Holding Techniques
   1. Thought Field Therapy (Callahan) or Energy Tapping (Gallo)
   2. Emotional Freedom Techniques (Craig)
   3. Negative Affect Erasing Method (Gallo)
   4. Be Set Free Fast (Nims)
   5. Rapidly Integrated Transformation Technique (Beck)
   6. Miracle Acupressure Tapping Technique (Friedman)
   7. Touch And Breathe (Diepold)
   8. Tap And Soft Touch Energy Technique (Friedman)

B. Meridian and Chakra Holding and Releasing Techniques
   9. Tapas Acupressure Technique (Fleming)
   10. Acupressure Chakra Technique (Friedman)
   11. Spiritual Kinesthesiology (Mountrose and Mountrose)
   12. Holographic Repatterning (Wordsworth)

C. Chakra Holding and Releasing Techniques
   13. Matrix Work (Clinton)
   14. Forgiveness And Chakra Energy Shift (Friedman)
   15. Light Imagery and Grateful Heart Technique (Friedman)
   16. Pranic Healing (Kok Sui)

D. Creating and Intending Techniques
   17. Creating, Allowing and Receiving Technique (Friedman)
   18. Creating and Manifesting What You Want (Friedman)
   19. Technologies for Creating (Fritz)
   20. Science of Deliberate Creation-(Abraham-Hicks)
   21. Soul's Intention (Young-Sowers)

E. Meditation, Imagery, Relaxation, Trance, Hypnosis (MIRTH) Techniques
   22. MIRTH Techniques (Friedman)

F. Inspiring and Imparting Wisdom Techniques
   23. Angelic Messenger Cards (Young-Sowers)
   24. A Course in Miracles Lessons (Foundation for Inner Peace)
   25. Attitudinal Healing Principles (Jampolsky).

Case Study

Brenda (name changed) was a 28 year old and single when she came in to see me. She had been raped 3 years earlier and in addition believed she had been molested by her father when she was a child. She was experiencing intense family problems, mainly with her father, and work conflicts with her colleagues. At intake Brenda had a stress score of 115 (22 is average), a well-being score of 40 (63 out of 100 is average), an emotional stability score of 43 (65 out of 100 is average), an affect balance score of 42 (65 out of 100 is average), a cognitive balance score of 60 (80 out of 100 is average) and a self-worth score of 38 (62 out of 100 is average). Her NEO-PIR personality score on neuroticism was 69 which was almost 2 standard deviations from the mean of 50 while her depression, anxiety and vulnerability scores of 71, 70 and 72 were all 2 standard deviations from the mean of 50. Her PAI clinical scores on thought confusion, traumatic stress, identity and negative relations of 81, 77, 74 and 72 respectively were 2 standard deviations from the mean of 50 while her affective anxiety, affective depression and hypervigilance scores of 68, 66 and 66 on the PAI respectively were over 1 1/2 standard deviations from the mean of 50.

In addition to substantial sadness and depression Brenda was reporting a lot of anger and some guilt. She also indicated that she believed she was defective, helpless and powerless, imperfect, sickly and unhealthy, and a victim, who was not in control, couldn't identify or express her feelings and would always struggle in life. Brenda was moderately pessimistic but quite attractive and mildly hopeful.

At the end of the intake session I asked her the "one question/question", i.e., what was the one most important question she would like an answer to if she could get it. Brenda's "one question/question" was "will I ever get better and how long will it take". I said 'yes' she would get better and probably within 3 to 6 months though it could be shorter or longer. Then we set the 'miracle goals' for 3, 6 and 12 months using an imaginary 'magic wand". Her 'miracle goals' were to decrease her fear of being hurt and injured; decrease her depression, anger, guilt, sense of betrayal, disgust and fatigue; learn to identify and express her feelings; increase her self-confidence in general and especially at work; be more effectively and appropriately assertive; be more forgiving to herself and her family; increase her trust of strangers and generally increase her overall peace, contentment, joy, happiness, emotional stability and well-being.

At the end of the first session we did the "Psychological Uplifter" exercise. While she rubbed the sore spot, Brenda said the following statements three times each:

1. "Even though I have this depression, anger, hurt, work and family problems, I accept myself deeply and profoundly, and I am a good person."
2. "I love myself unconditionally despite my problems and limitations"
3. "I am entitled to miracles".

I gave her a handout of this exercise and encouraged her to practice it 10 to 20 times a day for the next few weeks. I also asked her to take one step toward reaching any of her miracle goals. Early in therapy I recommended that Brenda read Jerry Jampolsky's, "Let of Letting Go of Fear" and my "Creating Well-Being" book, both of which emphazises the healing power of forgiveness and letting go of judgments. The main integrative energy and spiritual therapy techniques I used with her during therapy were: the Miracle Acupressure Tapping Technique (MATT) which includes a forgiveness module; the Tapas Acupressure Technique (TAT); the Acupressure Chakra Technique (ACT); the Forgiveness and Chakra Energy Technique (FACES); the Creating, Allowing, Receiving Technique (CART); the MIRTH (meditation, imagery, relaxation, trance and hypnosis) technique and Spiritual Kinesthesiology (SK). The TAT and SK techniques were developed by Tapas Fleming and Phillip and Jane Mountrose respectively. All the others were developed by me, though some are variations of other well known techniques.

By the 8th session Brenda's had a stress score of 23 (22 is average), a well-being score of 65 (63 is average), an emotional stability score of 65 (65 is average), an affect balance score of 94 (65 out of 100 is average), a cognitive balance score of 85 (80 out of 100 is average) and a self-worth score of 63 (62 out of 100 is average). In addition her NEO-PIR personality scores on neuroticism, depression, anxiety and vulnerability were respectively 50, 50, 53 and 49, with a mean of 50, later in treatment. Her PAI clinical scores on thought confusion, traumatic stress, identity, negative relations, affective anxiety, affective depression and hypervigilance were respectively 49, 58, 47, 50, 60, 42 and 48, with a mean of 50, later in treatment. On almost all these measures she had decreased 1.5 to 2 standard deviations.

Brenda was much more optimistic and hopeful. She was much more assertive and self-confident. She was functioning very well at work and had received a substantial raise. Brenda was engaged to be married and at peace with her family, especially her father. She was relaxed, happy, loving and joyful and no longer fearful of strangers. Healing and therapy continued for a little while longer to further enhance these very positive gains.

Summary
The integrative healing approach from an energy and spiritual perspective (IHES) presented in this chapter draws from many wonderful theories, tools, and techniques with

the common aim of helping clients shift from the path of fear, conflict, grievances, unforgiveness, negativity, unhappiness and energy imbalance to a path of love, peace, compassion, forgiveness, happiness and energy balance. In this integrative healing approach from an energy and spiritual perspective, empirically-derived assessment tools, client self-reports, muscle testing and the therapist's intuition are all utilized along with a wide variety of techniques. In addition, the healer's relationship with the client is seen as a powerful healing force as the client is in fear and calling for help and love (–> Beaudoin, Sise, Weil).

Note

1. The material in this article is elaborated in more detail in a chapter called Integrative energy and spiritual therapy (IEST) to be published in Energy Therapy in Energy Psychology edited by Fred Gallo, Ph.D (2001, in press).

References

Beck, M. (1999). *Rapidly integrated transformation technique.* Tucson: Self-published.
Bradburn, N. (1969). *The structure of psychological well-being.* Chicago, ILL.: Bantam.
Callahan, R. (1996). *Thought field therapy and trauma: Treatment and theory.* Indian Wells, CA: Self-published.
Callahan, R. & Turbo, R. (2001).*Tapping the healer within using thought field therapy to instantly conquer your fears, anxieties, and emotional distress.* Chicago, IL: NTC/Contemporary.
Clinton, N., (2000). *Matrix manual.* Princeton, NJ: Self-published.
Costa, P. and McCrae, R. (1978). *NEO-PIR .* Odessa, Fla.: Psychological Assessment Resources.
Craig, G. & Fowlie, A. (1995). *Emotional freedom techniques: The manual.* Sea Ranch, CA: Self-published.
Diepold, J.(1998). *Touch and breath: An alternate treatment approach with meridian based psychotherapies.* New Jersey: Self-published.
Foundation for Inner Peace. (1975). *A course in miracles.* Glen Ellen, CA: Foundation for Inner Peace.
Friedman, P. (1980a). Integrative psychotherapy. In R. Herink (Ed.) *Psychotherapy handbook.* New York: New American Library.
Friedman, P. (1980b). *An integrative approach to the creation and alleviation of disease within the family.* Family Therapy, 7, (3), 179 to 195.
Friedman, P. (1981). *Integrative family therapy.* Family Therapy, 8, (3), 171 to 178.

Friedman, P. (1982a). Assessment tools and procedures in integrative psychotherapy. In A. Gurman (Ed.). *Questions and answers in the practice of family therapy.* New York: Guilford Press. pp. 46 to 49.

Friedman, P. (1982b). *An integrative approach to the assessment and outcome of psychotherapy.* Paper presented at the National Community Mental Health Center Conference, New York. pp. 1-18.

Friedman, P. (1982c). *Multiple roles of the integrative marital therapist.* Family Therapy, 9 (2), 109 to 118.

Friedman, P. (1989). *Creating well-being: The healing path to love, peace, self-esteem and happiness.* Saratoga, CA: R and E Publishers.

Friedman, P. (1990). *Creating well-being* audio cassette album. Plymouth Meeting, PA: Foundation for Energy and Spiritual Healing and Well-Being.

Friedman, P. (1992). *Friedman well-being scale and professional manual*. Palo Alto, CA: Mind Garden,

Friedman, P. (1994). *Friedman belief scale and research manual.* Plymouth Meeting, PA: Foundation for Energy and Spiritual Healing and Well-Being.

Friedman, P. (1996). *Friedman quality of life scale.* Plymouth Meeting, PA: Foundation for Energy and Spiritual Healing and Well-Being.

Friedman, P. (1997). *Friedman well-being scale and Friedman quality of life scale.* In Proceedings of International Society of Quality of Life Studies Conference and Annual Meeting. Washington D.C.: International Society of Quality of Life Studies.

Friedman, P. (1998). *Friedman affect scale.* Plymouth Meeting, PA: Foundation for Energy and Spiritual Healing and Well-Being.

Friedman, P. (1999). *Coaching workbook for creating, understanding and enhancing your well-being.* Plymouth Meeting, PA: Foundation for Energy and Spiritual Healing and Well-Being.

Friedman, P. (2000). *Integrative healing and the psychological acupressure techniques.* In Selected papers of the 7th annual Association of Specialized Kinesthesiology-United States conference and annual meeting. Philadelphia, PA: Association of Specialized Kinesthesiology-United States.

Friedman, P. (2001). *Friedman personal/spiritual growth scale.* Plymouth Meeting, PA: Foundation for Energy and Spiritual Healing and Well-Being.

Friedman, P. (2001). *Integrative energy and spiritual therapy.* In F. Gallo (Ed.) Energy Therapy in Energy Psychology, in press.

Fritz, R. (1991). *Creating.* New York: Fawcett Columbine.

Gallo, F. (2000). *Energy diagnostic and treatment methods.* New York: W.W. Norton.

Gallo, F. & Vincenzi, H. (2000). *Energy tapping.* Oakland, CA: New Harbinger.

Gallo, F. (1998). *Energy psychology: Explorations at the interface of energy, cognition, behavior, and health.* Boca Raton, FL: CRC.

Hicks, E. & J. (1992). *Abraham Speaks: A New Beginning I.* San Antonio, Texas: Abraham-Hicks.

Jampolsky, G. (1979). *Love is letting go of fear.* Berkeley, CA: Celestial Arts.

Jampolsky, G. (1999). *Forgiveness.* Hillsboro, OR: Beyond Words.

Mountrose, P. & Mountrose, J. (2000b). *Getting thru to your soul.* Sacramento, CA: Holistic Communications.

Nims, L. (2000). *Be set free fast training manual.* Orange, CA: Self-published.

Woodsworth, C. (1994). *Holographic repatterning: The Fundamentals*. Scottsdale, Arizona: Wordsworth Productions.

Woodsworth, C. (1994). *Holographic repatterning: Transforming unconscious patterns.* Scottsdale, Arizona: Wordsworth Productions.

Young-Sowers, M. (1993). *Angelic messenger cards.* Walpole, New Hampshire: Stillpoint.

Young-Sowers, M. (1984). *Agartha.* Walpole, New Hampshire: Stillpoint.

Young-Sowers, M. (2000). *Soul's intention.* Walpole, New Hampshire: Stillpoint.

6

The Monopoly Theory of the Universe and the Three Steps of Healing

Alan Handelsman

NOTE: *One of the things I consider myself good at is saying what I mean. However, I have failed here in a significant way. When I refer to "man," or "he" in this article, I never mean simply man or he. I mean man and/or woman, and he and/or she. Please remember that as you read.*

This article is not written as truth. Just as a possibility. After you read it, you may conclude (possibly with good reason) that I have much too much time on my hands. Maybe so. But as I read books that try to explain the universe and its meaning, I start thinking while I'm waiting for the light to change to green while driving to work. And I think about other ways of looking at the problem of meaning, and man's place in the universe. This is one possible explanation for one possible view. So... what if the universe is something like this:

> Picture yourself at a card table. One of those that folds up when not being used. There are three others sitting on the other three sides of the table. You are there to play a game. The old game of Monopoly. You open the box, and start setting up the game. The first order of business is choosing a banker. The next order of business is deciding (and sometimes fighting over) what "piece" you want to be. The piece you choose gives you some of your personality during the game.

In my house growing up we lost some of the pieces so soon that we only ever had a few to play with, so I cannot remind you of all of them. I do remember the race car, the top hat, the Scotty dog, the ship, the shoe, and the iron. While the ship was cool and very sleek, my favorite was always the race car. This, I believe, did not signify my quest for speed or thrills as much as the fact that moving the car from one space to another did not require lifting it. It was the piece one could move smoothly, with the least amount of effort and resistance.

So now the money is distributed, the pieces are on the board, and the game begins. In your heart, you know that no matter what happens or who wins at the end of the game, you put the board away, and nothing will change.

So why play? For amusement. For time spent playing the game goes by a bit faster. Because there is diversion with no risk. From the time before the game begins until the time after it ends, nothing will really change. No matter what happens on the board, the players' lives will not change in the hours of the game. Not really. The purpose of the game? Certainly not to make money, because Monopoly money cannot be spent outside of the game. For fame? Who, even among the four players, will remember the outcome the next day? For evolution or growth? While I expect someone to write a book called, Everything I Needed to Know I Learned While Playing Monopoly, I am not sure the rest of us were paying that much attention. Maybe we are playing simply to have fun. To enjoy the playing of the game itself. Just that. Just maybe.

Now the pieces start moving around the board. As we identify with the pieces, we get more and more involved with the moves of the game. The pieces buy, sell, and trade property. We, as pieces, make money and lose money. We advance, and sometimes get stuck. We go to jail, we win beauty contests, we make decisions, and live with the consequences. There usually comes a point when we begin to forget that this is simply a game. We get very emotionally involved. We begin to believe that when we make money we are rich... that when we lose money we are poor... that when we win a contest, we've earned it by something we've done... that when we go to jail, we are no longer free. We believe that when we take a chance, we are risking something. And we begin to fear. We fear that we will fail. And maybe most of all, we fear the end of the game, and what it will bring.

We also get angry at the other pieces on the board. Without those others, it would be smooth sailing (or racing) for us. "Why did the hat have to put that hotel on Kentucky Avenue?" we ask. "If only I'd gotten there first!" we mutter under our breath.

We have forgotten that we are the player as well as the piece. We have forgotten that our moves mean a lot in the context of the game, but in the player's context, our moves mean next to nothing. Our moves serve no purpose other than to amuse the player. We have forgotten who we really are.

Let's move back from the perspective of the piece to the view of the player. We, as the player, enjoy playing the game. Enjoy getting involved in the moves of our pieces. The fact that the pieces can make mistakes, and the worst that can happen is that we lose a game that is only for fun anyway, makes it that much more fun. We can take more chances with our pieces. We can even enjoy the anger and fear and despair and joy and resentment and hostility and tears and victories and grief and defeats and peace and strivings and setbacks of our pieces, because we know that as players, we are more than the emotions our pieces feel. We are more than our decisions and actions. We are more than our bank balance. And we are even more than the game itself.

When our piece goes to jail, and we have to wait three turns before we can escape, the piece feels trapped, but the player says, "Good! Now I can go to the bathroom, and then get a sandwich!" For the piece, jail means restriction. For the player, jail means freedom! Depending on your perspective, the same event or situation can have different meanings, even opposite meanings. The event itself is meaningless, until you look at it from a particular perspective. If you know that you have different perspectives available, you can then choose the meaning you want the event to have at any particular time. You can even change the meaning as time passes and the circumstances change.

This is not to say that the game is not real. This is only saying that the game isn't the only thing that's real. Think of a time when you could not go to work because of an injury or illness. With this extra time you had, maybe you were able to think through some ideas that were only vaguely formulated until then, or you read a book, or finished a long delayed home project. So, during the time of your recuperation, were you less free because you were restricted from going to work, or more free because you were able to accomplish tasks that you couldn't have until then? Is there a "right" answer to that question?

Have you ever cursed yourself for not leaving the house in time to get where you were going, and before you leave receive an important telephone call that you would have missed if you'd left on time? Sometimes it is difficult to label an event or action as good or bad until more information is known, or another perspective is gained. Maybe, at least until the game is over, it is unnecessary to label any one move as good or bad.

At this time in the game the pieces have lost the connection with the player. And as a player, a curious thing happens. When the piece forgets who it really is, a cloud appears on top of it. Imagine playing the game, and every now and then, there is such a thick cloud over your piece that you cannot move it. As much as you look for it, and want the best for it, and care, you cannot locate it until the piece itself remembers who is really doing the moving. As the player in this situation, there is nothing you can do without the cooperation of your piece.

The relationship between the player and the piece is not as much one of master and servant as of teammates. Without either one, there simply is no game. They are partners, both working for the same goal. What happens to either one, happens to both. When they are disconnected, neither one can continue the game. When they are connected, both reap the benefits. Even as they perform slightly different functions in this game, they are one.

As soon as the piece remembers that it needs the player's help, that it really is the player, it is like a little light goes on above the piece which lifts the fog. The player once again sees its piece clearly, moves it along, and the piece is back in the game. Have you ever felt stuck in your own life? Have you ever felt invisible? Like nothing you do is working? Then, have you ever asked the Universe for help, or prayed? Have you ever experienced a healing? And after you get connected to "the Source" again, doesn't it seem that things start to "click" again? That you are back "on the right track?" Do you notice that you begin to get unstuck, and that things in your life begin to work again?

We decide to have some fun, to amuse ourselves. We take out this game, engage others to play with us, and then quickly after the start of the game, we forget that it's a game. We forget our purpose. We forget that we asked our opponents to participate. And most of all, we forget who we really are, and that we will survive long after the game is history.

You might ask, "Yes, but if I am one of the four players around this table, at the end, I might end up with all the money, or none of the money. And while I cannot spend it, won't I have this bitter memory of the game if I end it on the 'losing' end.? Won't I have regrets about how I played the game that will last at least a little while after the game has been put in its box?" Good questions. But now take a few moments as you sit at the table at the end of the game. Look at the other players on your right and left, and then directly across from you. If you look closely, ...very closely, you will see that they are all you! You have simply separated yourself so that you could have that much more fun playing the game.

Imagine yourself now on a tennis court. You serve the ball over the net and no one hits back. What happens? Nothing. No game. Or maybe you put a very young child across the net. You get the ball returned, but in such a fashion that you know for sure you will always win. Yes, you now have a game, but how long will it be until you get so bored that you stop playing anyway? The only way to sustain the fun and interest in a game is to choose a competitor that has the ability to beat you.

And if you choose to play the game at all, and you choose an opponent who can beat you, this is where acceptance, the first step of healing, comes in. Since this is just a game, and your opponent is really you anyway, and the person with the high score doesn't win much and the person with the low score doesn't lose much, doesn't that make it pretty easy to accept the events and situations of the game?

So now a shot from you opponent comes whizzing by your ear on its way to dropping just inside the line for a point against you. Without the knowledge that you are more than the game your are playing, your response may be anger: "What a jerk he is to have to hit the ball so hard." Or grief, "If only he hadn't hit it back so hard." Or guilt: "If I had only hit the ball to his backhand, he wouldn't have done that to me." Or fear: "If he does that again, I'll lose for sure." Or hostility, "I'll show him. I'll kill him on this next shot." Or defeat: "There's no way I can beat him." Or indifference: "What's the use of hitting the ball at all?" Maybe there are other reactions you can imagine...or remember.

However, if you know you are "connected" to who you really are, and know that this opponent is one of your own creation, and you know that nothing changes from beginning to end, and that no matter what the score, you are safe, at peace, and divine, that after you close up the board or walk of the court, the "player" is still around, then there is only one basic reaction when that ball goes whizzing by your ear, or painfully into your gut. You look your opponent in the eye, smile, and say, "Nice job. Well done."

That is acceptance. Of your opponent, of the game itself, of your role in creating it, of yourself, of the source of all that is. You can accept anything, because you know that there is nothing that has happened, and nothing that can happen that can change who you really are.

And when acceptance is felt, the second step to healing is almost complete. That is forgiveness. How easy would it be to forgive an opponent if you recognize that he is only doing what you asked him to do? And when you recognize that you were never in any real danger? And when you know that they are just playing their part of the game? What if you saw each opponent, and each event in your life as simply something to help you get better at playing the game in some way? Wouldn't it become easier to accept and forgive?

Then, it is time to forgive yourself. But if you created all of this, and you know that every single one of your actions and reactions was simply a move of your piece in a game, what is there left to forgive? What have you lost because of any move you've ever made in the game? Did you make a mistake, and end up in jail on the Monopoly board? Remember that to the player, who you really are, being in jail meant freedom. Was that really a mistake?

If there is really anything for which to forgive yourself, it would be simply for forgetting. For forgetting who you really are: the creator of your own reality. You are the creator and player of the game. Can you forgive yourself for forgetting that?

If so, it is time to move on to the third step of healing. This step happens when you stand in front of your opponent on the tennis court, or across the Monopoly table, and react to his winning shot or move by saying, "Nice going. Well done. Thank you for a great game. I couldn't have played without your help. Thank you for playing, for playing so well, and for letting me play." Now you have achieved the third step – Gratitude.

You can be grateful for all those people who helped you play your game. You can be grateful for the sacrifices that they sometimes made so that you could experience what you did, and learn what you did, so that you could have more fun playing your game, and in turn help others to have more fun with their games.

What does all this have to do with energy psychology? Maybe energy gets blocked when a person forgets who he really is, and the game he chose to play. Maybe what we are doing by all the tapping and holding and tuning and balancing is simply helping the person turn that little light on, so that the player of the Monopoly game can take him to a place where he can begin feeling better again. Maybe we are helping the "piece" acknowledge and accept the help of his "player" so that he can feel like he has a shot at winning this Monopoly game, even if the meaning of the game has changed somewhat. And maybe, as the piece and the player reunite, our client can enjoy playing the game again. Maybe our client can even begin to feel that not only does he belong in the game, but that he actually created it. Maybe, by helping our client face and eliminate his anger, fear, guilt, grief, and pain, we act as a mirror to help him see and remember who he really is. When the pain subsides and he begins to experience acceptance, forgiveness and gratitude, then there has been a true healing. What a gift for the one who is healed, and what a gift for us

7
Qigong and Energy Psychotherapy: Foundations of Energy Psychotherapy Healing

Larry Stoler

Energy psychology and psychotherapy give every therapist the tools of a master healer. Remarkable healing, transformational healing is no longer a province of only those born with the healing gift. Can there be any doubt that our increased effectiveness is directly result of using these superior tools? Is it not like the difference between playing a Steinway or Stradivarius as compared to playing lesser instruments? The musical artistry emerges with more clarity and power with these great instruments. So, too, our healing abilities come through more directly using energy psychotherapeutic approaches.

The energy psychotherapies advance our healing skills because they more reliably lead to complete elimination of the problem, and because each method is accessible based on a series of learnable steps. It increasingly appears that we are discovering the blueprints for healing.

As therapists, we primarily focus on the blueprints for psychological and emotional healing. Yet, we observe that these methods can bring relief to physical symptoms as well. Are we also developing reliable blueprints for physical healing? (–> Luthke, Nicosia)

As much excitement as these methods generate, the fundamental understanding about why they work remains a mystery. Are there any principles that would help us understand why "tapping" and "TAB-ing" both work? Why would EFT, EDxTM, TAT, BSFF, TFT, Matrix (and others) all work? How do we explain surrogate and distant healing effects? How are they related to the more common face-to-face treatment results?

What I will be proposing in the body of this paper is that our understanding of all these questions and more can be furthered by examining another related healing practice, medical Qigong ("chee-kung"). I will focus specifically on Chilel Qigong, a healing method used by more than 10 million people worldwide that I have been studying intensively and now teach.

First, let me share with you in more detail why it makes sense for energy psychotherapists to study Qigong in general and Chilel Qigong in particular.

The main element unifying all the energy psychotherapies is the premise that these therapies correct disturbances in the human energetic field. EFT, EDxTM, TFT, TAT, BSFF, NAEM (–> B: Abbreviations) and other methods claim to make energetic changes via the acupuncture meridian system. Matrix work does energetic balancing through the chakra system. Comprehensive systems, like Donna Eden's, use the meridian and chakra system along with others (–> Eden & Feinstein, Hover-Kramer, Luthke).

Meridian-based therapies are built on a foundation of Traditional Chinese Medicine. In TCM, the vital role of Qi ("chee") is understood. Simply put, health is synonymous with vibrant, balanced and flowing Qi. Illness occurs when Qi is depleted, stagnant or perturbed. Thus, all illness can be linked to disturbed Qi. Qi, then, can be thought of as a life force or spirit that is the essence of all things. Practitioners of Chinese Medicine use methods to cultivate and strengthen Qi. These methods are called Qigong. Qigong can be used for self-development, self-healing and for healing others. Martial Qigong (T'ai Chi, for example) focuses on the cultivation and development of Qi for self-defense.

A formal definition of Qigong is provided by Kenneth Cohen in his excellent overview, *Way of Qigong: The art and science of Chinese energy healing*: "Qigong is a wholistic system of self-healing exercise and meditation, an ancient, evolving practice that includes healing posture, movement, self-massage, breathing techniques, and meditation" (p. 4). There are hundreds of Qigong methods and schools in China today.

Chilel Qigong is a particularly important and relevant Qigong method. My interest in Chilel Qigong emerged from several parallel pursuits. For one, I have long been interested in phenomena of unusual and "miraculous" healing. Thomas Harpur's book, *The Uncommon Touch*, in which he profiled leading healers, such as Oskar Estebany was particularly influential. From this book and others like it and from my own growing experience in energy psychotherapy, I understood that profound and even instant physical healing was possible. Larry Dossey's work, in particular his book, *Reinventing Medicine* has been pivotal. Dossey offers rich data supporting his claim that a thorough understanding of healing must incorporate non-local (i.e., distant) healing phenomena.

Another pivotal influence was Dr. James Gordon's book, *Manifesto for a new medicine*. In his book, Gordon emphasized the importance of having a daily healing practice, and synchronistically at this time in my life, the message took. In the past, I had attempted meditation, yoga, Aikido, and self-hypnosis but could not make a practice stick.

A colleague of mine in Chicago introduced me to Chilel Qigong. I was drawn to it immediately. Why? Because it was accessible; it involved meditation through movement (rather than sitting meditation); it promised to help strengthen my Qi and my healing capabilities, and it had an impressive healing track record. Chilel appeared to offer a developed blueprint, a curriculum, for healing.

Chilel Qigong was developed by Dr. Pang Wing, a Qigong grandmaster (i.e., healer) and Western trained physician. In 1988, Pang opened the Huaxia Zhineng Qigong Clinic & Training Center ("the Center"). The Center serves as the cornerstone of Chilel Qigong practice. It is estimated that at least 10 million people practice Chilel worldwide. It is the largest medicineless hospital in China. Some 4,000 people live there, including doctors, students (aka, patients), Chilel teachers, trainees, and others. Upon entering the Center, students are given thorough Western medical evaluations. While at the Center, treatment consists entirely of Chilel Qigong methods done individually and in groups.

Pang conducts research and publishes outcome data on patients coming to the Center. This is data on patients presenting with a wide range of illnesses (more than 180 diseases), including cancer, diabetes, asthma, coronary artery disease, Lupus, and paralysis. Data published in 1991 covering 7,936 patients showed an overall healing rate of almost 95%. This is comprised of 15% who were completely cured, 38% who were greatly improved, and 42% who were improved. This is after a 24 day stay at the Center. (This information is from Luke Chan's introductory book on Chilel, *101 Miracles of Natural Healing*). Similar remarkable healings are occurring now among Chilel practitioners outside China.

For example, at a 6-day retreat I attended in October, 1999, our group emitted Qi to help heal a woman who suffered from polycystic kidney disease. This is a chronic, debilitating disease that leads to swelling of the kidneys and liver along with high blood pressure, and internal bleeding. The woman we worked on looked pregnant due to huge swollen cysts. We did group healing in the evening, and the next morning she was amazed to show us that her pants were falling off because the swelling had disappeared and her body returned to normal.

Chilel healing is thought to work through the action of one particular form of Qi, *Wan-yan* Qi. Wan-yan Qi permeates all of nature, it literally fills the entire universe. Wan-yan Qi is synonymous with love and compassion. Through practice, Chilel practitioners learn to collect Wan-yan Qi – and love and compassion – bringing it from the universe into their bodies (–> Eden & Feinstein). Chilel practice opens blocked meridians, allowing this healing Qi to flow through the body.

How does this lead to healing? Wan-yan Qi is the basis for all things. There is a famous Qigong saying: "Where Qi gathers, matter appears". Master Qigong practitioners make this evident by emitting Qi and healing bones instantly, dissolving tumors in real time, demonstrating that Qi repairs cracked eggshells. As noted, Qigong healing is ancient. While the term "Qigong" connoting healing approaches, is relatively recent on a Chinese scale-- probably introduced between 1368 and 1644 during the Ming Dynasty -- it was introduced in its current sense, involving Qi cultivation in the mid-1930s. However, qigong-like methods have been traced to at least 1028 B.C. Modern China has had an ambivalent attitude about Qigong methods. Initially after the founding of the People's Republic of China, Qigong was openly promoted and studied. During the Cultural Revolution (1966-1976), this changed and Qigong was prohibited. Most recently, the government has again been interested in Qigong. (from Kenneth Cohen's, *The Way of Qigong*, pp.12–22). The Chinese government recognizes that Qigong can play an important role in the health care policy for a nation of 1.2 billion citizens. In addition to the Center, there are numerous other hospitals and medical settings in which Qigong healing is practiced and researched. Indeed, the Chinese government promotes Qigong because of its effectiveness in promoting health, maintaining wellness, and combating chronic disease. Chilel Qigong is the number one Qigong method promoted by the government for this purpose.

By looking closer at the principles of Chilel practice, the relevance of Qigong to energy psychotherapy will be more readily seen. At the Center, Chilel healing occurs in these formats: independent practice – students (patients) doing the various Chilel exercises on their own, often for extended periods of time; group healing sessions – students practice the exercises in groups; and through external laying on hands or emitting Qi for healing others. In addition, at the Center, students live in groups and are involved in a total healing environment that includes eating food prepared by people healed at the Center.

The actual practice of Chilel involves the following components:

1. Belief: Qi healing can take place even when people don't "believe" it, but self-healing requires more of a commitment – a belief that the method will work. Otherwise, why persist in doing something that doesn't show immediate results?

2. Organizing a Qi-field: The idea that individuals can be linked together in a healing energy field (–> Feinstein) is central to Chilel. Connecting to this Qi field is accomplished by deliberate intention (–> Nicosia). The Qi field is understood to be comprised of an abundance of wan-yan Qi, or loving, healing Qi. Practicing within the Qi field means that even while doing Chilel alone, one is linked to millions of others. In Chilel, one learns to expand consciousness to connect to Universe, Infinity, the great One. All Chilel practice, including individual practice, occurs within this Qi field.

3. Facilitating Qi for healing: After organizing a Qi field, the next step is to direct Qi into the field by exchanging Qi with the Qi field through a series of release and absorb movements. Qi healing either for yourself or others occurs by moving Qi with your mind through affirmations, such as "Healing Qi is plentiful inside", "All meridians are open", "All illnesses are gone", or "Every cell in the body is healthy". External Qi healing is done by connecting with universal Qi, Wan-yan Qi, not by using up one's personal Qi.

Chilel is a highly focused, condensed Qigong form. It is an adaptation of numerous Qigong styles. As such it includes methods that are active (e.g., Lift Qi Up, Pour Qi down Method, Wall Squatting), and methods that are tranquil (e.g., Three Centers Merge Standing Meditation). It is versatile and adaptable, so that it can be practiced by people who are seriously ill or who have significant physical disabilities.

When physical practice is limited, the Chilel practitioner relies on using the mind to direct Qi. Later as physical health returns and mobility improves, mind, Qi and body are linked more powerfully.

While Chilel healing occurs by collecting Wan-yan Qi, there is considerable focus on meridians and body energy centers. So, in the Lift Qi Up, Pour Qi Down Method, you direct Qi to 3 energy centers, the Upper, Middle and Lower Dantien areas. The Lower Dantien is in between the navel and lower back, between the navel and *mingmen*. The Middle

Dantien is across the rib cage and through the heart and lung region at the level of Spleen 21, a point called *dabao*. Energy Psychotherapy practitioners recognize this as the under the arm point. The Upper Dantien is in the head at the level of the eyebrows, between *yingtang* (in between the eyebrows) and *yuzheng* opposite on the back of the head. Other acupuncture points are used as well.

After practicing Chilel for some time, I began to see that the energy psychotherapies could be understood as a form of focused or psychological Qigong.

Aren't thought field disturbances similar in principle to the patterns of disturbed Qi that are understood to cause illness? Moreoever, are we not doing qigong when our clients tap or hold meridian points? Throughout the different Chilel methods, the instruction is to deliver Qi into that area. Aren't the reports of surrogate or distance energy psychotherapy healing essentially the same as emitting Qi as in Chilel and other Qigong forms. There is an abundance of evidence for Qigong healing done at a distance.

Knowing Chilel has opened up a number of novel ways to adapt existing methods to help people overcome problems. Here is one example: Using EFT as the model, I began treatment by organizing a Qi field with the client as if we were beginning a Chilel session. Next, I followed the basic EFT approach, starting treatment by doing the Setup (rubbing the sore area on the upper left chest or tapping the side of the hand and using the phrase, "Even though I have (this problem), I deeply and completely accept myself". Then instead of doing the EFT tapping sequence, I had the patient send Qi into the Upper, Middle and Lower *dantien* areas as follows:

I had the patient hold the problem in mind. Then, I asked the patient to place his (her) middle fingers in between the eyebrows (*yingtang*) and direct Qi into the head for a moment focusing on clearing disturbing thoughts, judgments, grievances and attack thoughts. Then, I asked the client to circle her hands around the head to the sides, over the ears to behind the head and bring middle fingers together at the back of the head (*yuzheng*) and again direct Qi into the head.

Next, I asked her to bring their hands down to the middle of the chest in the solar plexus region and direct Qi into the body, focusing on clearing all the emotional aspects of the problem. Then, I asked her to move the hands down to the sides following the edges of the ribs, to the side of the body, and then move the hands up the sides and direct Qi into the body at that point (*dabao*, Sp-21), focusing on opening up her heart.

Finally, I asked the client to move her hands to the navel, and place middle finger on the navel and direct Qi into this important energy center, focusing on eliminating all physical distress. Then, I have her to circle the hands around the waist to the back, where middle fingers converge in the middle of the back opposite the navel (*ming-men*) and again direct Qi there.

Then, as in EFT, I asked them to tell me how the problem seemed to them now. I find that I get the same kinds of responses to this method as I do when I do the customary EFT treatment.

This method has some advantages to EFT though. One is that most clients find the addition of organizing the Qi field both calming and powerful. Also, many clients enjoy the contemplative aspect of this approach. Others like the idea of directing Qi into global energy centers rather than individual points. Others like it because it connects so immediately with their Chilel practice.

Aside from using Chilel as healing method, and as a creative source for developing additional energetic healing approaches, I primarily regard Chilel as a means to build my own Qi, and to help me become more conversant with and sensitive to Qi generally. And as we deepen our grasp of Qi based healing methods, we will learn to rely more and more on a trained intuition to guide treatment (–> Feinstein). Chilel has been immeasurably helpful to me in building this capacity. I strongly encourage everyone involved in energy psychotherapy to consider taking up Chilel or some other Qigong practice.

Suggested Readings

Chan, Luke. 101 miracles of natural healing. Benefactor Press, Cincinnati, Ohio. 45241.
Cohen, Kenneth S. The way of qigong: The art and science of Chinese energy Healing. Ballantine Books, New York, 1997.
Eden, Donna. Energy medicine. Tarcher/Putnam. New York, NY. 1998.
Fromm, Mallory. The book of ki: A practical guide to the healing principles of life energy. Healing Arts Press, Rochester, Vermont, 1998.
Gach, Michael Reed. Acupressure's potent points: A guide to self-care for common ailments.Bantam Books, NY, NY. 1990.
Gordon, James S. Manifesto for a new medicine. Addison-Wesley Publishing Co., Reading, Mass. 1996.
Harpur, Tom. The uncommon touch. McClelland & Steward, Inc. Toronto, Ontario. 1994.

Kit, Wong Kiew. The art of chi kung: Making the most of your vital energy. Element Books, Boston, MA, 1993.

Tiller, William A. Science and Human Transformation: Subtle energies, intentionality and consciousness. Pavior Publishing, Walnut Creek, CA. 1997.

δ

What Moves Us

Willem Lammers

The French psychoanalyst Lacan has warned us, not to want to understand too fast. The transition from a materialistic world view to a more complex one is connected to fundamental insecurity, and at the moment we're only beginning to find a language that fits our Western mind as well as the phenomena healers and mystics have been reporting for ages. We need an empty space, a room for not understanding. Maybe this book should contain some more blank pages, to be filled with new discoveries and personal experiences of the reader.

Human beings are complex, goal-oriented, interactive energy systems, which function at all the frequencies mentioned. These goals can geared toward biological survival, like eating and drinking, avoiding danger and ensuring reproduction. They are also oriented towards a higher level, like spiritual development, with many levels in between.

But what is energy? In the Western world, energy, derived from the Greek ενεργεια, "working inside", has developed a mechanisticc, materialistic meaning. The higher cause has disappeared from everyday language and we have imported new concepts to cover this meaning. Mankind in every culture has had a word for this ultimate cause. The Greek had the the word φυσις (physis) for what make things grow and develop, the Egyptians called it *Ka*, the Hawaiians *Huna*, the medieval healer Paracelsus *archaeus* and at last, in our culture, the French philosopher Henri Bergson called it *élan vital*. The concept didn't have many friends in the beginning. Freud recognized Eros and Thanatos, but found Eros and Thanatos, drives towards sexuality and death, but he considered an inherent creative power in nature as "a pleasant illusion".

There are also other voices: Golas (1972) writes:

It's important to note that energy is not a quantity of anything "objective". Energy, like space and matter, is what a lot of live beings are doing. Energy beings usually react to their neighbors in a way that is often predictable and apparently automatic, like falling dominoes. While relating to space beings, energy beings will appear to be high, vibrating rapidly, with a sense of increasing subjective freedom. Oriented to mass beings, they will be low energy, vibrating slowly with a growing feeling of subjective compulsion and disorder.

All forms of energy, potential as well as in motion, are organized according to governing principles which nowadays we call fields. Fields allow energy to be transmitted, absorbed and conducted. Energy exists at the material and physical level, like in light, sound, heat, magnetism, color, electricity, chemical reactions. These phenomena can be described and measured with the help of the instruments of orthodox science.

Energy also exists in spirit as consciousness, in mind as thoughts, in emotion as feelings, and in energy exchange as communication. In our world of today, we talk about subtle energies. They are said to contain the intelligence or information which provides patterns for the organization of matter.

Subtle information forces in nature

- can penetrate everything
- cause instantaneous reaction at incredible distances
- do not behave according to known formulas
- cannot be measured by conventional electronic test equipment
- and represent a completely new spectrum.

Would Odysseus ever have reached Ithaca without access to this ultimate resource?

8

An Introduction to Thought Energy

Greg Nicosia

We all readily agree that our thoughts are real, but in fact, we grossly underestimate the power of our thought in the manifestation of our own life experience. We are preoccupied with the 4- dimensional world, on that which we see around us in time. We have little explored and examined the realities of the immaterial world, for example, the realm of thought, as you know it. But, the advent of quantum mechanics has changed the scientific exploration of thought energy, and the physics of today is much stranger than any fiction you have imagined. For example, the newest man-machine hybrid is not the bionic man; it is the intentionally imprinted electronic device. That's right, electronic devices whose effects are programmed by human intention. Stranger still is the use of intention today to alter the functioning of an electronic device last week. Thoughts are real and they exist far outside of your head. Thoughts affect the physical world and are not bound by the constraints of time and space. And so we must transform our conception of time, space and very nature of reality to understand the power of thought energy and the conscious intention that directs it (–> Brucker). Once this quantum leap is made, it is only a small step to see thought energy as an effective activator of the bioenenergy system and as a common denominator and mechanism of action involved in the healing effectiveness of a wide variety of bioenergy based therapies.

The first step in the transformation of our understanding of reality as we know it is the breaking of Einstein's limitation upon the speed of light. Einstein certainly catapulted us into a New World of quantum mechanics, but quantum mechanics actually far exceeded what Einstein could accept. Einstein believed that the speed of light was constant and could not be exceeded. Indeed, just this year light has literally been brought to a standstill. In the twentieth century, most physicists were contentedly waiting for the Grand Unification Theory to be unveiled, or come together, and explain all four known forces of the universe: the weak and strong nuclear forces, electromagnetism and gravitation. If all of these forces could be explained by a single theory, it has been believed by physicists that we would then have the theory of everything. Unfortunately, or fortunately as the case may be, there is a growing body of evidence that tells us that we do not know all of the forces of the universe.

This begins with Einstein, Pudolsky and Rosen's famous EPR experiment proposal known as the EPR Paradox, that challenged quantum mechanics' prediction that something, in this case information, could go faster than the speed of light. Einstein thought that was impossible. In this experiment, a photon is split into two photons by passing it through a special crystal. These two photons are then called *entangled*, because whatever happens to one of them, exactly the same thing happens to the other. If one of the entangled photons passes through a polarized filter, than so does the other one. Or, if you change the spin of one, the other one similarly changes the direction of its spin. Einstein, Rosen and Pudolsky proposed to take a photon that was entangled and shoot the photons in opposite directions, so that they were each traveling at the speed of light away from each other. Now, these entangled photons are traveling away from each other at twice the speed of light. Then, if one of the characteristics of the first photon were changed, this same characteristic can be measured for the other entangled photon. In 1950, Albert Bell, a mathematician, proposed Bell's Theorem, which mathematically proved that, indeed, this could not logically be the experimental outcome, otherwise photons would be communicating in a fashion akin to telepathy! In 1972, Clauser and Stewart were the first to experimentally provide evidence that – at twice the speed of light – changing the spin of one entangled photon here immediately changed the spin of the other observed elsewhere.

More recently, several more definitive experiments have been performed. In one experiment (Gisin, 1997) performed in Switzerland, the entangled photons were sent down in fiberoptic cables to different cities, seven miles apart. When the photon reached the end of the track, so to speak, in one city, it passed through a device that allows different paths to be taken. The entangled particles followed the same paths apparently knowing which path the other had taken. For these entangled photons, the minimum speed of information transmission was calculated to be not less than 10,000 times the speed of light. Virtually instantly information is instantly communicated between them. Theoretically it does not matter how far in the universe these entangled photons are separated.

Still, some physicists disputed the breaking the speed of the light barrier and made arguments about the common ancestry of the entangled photons being responsible in some way for the experimental results. The issue was finally put to rest by the experiment which has come to be known as the Teleportation experiment (Bouwmeester, 1997). In this experiment, two particles are entangled by being passed through a crystal, and are then sent in two different directions. One of these is now entangled with yet another particle, which changes one of its characteristics. Then the other originally entangled particle is measured at its remote location. Low and behold, the other entangled particle has also received the new information that the second particle gave to the originally entangled partner. What we now know is that at a photon level, teleportation can be accomplished at speeds exceeding the speed of light.

There is also the phenomenon of quantum mechanical tunneling that Albert Einstein called "spooky". Again a prediction of quantum theory proved to be true: When we shoot particles at an impenetrable barrier, simply by quantum mechanic probability, some of them appear on the other side. Not only do they appear on the other side, but the larger and thicker you make the barrier, the faster they travel through it. If you make the barrier thick enough, the particles travel much faster than the speed of light to get to the other side. These are not only theoretical predictions, or limited to experimental findings. In fact, this particular notion of tunneling has already been operationalized in the productions of capacitors that high tech industries use, because it allows for information to be transduced faster than the speed of light.

It is now very clear that some things are moving much faster than the speed of light and, as demonstrated by quantum tunneling, seem to obey conjugate or inverse rules of a faster than light "reverse" world. William Tiller (1997, –> Diepold) delineated the physics of a ten-dimensional universe in which higher order dimensions are characterized by a mirror image principle. Here, light, which is both a particle and wave serves as a boundary between the physical world of sub–lightspeed (c) particles and the conjugate physical or etheric world of waveforms with velocity > c that move slowest in a vacuum and speed up in dense physical matter. In these inverse space-time etheric dimensions, negative temperature, levitation, magnetic monopoles are the Fourier Transform of the physical universe.

Tiller proposes an 11-space energy that can be viewed as initially slowing down and precipitating out a 10-dimensional grid with internodal spacing of 10–29 meters. This 10th dimension of mind level, thought, informs and activates a 9-dimensional structure of etheric substance and emotion that imparts a magnetic particle quality ultimately attracting from the universe that to which it is connected. A further quantum jump or slowing down from the 9th dimension yields the two 4-dimensional conjugate universes of etheric and physical substance. Basically, for everything with which we are familiar in the physical world there is an energetic etheric template (–> Luthke), a mirror image of inverse space/time and frequency.

A concrete physical representation of the conjugate universe is found in the light diffraction experiments, from which we initially learned that light is both a particle and a waveform. The interference patterns obtained when photons are passed through a two-slit template are similar to those obtained by dropping two pebbles in the water simultaneously. When they hit the water, what you see is that some of the waves cancel each other out, some of them add together and an interference pattern of lines appears (Figure 1; Tiller, 1997a).

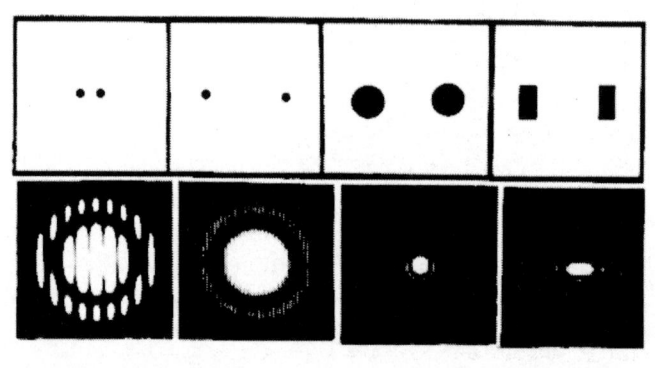

Interestingly enough, if you move the two slits apart, the interference pattern lines become closer together. If you make the slits bigger, the interference pattern becomes smaller. If you orient the slits at an angle, the resulting diffraction pattern appears at the inverse angle. Most interestingly, if spiral templates are employed, the resulting interference patterns are the mandalas that have been known from ancient times to represent the chakras, complex spinning patterns of energy in the wave form world, made simply by passing light through a spiral pattern (Figure 2, Tiller, 1997a).

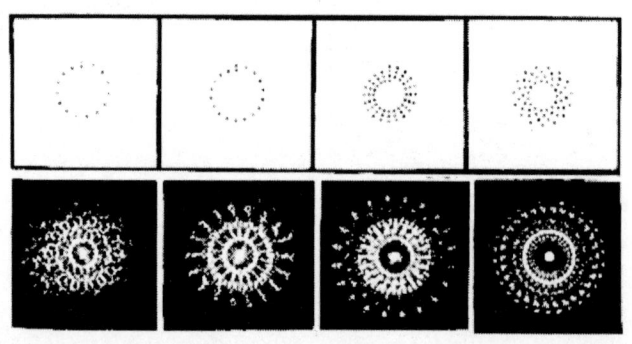

In sum, Tiller's model of a ten-dimensional universe provides a framework in which human beings' non-physical dimensions of intentionally directed thought and emotion are manifesting physical reality and life experience (–> Brucker, Feinstein). Furthermore, Tiller provides us a detailed analysis of a mechanism, the bioenergy system that allows for communication between the physical and nonphysical aspects of our being. Examining the ion pumping potential of an acupuncture meridian point reveals a cross-section that looks like an umbrella. Looking down on the skin, this umbrella appears to be a circle, an acupuncture point, when viewed in terms of its electrical conductivity. More importantly, that means that an acupuncture meridian point is a biologic bipolar antenna (–> Diepold). Thus, humans possess a series of antennae connected to each other in each and every meridian forming an integrated system covering a wide range of frequencies, very much like the arrays of radio telescopes that we use to plumb the depths of the universe. Ultimately, the human being is the most sophisticated information, transmission and reception device ever conceived. We are continuously receiving, transducing and sending information through the antenna system called meridians. This begs the question: Where are we sending this information or from where are we receiving it?

Perhaps this communications system is simply for communication within our multidimensional self. However, recent research evidences more far-reaching effects of this thought energy driven system. Indeed, over the last 70 years an impressive body of experimental data including nearly 2.6 million trials has been generated, evidencing concurrent direct mental influences, or what might be called "real-time psychokinesis (PK)" mind over matter effects. These studies typically involve electronic random event generators operating on the basis of radioactive decay or thermal noise in semiconductor components that are influenced by human thought intending a desired outcome (Radin and Ferrari, 1991). More recently, human intention has been demonstrated to reliably imprint electronic devices which in subsequent research effect the imprinted intention (Tiller, 2000a). These intentionally imprinted effects were also obtained at locations 150 feet distant from the experimental chamber as well as in close proximity to the imprinted electronic device (Tiller, 2000b). Once the phenomenon of intentionally imprinted electronic devices is appreciated, it seems rather trivial to assert that we can influence one another, and even intentionally activate bioenergy systems at remote locations (e.g. Vasiliev, 1976; Braud, 1990, 1992; Benor, 1993).

Now, that *thought* is out of the box of our heads, and its nonspatial locality is evidenced, inverse space-time is just a heartbeat away, or did it arrive yesterday? Braud (2000) recently reviewed the retroactive or time-displaced intentional influence on random number generators first proposed and examined by a theoretical physicist, Helmut Schmidt. Quantum mechanics involves a number of paradoxical phenomena including the observer effect. Basically, until an event is observed, it does not really exist in any particular state. Its state is simply given by a collection of probabilities. Once it is observed, the probability of what it is observed becomes one and the probability of all other possible states goes to zero. Until it is observed, there is always a probability that any of its possible states can manifest. In recent studies of retroactive PK, individuals were asked to intentionally influence series or events that had *previously* been produced by random event generators, printed out, sealed unseen and held by an independent supervisor. As incredible as it may seem, strong evidence for retroactive PK is obtained from these studies (e.g. Schmidt, 1986,1990, 1993).

The idea of or search for higher dimensions was ridiculed in scientific circles just two years ago. Today it has become the focal point of research for particle physicists who are now trying to find the door to the higher dimensions at CERN and other particle accelerating facilities. Cosmology has now produced two independent lines of research (e.g. Miller, 1999) evidencing a flat universe expanding at an accelerating rate, indicating the existence of an unusual kind of energy evenly distributed throughout the universe. This "funny energy" corresponds to something that has an antigravitational effect pushing on the fabric of space-time and dominates the cosmos. Could this be the cosmological constant first invoked by Einstein, who later said that he thought it was his biggest blunder? This constant is associated with a sea of evanescent or virtual particles and antiparticles populating empty space that are now known to produce the Casimir force. Today's physics continues to bring forth more evidence of higher dimensional phenomena. In fact, Schultz and Smith (2000) recently unveiled a device with no moving parts within which electromagnetic radiation acts contrary, reversed, to the way it does in ordinary matter. There is at last a portal through which the higher dimensional world can be explored!

At this point in time, our science tells us that thoughts are real. Thoughts are measurable outside of our heads and they exert a real influence on people and objects that is not bound by time or space. Thought and the intention that directs it appear to be a ten-dimensional phenomenon integral to the process of creating manifest reality and life experience. We are all truly awesome creatures possessing both physical and nonphysical, spiritual dimensions that allow us to create the realities we experience through the act of its observation.

Thought Works! Indeed it does and it can be used and directed in many different ways. Our intentionally directed thought is sufficient to activate a meridian point (–> Diepold, Stoler) and thus it becomes possible to use it as an integral part of the variety of thought field therapies that have proliferated during the past decade. As part of both the diagnostic and treatment process, intentionally directed thought may substitute for the physical acts involved in these therapies and when combined with surrogate testing, frees our healing efforts from the bounds of space-time. Just think of it, we can heal our wounds yesterday.

But first we must conceive and be aware of it, and have the requisite experience that allows us to believe it. Similar arguments and scientific data can be marshaled evidencing the effects of intentionally directed thought upon the chakra system. And, in similar fashion chakra-based therapies can be effected through the use of intentionally directed thought. Indeed, it is the power of the intention to heal carried by the thought that generates a physical action that causes the beneficial result of the specific acts involved in the healing methods used in energy psychology. Recall Tiller's early research on biologic radiation detectors where the intention and not the physical placement of the hands was the critical variable. Simply tapping a meridian or moving our hands around a chakra without the intention of activating the healing effects of the bioenergy system is useless.

Indeed, if accompanied by malintention the same physical acts becomes harmful. We are all creators, awesome creatures of multiple dimensions. Even the drunk lying on the sidewalk possesses these same attributes and power, although he does not have this awareness. In fact, few people possess this fundamental knowledge of what they are.

As practitioners of energy psychology, increasing this awareness, both personally and professionally is part of our labor. We are a growing army of energy healers. We are growing in our awareness, and our common denominator is the power of our thought energy and the healing intention that directs it.

References

Benor, D.J. (1990). Survey of Healing Research. *Complimentary Medical Research*, 4 (3), 9-33.

Benor, D.J. (1993). *Healing Research*. Vols 1-4. Munich, Germany: Helix Verlag.

Bouwmeester, D. andZellinger, A. (1997). Nature, cited in (1998) *Instant Transport: Achieving quantum teleportation in the laboratory*. Science News, 153, 41.

Braud, W.G. (1990). Distant mental influence of rate of hemolysis of human red blood cells. *Journal of the American society of Psychical Research*, 84, 1-24.

Braud, W.G. (1992). Remote mental influence of electrodermal activity. *Journal of Indian Psychology*, 19 (1), 1-10.

Braud, W.G. (2000). Wellness implications of retroactive Influence:exploring an outrageous hypothesis. *Alternative Therapies*, 6 (1), 37-48.

Dibble, W. and Tiller, W. (1997). Development of pH and temperature oscillations in water containing ZnCO3 crystallites using intention imprinted electronic devices. *Subtle energies and energy medicine*,8(3), 175-192.

Miller, J. (2001) A dark force in the universe. *Science News*, 159, 218-220.

Radin, D. and Ferrari, D. (1991) Effects of consciousness on the fall of dice: a meta-analysis. *Journal of Scientific Exploration*, 5, 1-24.

Schmidt, H., Morris, R. and Rudolph, L. (1986). Channeling evidence for a psychokinetic effect to independent observers. *Journal of Parapsychology*, 50, 1-15.

Schmidt, H., Morris, R. and Hardin, C. (1990). Channeling evidence for a psychokinetic effect to independent observers: an attempted replication. *Mind Science Foundation Research Report*. San Antonio, Texas: Mind Science Foundation.

Schnidt, H, and Braud, W. (1993). New PK tests with an independent observer. *Journal of Parapsychology*, 57, 217-240.

Tiller, W. (1997a). *Science and Human Transformation*. Walnut Creek, CA: Pavior Publishing.

Tiller, W., Dibble, W. and Kohane, M. (1997b). Towards objectifying intention via electronic devices. *Subtle Energies and Energy Medicine*, 8 (2), 103-123.

Vasilev, I. (1976). *Experiments in Distant Influence*. New York, NY: Dutton.

9

At Play in the Fields of the Mind: Personal Myths as Fields of Information[1]

David Feinstein

Mythological symbols touch and exhilarate centers of life beyond the reach of the vocabularies of reason and coercion.
– Joseph Campbell (1968, p. 4).

The recognition that personal myths shape individual behavior in a manner analogous to the way cultural myths influence social behavior has been gaining currency within psychology. Myth is grounded in the quintessential human ability to address the large questions of existence using symbolism and narrative. While a myth – to be plausible for contemporary individuals – must be aligned with our capacity for rational thought, mythmaking is as much with us today as it was thousands of years ago. The symbolism of an individual's guiding mythology can, in fact, be discerned using established psychological techniques for uncovering unconscious processes, including interviews, dream analysis, free association, structured fantasy, and projective instruments.

This paper builds on the author's earlier work[2] while expanding the personal mythology construct, suggesting that personal myths function not only as biochemically-coded models of reality, but also as fields of information—natural though non-visible elements of the physical universe—that impact consciousness and behavior. Just as some neurologists have proposed that "mental fields" complement brain activity in unifying experience and some biologists have proposed that "morphic fields" complement the action of the gene in giving form to an organism, this chapter develops the thesis that myth-carrying "fields of information" complement the physiological bases of consciousness in storing symbolic content and maintaining psychological habits.

The Nature of Personal Myths

Personal myths are organizing models that shape perception, understanding, and behavior. They emerge from four sources: biology, personal history, culture, and transcendent experiences. Comprised of postulates about oneself, one's world, and the relationship between the two, personal myths are internalized models of reality that explain the external world, guide individual development, provide social direction, and address spiritual questions in a manner that is analogous to the way cultural myths carry out those functions for entire societies. These internalized guiding models address immediate as well as eternal concerns, and they are both descriptive, furnishing explanations, and instructive, generating motivation (–> Carrington, Shaw, Weil).

As organizing models, personal myths are continually being compared with experience. When a mismatch is detected between an inner model and an experience, perceptions may be changed to match the model (i.e., Piaget's *assimilation*) or the model may be changed to match the experience (Piaget's *accommodation*). The evolution of internal models, a process that occurs largely outside the individual's awareness, is a primary focus of psychotherapeutic intervention. By framing internal models as personal myths, the dynamic, "storied nature" (Sarbin, 1986) of human cognition comes to the foreground. In addition, recognizing the essential mythological nature of the psyche extends the boundaries of scientific language, allowing it to more readily incorporate the larger cultural and spiritual dimensions of human experience.

Like beliefs and attitudes, personal myths are rooted in the individual's biochemistry. They are biochemically-coded models of reality. This chapter considers evidence that biochemical theories of information storage and retrieval are not sufficient in themselves for explaining the way personal myths function, and it develops the hypothesis that personal myths, in addition to their biochemical infrastructure, are also embedded in fields that store information and maintain habits.

Fields of Information

A field is a domain of influence, presumed to exist in physical reality, that cannot be observed directly, but which is inferred through its effects. Although they elude direct inspection, the four established fields of physics – gravitational fields, electromagnetic fields, and the strong and weak quantum matter fields – are known to exist because of phenomena that can be observed. They are understood as material though elusive forces in the physical universe.

Findings from several areas of science are converging to cause some investigators to postulate a variety of fields, different in nature from the four established fields of physics, but similar to one another in that each is conceived of as carrying information that influences consciousness and behavior (–>Nicosia). Neurologists, for instance, are proposing that previously undetected fields may be involved in brain function. The ability of neurons to broadcast signals to one another has been identified by Schuman and Madison(1994) at Stanford Medical School. Their "neural broadcasting" theory suggests that information can be transmitted from a single neuron to neighboring neurons that are not electrochemically connected via axon and dendrite: "The formation of synaptic changes previously thought to be restricted to synapses onto a single cell can also result in synaptic changes at nearby synapses" (p. 535). The investigators speculate that "the presence of synaptic activity may work in concert with other factors" (p. 535), and it is entirely plausible that these unidentified "other factors" involve the influence of neural fields. Libet (1994), another prominent neurologist, has in fact hypothesized a mental field "which is produced by, but is biologically distinct from, brain activity" (p. 119). This construct is formulated as a "testable field theory of mind-brain interaction. These mental fields "cannot be observed directly by external physical means" (p. 121), and their properties differ significantly from those of any currently known physical field in such dimensions as their ability to alter neuron function and to unify subjective experience. Physicists, meanwhile, have been discussing correspondences between consciousness and quantum fields for well over half a century (e.g., Bohm, 1951; Edington, 1929). Penrose (1994), for instance, that many of the brain's capacities can best be explained by postulating that consciousness operates according to the principles of quantum mechanics. While quantum theories of consciousness might place many difficult questions about the brain and the mind into a compelling new context (e.g., Friedman, 1994; Wolf, 1994; Zohar & Marshall, 1994), the question remained unanswered whether parts of the brain small enough to be governed by the laws of quantum mechanics could be complex enough to exert a discrete influence on consciousness. Hameroff (1994), an anesthesiologist, has proposed that the microtubule is the brain component that operates at the quantum level while affecting consciousness. A microtubule is composed of long, thin hollow tubes of protein about a ten-millionth of an inch in diameter that form meshlike networks throughout each cell. A single electron sliding back and forth along the microtubule's length determines the microtubule's configuration and function. Significantly, the action of anesthetics such as ether and halothane is that they temporarily incapacitate the microtubules, turning off consciousness with minimal disruption to other brain functions. Since microtubules are small enough to operate according to quantum principles and are directly involved with consciousness, Hameroff believes they are the link between consciousness and quantum mechanics. Complementary theories, emerging from neurology, physics, anesthesiology, and systems theory, biology, physiology, neuroanatomy, medicine, psychology, and energy healing have postulated the existence of information fields that might influence consciousness and behavior, based on findings from within their respective disciplines. Beyond such scientific speculation, a number of time-honored traditions in both the East and the West refer to a more subtle counterpart to the material body, referred to variously as the "aura," "subtle body," "pranic body," or "etheric body" (–> Eden & Feinstein, Hover-Kramer, Luthke, Nicosia). Several features are shared by reports (summarized elsewhere[1]) of:

1) human activity influencing mechanical devices from a distance (–> Brucker),
2) distant effects of visualization, prayer, and meditation on consciousness, healing, and even the activity of blood cells in test tubes,
3) the extraordinary mental abilities of prodigies and savants,
4) systematic investigations of telepathy,
5) similarities in myths and symbols across cultures, and
6) the parallel symbolism observed in clinical situations and in nonordinary states of consciousness: evidence suggesting the existence of each of these phenomena, while not always unequivocal, has been accumulating; each seems to involve the procurement of information in a manner whose mechanisms are difficult to explain in terms of known physiological structures; and the effects observed are consistent with a "field of information" hypothesis.

Mythic Fields

Mythic fields become established when new patterns of understanding and motivation are initiated and repeated. Once established, they tend to maintain the psychological habits that typify the individual—the person's characteristic forms of emotion, thought, and behavior. The influence is bi-directional: field follows form and form follows field. Psychophysiological forms and mythic fields are linked by resonance. Sheldrake (1988) explains that "characteristic rhythmic patterns of activity within the nervous system" (p. 151) may enter into resonance with a morphic field. Interestingly, when a group of neurons becomes linked through mental activity, the neurons themselves behave like a "field" (Pearce, 1992, p. 16), with all the cells vibrating as a single frequency or "phase-coherent oscillation" (Edelman, 1992, p. 95). The individual's mythic field presumably resonates with these neurons in a process of mutual influence.

In my own formulation, I first conceived of the mythic field as a subtle form of energy that exists within the dimensions of Newtonian space-time. More recently, in trying to account for the anomalies described earlier, I have come to believe that mythic fields must sometimes embody properties that are associated with quantum fields, such as nonlocality. Even without visual or auditory cues, a sensitive individual can often detect changes in another person's mythic field, experienced as an altered energy or vibration ("before I even pulled into the driveway, I could feel that he was angry"). People who work in the "new" discipline of energy medicine are particularly attuned to this realm. The following is excerpted from an interview I conducted with my partner, Donna Eden, a mind-body healer known for her ability to see and feel the body's energies and, based upon what she sees and feels, to identify physical problems in a manner that reliably corresponds with medical diagnoses. She described the way she experiences what I refer to as personal myths and personal fields of information:

> In shifting from one myth into another, the vibration of the person's field changes and the field's colors change. When a person is under emotional stress, the energy tends to take on the stamp of an old myth that is oriented toward emotional or physical survival, usually some version of fight or flight. When one of these survival-oriented myths is activated, I see its energy originating in the root chakra. The old myth sits like a fountain in the root chakra, with the field that comes out from this fountain surrounding the person's body.
>
> At other times the old myth quiets down. While I can still see its energy, I can also see the energy of other myths come in. When a new myth has become more than an idea and has begun to take a stable physical form, it begins to infiltrate the auric bands, changing some of their colors. Its energy will be less dense and move more quickly than the energy of the old myth. As a new myth begins to take hold, at first it looks faint to me, but with time it becomes more distinct.
>
> What you call the conflict between an old myth and an emerging myth often isn't so much that the two fight one another but that the old myth is simply fighting for its survival. When a myth doesn't work anymore, a point is reached where its energy gets very murky. I can see the energy of an old myth doing all it can to hold on, like hot tar. If it gets stuck that way for a long period, physical illness often follows (personal communication, February 28, 1995).

A small body of evidence suggesting a relationship between subtle vibrational patterns in the body and disease states is, in fact, accumulating (e.g., Hunt, 1995), and the paradigm underlying energy medicine (Eden, 1999) or vibrational medicine (Gerber, 1996) complements the line of reasoning presented here (–> Luthke, Stoler).

Clinical Implications: Shift the Field, Change the Myth

More than half a century ago, Rollo May (1939; 1989) observed that "both the counselor and the counselee are taken out of themselves and become merged in a common psychic entity. The emotions and will of each become part of this new psychic entity" (p. 67). One of May's students, Larson (1987), a psychologist who has studied this "new psychic entity," describes a striking incident from her own clinical work:

> A new client entered my office for the first appointment. I spontaneously began experiencing very subtle, unusual sensations in my own lower torso. Prior to this appointment I had completed a deep relaxation exercise, so I was quite aware when the subtle, tingly sensations began. I first reflected inwardly trying to discover the source of the mysterious sensations. I asked myself if the new client reminded me of someone I had previously known. I searched myself to ascertain if my own personal memories were related to the tingly sensations. Then I bracketed the experience noting it, watching it, and reflecting further upon it. Finally, my curiosity was overpowering. At a seemingly appropriate point, I described my experience to the young woman client, and asked if my experience had some meaning for her. The young woman immediately replied, "Oh yes, I have cancer of the cervix, and I've been having chemotherapy there." (p. 323).

Investigating this phenomenon, which she terms "psychotherapeutic resonance," Larson found that many therapists report a momentary merging of the boundary between themselves and a client that in its intensity exceeds empathy and rapport (see also Sterling & Bugental, 1993, on the "meld" experience of therapist with client). In psychotherapeutic resonance, the therapist evidences immediate non-verbal understanding of feelings the client has not acknowledged, may directly experience physical sensations the client is experiencing, and the therapist and client become synchronized in even tiny movement patterns. Is the therapist unconsciously tuning into a subtle field of information carried by the client?

Early in my career, I had the good fortune of observing first hand the therapeutic mastery of Milton Erickson, Alexander Lowen, Peg Mayo, Carl Rogers, and Virginia Satir. I was many times present when one of these gifted clinicians would provide a demonstration for trainees. Their skills sometimes seemed uncanny. How did they know what this person needed? I would study transcriptions of their clinical work, hoping to discern their secrets. The most interesting pattern I could detect was their ability to offer a creative and unexpected intervention at the moment of therapeutic opportunity, impossible to acquire by studying transcripts, and often quite different from their trademark techniques, yet strikingly attuned, plausibly through resonance, to the client's unique needs. I have witnessed Carl Rogers being decidedly directive ("Steven, I don't think you should marry her!"); Virginia Satir cut to the core of a psychodynamic conflict with no reference to the person's family or family of origin; and Alexander Lowen get to the heart of a problem with no mention of the person's posture or bodily tensions. If their interventions were not based on their established clinical approach, to what, I wondered, were they attuning themselves? I have come to think of this elusive "what" as the client's mythic field. I believe, in fact, that many effective therapists are high in "psychotherapeutic resonance," able to spontaneously attune themselves to the client's "field," accurately obtaining information that is not transmitted through even the most subtle sensory cues.

Many phenomena that are difficult to account for in psychotherapy, such as the enormous power of projective identification (e.g., a seasoned child psychiatrist observed that she knows she is dealing with a victim of child abuse when she experiences an irrational "impulse to abuse the child" – cited in Gabbard, 1994, p. 71), have been attributed to "subtle sensory cues." I would reverse the argument – wherever subliminal sensory cues are the explanation of last resort, consider the possibility that a field of information is also involved. I myself have learned, when in a clinical situation and unsure about what I should do next, to quiet my inner chatter, shift my attention to the "field" the client brings into the room, and allow it to inform my responses. This often results in the subjective experience that I am tuning into a normally imperceptible atmosphere carried by the client. After consciously shifting my attention to the client's hypothetical "field," new understanding and interventions may come in a flash. Such moments of insight sometimes seem to tap into information about the client to which I do not have any apparent access but that is subsequently confirmed. Whether shifting my attention to the client's "field" is a way of actually attuning myself to a dimension of the clinical situation that transcends sensory cues or is just a helpful bit of self-deception, I believe the maneuver makes me a better therapist.

Focused imagery that brings a person into the past to rework early emotional distress and trauma can be designed to mimic some of the healing functions of dreams and to help transform the psychodynamic bedrock of a dysfunctional myth. A man was able to trace his abusive impulses toward his son back to his own experiences of abuse. He was guided to visualize himself as a child in his primal drama with his own father. In this rendition, however, his adult self was also there. The adult self persuaded the father to shower his son with the love and emotional support that the father at some level – buried beneath his own conflicts – held but did not express (in extreme cases, the person's fantasy may have to eliminate the parent altogether and have the adult self provide the parenting directly; in any case, coming to a productive scenario is a significant piece of the therapeutic work). In the presence of that imagined emotional support, he could sense a shift, the genesis of the field that might have existed had he actually received the love being fantasized. This is a procedure for deep transformation that I call "Rewriting History through the Emotionally Corrective Daydream." A daily ritual to strengthen his new personal myth, and the field associated with it, might project him into an imagined future where he is living from a guiding myth that supports constructive responses to his son at the moments of greatest stress. Because repetition, according to Sheldrake (1988), increases the strength of a field, by frequently evoking in his imagination the sensations and images associated with his new myth, he can presumably increase the habit strength of this fledgling myth until it becomes readily accessible. Based on preliminary clinical observations (Feinstein & Krippner, 1997), therapeutic rituals for directly embedding a new mythology (–> Carrington) can be designed around the presumed influence on the mythic field on each of the following:

- setting an intention to initiate constructive changeimagery journeys to the past that psychodynamically rework dysfunctional myths imagery journeys that seed the future with a more constructive guiding mythology visualizing the qualities of this new myth
- shifting internal speech to support the new mythbehavioral rehearsal to anchor the new myth.

Conclusion

The evidence for telepathy, the distant effects of visualization, and the other "anomalies" summarized in this paper suggests that consciousness is not just an epiphenomenon emerging from biochemical events any more than the evening news originates only in the television set. The news is produced by both the television set (a "bottom-up" influence) and the television signal (a "top-down" influence). Personal myths are also produced by "bottom-up" and "top-down" influences. Neurons, like the components of a TV, exert a bottom-up influence, from the brain up to the developing story. Fields of information, like the TV signals, exert their influence from the top, down to the developing story. Neurons and fields seem to operate in tandem, like the TV set and the signal. Personal myths reflect both the brain and the field, just like the TV program is a reflection of both the TV set and the signal. Personal myths, as biochemically coded organizing models, exert a "bottom up" influence on consciousness and behavior; personal myths, as fields of information, exert a "top down" influence.

The hypothesis that mythic fields influence feelings, thoughts, and behavior, if supported, would hold far-reaching implications. While we know with relative certainty that Lamarck was wrong to believe that a person's experiences create biological changes that are then passed along through the genes, the possibility that those experiences create changes in a field of information that is part of the child's intellectual "amniotic fluid" gives a new twist to Lamarckian interpretations. An understanding of the way mythic fields act upon the psyche would make it possible to more proficiently tailor, for desired change, techniques that utilize ritual, visualization, focused intention, and behavioral enactments. An understanding of the more subtle physical realms that influence mental structures would also provide a stronger empirical foundation for investigating the higher mental processes that have long been the concern of humanistic psychologists. More dramatically, the idea that fields of information affect consciousness would augment our understanding of collective myth-making, suggesting in fact a physical infrastructure for the fashionable idea that a "global brain" (Russell, 1995) is now emerging. Since experimental evidence has linked mental activity with "non-local" fields of information, it is not a huge leap to postulate that – just as two aligned magnets form a shared field – an idea that is held by many people would exist in concert with a collective field of information. Such a collective field would presumably intensify if the numbers holding the idea increased, as when an image is multiplied via satellite (Feinstein, Mortifee, & Krippner, 1998). With electronic communications media, we are, in fact, able to interact more consciously than ever before with the fields that underlie our collective thoughts, to recognize them as tangible if subtle entities, and to open novel approaches for participating in their evolution.

Notes

1. This paper is excerpted from a substantially longer chapter scheduled to appear in The Handbook of Humanistic Psychology, James F.T. Bugental, et al (Eds.), Sage Publications, in press. An earlier version appeared in the Journal of Humanistic Psychology,

1998, 38(3), 71–109. The full text of that article can be downloaded from www.innersource.net. The complete citation material for references in this excerpt can also be found there.

2.   David Feinstein & Stanley Krippner, The Mythic Path (New York: Tarcher/Penguin Putnam, 1997).

References

Bohm, D. (1951). *Quantum theory.* London: Constable.
Bohm, D. (1980). *Wholeness and the implicate order.* London: Routledge and Kegan Paul.
Edelman, G.M. (1992). *Bright air, brilliant fire: On the matter of the mind.* New York: Basic Books.
Eden, D. (1998). *Energy medicine.* New York: Tarcher/Putnam Penguin.
Edington, A. (1929). *The nature of the physical world.* London: Dent. Editorial
– (1981). *A book for burning?* Nature, 293, 245 - 246.
Feinstein, D. (1979). Personal mythology as a paradigm for a holistic public psychology. *American Journal of Orthopsychiatry,* 49, 198 - 217.
Feinstein, D. (1997). Personal myths and psychotherapy: Myth-making in psychological and spiritual development. *American Journal of Orthopsychiatry,* 67, 508-521.
Feinstein, D. (in press). *Archetypes.* In A.E. Kazdin (Ed.). *Encyclopedia of Psychology.* New York: Oxford University Press.
Feinstein, D., & Krippner, S. (1997). *The mythic path.* New York: Tarcher/Penguin Putnam.
Feinstein, D., Krippner, S., & Granger, D. (1988). Myth-making and human development. *Journal of Humanistic Psychology,* 28(3), 23 - 50.
Feinstein, D., Mortifee, A., & Krippner, S. (1998). Waking to the rhythm of a new myth. *World Futures,* 52,. 187-238.
Friedman, N. (1994). *Bridging science and spirit.* St. Louis: Living Lake Books.
Gabbard, G. O. (1994). *Psychodynamic psychiatry in clinical practice.* Washington, DC: American Psychiatric Press.
Gerber, R. (1996). *Vibrational medicine.* Santa Fe, NM: Bear
Hameroff, S. (1994). Quantum coherence in microtubules: A neural basis for emergent consciousness? *Journal of Consciousness Studies,* 1(1), 91-118.
Krippner, S. (1975). *Song of the siren: A parapsychological odyssey.* New York: Harper & Row.
Larsen, S. (1976). *The shaman's doorway: Opening the mythic imagination to contemporary consciousness.* New York: Harper & Row.
Larsen, S. (1990). *The mythic imagination: Your quest for meaning through personal mythology.* New York: Bantam.

Larson, V.A. (1987). An exploration of psychotherapeutic resonance. *Psychotherapy*, 24, 321-324.

Libet, B. (1994). A testable field theory of mind-brain interaction. *Journal of Consciousness Studies*, 1(1), 119-126.

Lukoff, D. (1997). The psychologist as mythologist. *Journal of Humanistic Psychology*, 37(3), 34-58.

May, R. (1989). *The art of counseling* (rev. ed.). New York: Gardner Press. (Original work published 1939)

McAdams, D. P. (1993). *Stories we live by: Personal myths and the making of the self.* New York: Morrow.

Pearce, J. C. (1992). *Evolution's end: Claiming the potential of our intelligence.* San Francisco: HarperCollins.

Penrose, R. (1994). *Shadows of the mind: A search for the missing science of consciousness.* New York: Oxford University Press.

Piaget, J. (1977). *The development of thought: Equilibrium of cognitive structures* (A. Rosin, Trans.). New York: Viking.

Russell, P. (1995). *The global brain awakens: Our next evolutionary leap.* Palo Alto, CA: Global Brain, Inc.

Sarbin, T.R. (Ed.). (1986). *Narrative psychology: The storied nature of human conduct.* New York: Praeger.

Schuman, E., & Madison, D. (1994). Locally distributed synaptic potentiation in the hippocampus. *Science*, 263, 532-536.

Sheldrake, R. (1981). *A new science of life: The hypothesis of formative causation.* Los Angeles: Jeremy P. Tarcher.

Sheldrake, R. (1988). *The presence of the past: morphic and the habits of nature.* New York: Random House.

Sheldrake, R. (1994). *Seven experiments that could change the world.* London: Fourth Estate.

Sheldrake, R., & Bohm, D. (1982). Morphogenic fields and the implicate order: A conversation between Rupert Sheldrake and David Bohm. *ReVision*, 5(2), 41 - 48.

Sterling, M.M., & Bugental, J.F.T., (1993). The meld experience in psychotherapy supervision. *The Journal of Humanistic Psychology*, 33(2), 38 - 48.

Tiller, W. A. (1993). What are subtle energies? *Journal of Scientific Exploration*, 7, 293-304.

Wolf, F.A. (1994). *The dreaming universe: A mind-expanding journey into the realm where psyche and physics meet.* New York: Simon & Schuster.

Zohar, D., & Marshall, I. (1994). *The quantum society: Mind, physics, and a new social vision.* New York: William Morrow.

Comments by Stanley Krippner, Donna Eden, and Richard Alexander on earlier drafts of this paper are gratefully acknowledged.

10

The Phenomena of Psychokinesis

Marla Brucker

If you believe you can or you believe you can't, you're right.
– Henry Ford

I want to welcome you to a new adventure. How many of you have bent spoons or forks before, other than the silverware being caught in the garbage disposal? Of course we might have tried bending them, but I am sure not without great effort. As you learn these new techniques you will begin to realize your greater potential, by moving beyond your limitations and begin to tap into the unused 90% of your mind's power and. A shift does occur.

Psychokinesis (PK) is the ability of the mind to have a noticeable affect on physical objects. You will be amazed as the metal object you are holding begins to bend in your hand, just by the power of your intention. It *will* happen!

In this incredible hands on training, you will become more adept in tapping into the inner resources of your mind, as you begin to make things happen. You will learn the fundamentals of how the mind can transfer energy of thought, into the goal of your intention, in this case the item you wish to bend (–> Nicosia).

Intention as we know it, is thought, meaning and purpose directed towards a goal, which resonates as vibration with the amplitude of frequencies. Vibration can be increased and intensified with the power of one's mind. Conditioning of the cells to reverberate in relation to specific thoughts, with the ultimate goal being the intention of our desired outcome (bending metal), creates a change in the object's vibrational frequency all the way down into the molecular (cellular) level. Therefore, the material in the metal becomes soft, making it easy to bend. This process termed (by Jack Houck, a renown psychokinesis specialist), as "warm forming". Bending can thereby be accomplished with little or no physical effort.

Since the human brain is both a transmitter and a receiver of information, it is also important to look at how brain wave frequencies produce change in the vibrational movement of molecules, whereby bending can occur. Researchers believe that various altered states of consciousness not only increase a person's control over their mind and body, but also breed a multitude of newfound psychic experiences. It is at the deeper "evolved" levels of the mind that many "psi"(energy) events like thought transference and mind-moving matter takes place.

Learning how to manage brain wave frequencies can give us insight into how our body and mind are affected when we enter into different states of consciousness, and how to utilize each state to our benefit. The brainwave frequencies of beta (13 to 26 cycles per second) and delta (0 to 4 cycles per second) are at the extreme ranges. Beta, being associated with normal conscious levels of brain activity, and delta states associated with deep, non-dreaming state of sleep, are not beneficial in accessing a warm forming affect. Whereas, those of us functioning at an alpha (8 to 13 cycles per second) and theta (4 to 8 cycles per second) range seem to have more energy, broader awareness and focus ability. It is at these mid-range frequencies that one perceives information that they oftentimes didn't even know they had access to. Therefore, accessing an alpha or theta state, with mental static and internal dialogue turned down, a person is more receptive to the PK phenomenon.

Materials get soft by temperature. Temperature is no more than vibration, the vibration of molecules, and all molecules vibrate at certain frequencies. Through concentration we can set up frequencies of vibrational energy that are systematically in sync with the frequencies of the material. When connected with the vibrational frequencies more energy is generated and temperature increases, causing the material to vibrate faster thereby creating an annealed (make less brittle by heating and slow cooling) state.

Metallurgical analysis of worm-formed metal has shown that the two most important characteristics of metal that is easily bendable are the number of dislocations (moving out of the usual proper place) it contains, and a low thermal conductivity acting as transducers to receive this energy. When a large portion of the metal has soft grain boundaries or borders, the grains are free to float or slip and the metal then temporarily looses its firmness and rigidity. Although scientists are still questioning how the mind could arrange putting "energy" into the metal, it does seem to use the dislocations as a transducer. With no place to go, the energy turns into heat and melts the grain boundaries. With most of the grain boundaries molten, (liquefied by heat) for a few seconds, the metal thereby looses it structure and can be easily formed. Sometimes the person bending reports that the metal becomes warm as if heat were coming from the inside of the metal. It is postulated that with intention and the desire to bend, the mind is creating the conditions for energy of unknown form to be deposited along the "brain" boundaries of the metal.

Although an increasing amount of data suggesting that the above process is what most often happens in the metal, how the mind or subconscious converts the goal (intention) into thermal energy along the grain boundaries still remain a mystery. The key factor in this process is the power of one's mind and one's intention to accomplish such a task, therefore getting an unconscious connection between the individual and the metal they are planning to bend is essential.

Another important aspect in bending is that the individual must consciously be willing to bend the metal. He/she must make a mental connection with the object to be bent and deliberately will it to bend. After a brief interval the material becomes soft from internal heating, by connecting through thought and an altered state of consciousness, thereby changing the molecular structure. Then with a little force the bending will occur. Some pieces of stainless steel tableware that have been "warm formed" have broken with a loud popping sound. Some other objects that have large internal stresses and a number of dislocations (silver plate and sterling silver) have bent while just being held in one hand without the use of the other.

There is just a short time span that the metal becomes and remains soft. The key to bending is knowing when the metal looses its structure (i.e., becomes rubber-like) and is ready to be bent, during which time they can form the silverware into creative distorted shapes. A study, reported in The Geller Papers, 1975, states that there are certain emotional and/or sensory feelings that people might experience when the metal begins to loose its structure and is ready to bend, listed below are the results of the study.

Sensory or Emotional Feelings	Percentage
1. Feelings of warmth or tingling	13.87
2. Other emotional experiences	17.52
3. Tingling, warmth and other emotional experiences	8.71
4. No sensory or emotional experience	56.29
5. Unknown	3.65

One of the first things that reveal its self while working with groups is that the psychokinesis phenomena cannot always be produced unless all who participate are in a relaxed state. Otherwise feelings of tension, stress and even fear on the part of any of those present generally communicate itself to the whole group, and chances of success are significantly reduced. The entire process happens most easily when all those present and participating actively want the bending to occur. In addition, matters seem to be greatly enhanced when the experimental arrangement is aesthetically or imaginatively appealing to those desiring to bend, as well as the psychokinesis facilitator. What transpires next is often surprising and unexpected.

When the mind interacts with matter it is necessary for the group (or individual) to concentrate on the metal intended to be bent, and then command it to bend. In some unspecified manner, the system translates this intention, or thought into the physical mechanism necessary to accomplish that goal. The intensity of the specified command, expressed out loud or within oneself is important. Creating a positive emotionally intense situation or feeling helps for the "warm forming" to occur. Most of the energy used in accomplishing a PK experience comes from a person's intention coupled with the energy within themselves and the object being affected. The actual energy required by the person to connect his/her mind to the object and command it to bend is small.

One may observe what is referred to as the "first time effect". A person may get dramatic results the first time they attempt bending, but have more difficulty doing so the next time they try. This occurrence is due to over analyzing what they have just done and failing to understand it. Some people become a little frightened and/or their resistance just gets in the way again.

It is important to understand the components of psychokinesis, especially when working with groups.

1) Grounding Oneself – (The action of connecting oneself metaphorically to the ground, creating a balance within). The majority of energy used in accomplishing PK comes from within the mind. Creating a peak emotional experience with a clear focus will help direct thoughts and energies towards the intended object.
2) Muscle Testing – Thoughts, colors and even food can affect the body's energy system, either by weakening or strengthening it. Understanding how our body responds to different stimuli provides us with a better perspective on

how we can direct our energies towards our goals (of bending) and create a more profound effect in our own lives.
3) Visualization – An important way to influence the psychokinesis is by thinking. Since the brain uses images and symbols to think, visualization becomes an essential component to the PK process.
4) Building group dynamics – The influence of group energy creates a higher vibrational energy, thereby the softening of the metal can occur at a more rapid rate. Learning how to let go – it's important to let go of our own resistance, skepticism, inhibitions, doubts and fears that often limit us from accomplishing this psychokinesis phenomena, as well as our goals. The process of letting go allows us to open up to new possibilities.

The attempt to concentrate in order to obtain the desired results can at times interfere with the relaxed state of mind needed to produce such a phenomenon. What actually takes place happens at the subconscious level. Once the intention to do something has been firmly established, the conscious function of the mind need to let go of trying, otherwise that becomes more of a hindrance than help. Letting go, versus allowing oneself to accomplish this goal, is oftentimes more difficult than the bending. Therefore it is important to remember that relaxing the mind while focusing and concentrating on the task will help a person achieve their desired outcome in a more profound way.

Commanding the metal to bend, laughing, remembering a peak emotional experience and even listening to wonderful upbeat music helps enhance the emotional level in a group. The next step is to release and then "let go". This procedure helps create a distraction among the group in order to minimize an individual's intense concentration, thus assisting the release or letting go process.

It is important for the group to:

- Be relaxed and open minded
- Be cohesive and excited
- Get a point of concentration and focus in their head, and then connect with the metal
- Intensify the focus and bring up a mental picture of the metal softening and bending
- Bring that focused intention down through their body and into the hand that is holding the metal, then sending it into the silverware at the point you intend to bend it

- Command it to bend
- Release the command and just let it happen.

The group is instructed to shout once the bending begins to occur so that others can observe that process. This also helps in breaking their intense concentration, thus enabling them to bend theirs as well. This break in attention helps release one's resistance, opening the mind's capacity to organize the methods for achieving that person's goal of bending.

It is conceivable that the emergence of awareness of our own (and others) powerful energy can take us far beyond what we currently perceive. Although scientists often questions whether the human body can effortlessly emit such a powerful source of energy, energy like this – properly understood and harnessed – could offer vast new potentials.

This process can also be used in helping to overcome obstacles and has even help heal oneself by tapping into their hidden resources and directing their intention on that specific outcome. Suppose there is some unknown force, energy or mode of connection between the brain and metal object, then we may also suppose that the PK power of the mind interacting with matter may function in the same way people heal themselves from terminal illnesses, or walk again after being paralyzed. There is an unconscious connection. Many people who experience the "warm forming" affect begin to discover ways of having more control of what happens in their life.

Everything we need is already within us, we just have to access it, and then learn how to use it. This workshop will help you realize and recognize more of your greater potential as you begin to move beyond limitations. A shift does occur, allowing you to begin to tap into the unused portion of your mind's power, which becomes a powerful component for healing professionals.

You are all unique. Your particular footprints have never walked on the face of the earth before you. Nor will another voice sing your encouragements and praise to others with the particular sound and characteristics of the voice you possess. All of the contributions you leave behind will be unique as well...the things you have said, the acts you have performed, and the people you have touched. Know that you have made an impact on the world as those you have touched with your uniqueness is touching others and spreading that throughout impacting others. It remains for you to dream what you dare to dream, do what you dare to do and be what you dare to be. It is through your thoughts and intentions that you can enrich your life and control your destiny. You can rise to any height, and find peace, happiness, and unlimited power within you. You can become all that you want, and deserve to be. Ultimately, it all depends on your particular manner of thinking. Now, that you know how to think like a winner you are now be a winner. You can break through the success barrier simply by selecting your target and pursuing it with all your talents and abilities, and all the energy at your command. It is a journey like no other you can hope to have. I as your fellow traveler, wish you well on your quest into continued growth and self-discovery.

Man's mind, stretched to a new idea, never goes back to its original dimension.
– Oliver Wendell Holmes (1809-1894)

References

Geller, U.(1975), *Geller Papers*. Bosten. Massachusetts: Houghton Mifflin.

Houck, J.(1985). *A Conceptual Model of Paranormal Phenomena, Information Transfer and Mind-Brain Interaction*. United States Psychotronics Association, USPA Annual Conference Proceedings.

Houck, J.(1984). *PK Party History*, Psi. Research, Vol. 3, No. 1.

Hasted, J.(1981). *The Metal-Benders*. London: Routledge and Kegan Paul Ltd.

Targ, R., & Puthoff H.(1977). *Mind-Reach: Scientists Look at Psychic Ability*. New York: Delacorte Press.

Brown, M.H. (1997). *PK: A Report on the Power of Psychokinesis, Mental Energy that Moves Matter*. New York: Garber Communications Inc.

Braude, S. E. (1997). *The Limits of Influence*. Pennsylvania: University Press of America.

Rhine, L.E. (1993). *Mind Over Matter: Psychokinesis, Mysteries of the Unknown*. Boston, Massachusetts: Time Life Book.

Clark, A. V. (1990). *Psycho-Kinesis: Moving Matter With the Mind*. New York.

Averbach, L. (1976) *The Geller Phenomenon*. London: Aldus Books.

Awareness and Healing

Willem Lammers

In Ancient Greece, there was an understanding that one was required to worship all the gods and goddesses. You might have your favorites, but none of the remaining deities could be ignored. The god or goddess you ignored became the one who turned against you and destroyed you. So it was with the Trojan war, in ancient mythology. So it is with consciousness work. The parts of ourselves that we disown may turn against us (Rowan, 1993, p.118).

The Indian Jesuit priest Anthony de Mello (1990) says that, if we are to believe the mystics, reality is *whole*, but words and concepts fragment reality: The moment you teach a child the name of the bird, the child will never see that bird again" (p.121). Our task is to become aware of the split between ourselves and reality, to get into today. Otherwise "life is something that happens to us while we're busy making other plans" (p.114).

The French chemist Kekulé was ridiculed after he had discovered the structure of the carbon ring molecule: He told his colleagues he had dreamed of six monkeys in a dance, who grabbed each others' hands and feet and formed a circle. In my chemistry schoolbook, the carbon ring was still called the "monkey formula". Kekulé allowed his awareness to cross the rigid structures of the chemical formulas that were known until that time, and founded the new branch of science called carbon chemistry.

Awareness is the base of the art of healing. Healing means becoming whole. In my native Dutch language, it's even the same word. Illness, disease and distress show up when we are out of contact with the whole.

How can we actively (re)establish the contact with the *whole*? How can we learn the art of healing? In ancient times, it was clear that healing came from the gods, and they had their mediators. In our times it's more complicated. We learn theories, methods and techniques, and we tend to believe that some methods work better than others. That's one aspect, and maybe we need to do that to focus our intention (–> Nicosia). The other aspect of healing is *inspiration*, the "breathing in" we get, or the intuition, from the Latin *intuo*, "I'm looking inward". There is no healing without a connection to the inside and to the intentional, cohesive energy fields that create the world as we perceive it.

Many of us discover healing methods by a combination of knowledge and intuition, in a process that sometimes has an amazing quality of what Csikszentmihalyi would call "flow" (–> Hover-Kramer). Here I want to share my own experience in the development of the "Celtic Cross", a very gentle method to reinstall unity with the whole.

Many wise men in history have stated that our distress and disease comes from a loss of contact with the Whole. This loss manifests in the emergence of many different polarities. Polarities already show in Genesis, where Adam and Eve ate from the Tree of Knowledge, also called the Tree of Good and Evil. Bridging, or neutralizing, polarities means to reinstall the contact with the One Source. These polarities are present everywhere, in each aspect of our daily life: good and bad, warm and cold, I–Thou, inside and outside, North and South. They're a normal part of our life and we're used to perceiving the world in polarities. They offer safety, predictability and structure our world, and they cause a lot of our problems. Polarities also lie at the base of our primary emotions: Feelings of fear point towards power and powerlessness, anger polarizes between me and others, grief is the splitting of past and present.

I was pondering this, while I was teaching a seminar in Exeter, England. The training group was busily practising a newly taught method. For I reason I'm still not aware of, I opened my laptop computer, started the word processor with a blank page and started to write. Words seemed to flow automatically, and a new meridian-based method to bridge polarities emerged, without any effort from my side. I had worked this way before, but never before I got such a long, coherent message. The newly transmitted method made use of polarities, as I learned with our Yugoslavian colleague Zivorad Slavinski. The use of affirmations gives it has a ritualistic character, like Larry Nims' BSFF and my own Successive Point Process (–> Carrington). The eye movements are also found in NLP and Eye Movement Integration. The combination of tapping a point for a while and then holding it has been tested by many practitioners (–> Diepold), and has shown up on different mailing lists in the internet. The Governing Vessel and the Central Vessel represent the most important polarities in our bodies: activate/relax, top/down, left/right and front/back. The points used are also part of Gallo's Negative Affect Elimination Method (NAEM, Gallo, 1999) and Slavinski's Psycho-Energetic Auro Technology (PEAT). The "Celtic Cross" itself is an amazingly simple energy psychology synthesis. The procedure only minimally changed in the course of the month between the transmission and the writing of this chapter. It consists of a number of clearly defined steps:

- Focus on an issue.
- Move your eyes in the direction where the issue feels most present or problematic.
- Tap the point on the Governing Vessel on the Third Eye as long as you feel like it, and then hold it as long as you feel like it, while saying, "North is South".
- Tap the point on the Central Vessel between the nipples on the sternum (CV-17) as long as you feel like it, and then hold the point as long as you feel like it, while saying, "South is North".
- Tap the point under the left collarbone on the Kidney Meridian (K-27). Tap as long as you feel like it, and then hold it as long as you feel like it, while saying, "East ist West".
- Find the point under the right collarbone on the Kidney Meridian (K-27). Tap as long as you feel like it, and then hold it as long as you feel like it, while saying, "West is East".
- Find the point on the Central Vessel between the nipples on the sternum (CV-17) as long as you feel like it, and then hold the point as long as you feel like it, while saying, "In is out".
- Find the point on the Central Vessel between the nipples on the sternum (CV-17) as long as you feel like it, and then hold the point as long as you feel like it, while saying, "Out is in".
- Hold the right hind on the heart chakra and the left hand on the solar plexus as long as you feel like it, while focusing on the sentence, "LOVE IS".
- Focus on the issue you started with.
- Repeat the procedure until you reach a state of unity and balance.

In tapping and holding the different points, clients usually feel a bodily or emotional shift at the transition between tapping and holding or at the end of the holding phase.

The state of unity and balance feels like coming home, a heightened awareness of the world we're in, lifting boundaries and being in contact with what is. That state is wordless: We don't cut up the whole of reality to make concepts, using words to indicate different parts. We can see the world as it *is*.

References

De Mello, A. (1990). *Awareness*. London: HarperCollins.
Rowan, J. (1993). *Discover you subpersonalities and the people in it*. London: Routledge.
Slavinski, Zivorad (2001). *Psycho-Energetic Auro Technology (PEAT)*. Unpublished workshop manual. Beograd.

You will find references to the energy psychology methods mentioned in the reference section.

11

Getting On the Same Page: How All the Different Energy Psychology Approaches Fit Together[1]

David Grudermeyer

Nine Lineages That Birthed Energy Psychology

1. The Chakra/Prana Lineage (India)
Balancing, strengthening and aligning the chakras (the human energy field's "energy centers") has long been one of their keys to health, the benefits of which are now being documented by Western science and medicine. Yoga and Pranic Healing/Psychotherapy are parts of this lineage. Chakra treatments are also incorporated into Barbara Brennan's and Rosalyn Bruyere's healing approaches, and Carolyn Myss' diagnostic approach. These three innovators are among the grandmothers of chakra and biofield based psychotherapies.

2. The Meridians/Acupoints/Qi Lineage (China)
Balancing, strengthening and aligning the meridians and associated acupoints (the human energy field's "energy pathways") has long been one of their keys to health, the benefits of which are now being documented by Western science and medicine. Acupuncture, Qigong and Feng Shui are parts of this lineage. This lineage intersected with chiropractic and physical therapy traditions, through George Goodheart, to create the discipline of Applied Kinesiology (AK), the grandfather of the meridian-based psychotherapies (–> Durlacher).

3. The Aura Lineage
Balancing, strengthening and aligning the aura (the multi-layered "biofield" portion of the human energy field which envelopes the physical body) has long been considered a key to health, the benefits of which are now being documented by Western science and medicine.

4. The Nursing Lineage
Florence Nightingale, the British founder of modern nursing in the 1800's, was also a spiritual mystic who advocated the importance of treating the whole person in such a way that activated the person's intrinsic capacity for health. In 1970, Delores Krieger and Dora Kunz developed Therapeutic Touch (TT), bringing the treatment of the aura (biofield) into the realm of medical healing adjuncts. TT evolved in the nursing community to include chakra interventions of pioneers like Brennan & Bruyere as well, becoming known as Healing Touch (HT). Dorothea Hover-Kramer was a major figure developing HT. As a psychologist in addition to being a nurse, she is also the mother of biofield and chakra-based psychotherapy (which she termed "Psychoenergetics").

5. The Physical Therapy (PT) Lineage
The PT lineage utilized a diagnostic approach called Kinesiology to diagnose, though muscle testing, which muscle groups were in need of PT treatment, and to also evaluate if the PT treatment was producing the desired results.

6. The Chiropractic Lineage
In the mid 1960s, George Goodheart, D.C., hypothesized that diagnosing which meridians and acupoints needed treatment could be accomplished by adapting PT's Kinesiology diagnostic procedure to this purpose. His brilliant discovery led to the development of Applied Kinesiology and its offshoots, which have since become a major part of what is considered "standard of care" in the chiropractic field (–> Durlacher). Descendents that are chiropractic cousins of meridian-based therapies include John Thie's Touch for Health (TFH), Dennison's & Teplitz's Educational Kinesiology (Edu-K) and Brain Gym, Scott Walker's Neuro-Emotional Technique (NET) and Victor Frank's Total Body Modification (TBM). The Nambudripad Allergy Elimination Technique (NAET) is a derivative of TBM, and the Tapas Acupressure Technique (TAT) is a derivative of NAET.

7. The Psychology Lineage
American psychologist Roger Callahan and Australian psychiatrist John Diamond believed that AK might be developed into a psychotherapeutic intervention. In the course of studying with George Goodheart, they tried to collaborate together toward this end before

parting ways. Callahan built on AK to develop the Callahan Techniques. Diamond built on AK to develop Behavioral Kinesiology. These two seminal innovators are our treasured fathers of the meridian-based psychotherapies, which have come to be referred to generically as Thought Field Therapy. Derivatives and hybrids based on TFT include such methods as: James Durlacher's Acu-Power, Gary Craig's Emotional Freedom Techniques (EFT), Greg Nicosia's Thought Energy Synchronization Therapy (TEST), Fred Gallo's Energy Diagnostic & Treatment Methods (EDxTM), Judith Swack's Healing From the Body Level Up (HBLU), Larry Nims' Be Set Free Fast (BSFF), Lambrou's & Pratt's Emotional Self-Management (ESM), as well as a whole host of others. Asha Nahoma Clinton developed a hybrid of chakra and meridian interventions now known as Seemorg Matrix Work.

8. The Electromagnetic Field (EMF) Lineage
In 1935, Dr. Harold Saxton Burr, Professor of Neuroanatomy at Yale University School of Medicine, established that all living matter, from a seed to a human being, is surrounded and controlled by electrodynamic fields. This spawned a growing body of Western scientific research on human electromagnetic fields (and those of other animals), and the effects of astronomical electromagnetic fields, geophysical electromagnetic fields and artificial electromagnetic fields on the human electromagnetic field. The courageous pioneer, physician Robert Becker, further developed this field. Research has led to the development of devices to help keep the human energy field strong in the presence of artificial EMFs. EMF research is also helping us learn more about the causes of certain types of energy system disruptions that can be treated by energy psychology methods and their cousins from other allied health disciplines. The fields of geopathic stress, dowsing and *feng shui* are related to this lineage as well.

9. The Quantum Physics Lineage – the Physics of Non-Material Energy
Stunning research in the field of post-Einsteinian physics provides a scientific understanding of the underpinnings that may explain why energy medicine and energy psychology methods work. The proliferation of high tech medical diagnostic devices that conventional medicine now uses to evaluate the condition of the human energy system owes its theoretical credibility to quantum physics as well.

Put These Nine Lineages Together and What Have You Got?

A comprehensive picture of what constitutes our wonderful new field of energy psychology! The Association for Comprehensive Energy Psychology (ACEP) is a non-profit organization whose purpose is to provide ways to facilitate collaborative interplay among all these lineages. ACEP helps advance the visibility, credibility, treatment and research of interventions that directly and explicitly intervene with the meridians, chakras and biofield to treat mind-body, psychological, spiritual and peak performance issues. Individualized Energy Psychotherapy (IEP), developed by psychologists and ACEP co-founders David Grudermeyer, Rebecca Grudermeyer & Dorothea Hover-Kramer, is one of a number of training curriculums integrating diagnosis and treatment of all three of these aspects of the human vibrational matrix into a multidimensional energy psychology treatment approach.

Note

1. Excerpted from a substantially longer chapter in *The Desktop Guide to Energy Psychology Treatment* (2000), by the author.

12

Confessions From the Heart of Ethics[1]

Pati Beaudoin

Clinicians from most fields — social workers, massage therapists, physicians, psychologists, and other professionals trained in the health disciplines — are typically required to study and abide by an ethical code and standards of conduct (e.g. American Psychological Association, 2001). We are trained to think about such issues as practicing only within our areas of competence and maintaining professional relationships with patients[2]. While clinicians are often well-trained in thinking about these issues, seeing them from the heart may be more difficult. Instead, we often engage in discussions of ethics from a detached, intellectual perspective. I believe this is at least partially because we so often do not see the effects of our ethical lapses. The patient frequently does not bring the effects back to us, but instead brings them to family, friends or other therapists.

Having been in the position of friend or therapist of the person who is suffering the aftermath of a clinician's lapse, I have seen some of the pain we sometimes cause through these lapses. It is the direct experience of dealing with this pain that leads me to want to provide a heart perspective on why ethics is the most important consideration in the provision of energy work. Providing a heart perspective means illuminating the suffering our ethical lapses cause. I will do this by describing examples from my own experience, for it is my own experience that is close enough to the heart to touch others.

Competence
Clinicians are cautioned not to practice outside their areas of competence. Several years ago a colleague in a hypnosis consulting group described how he had "cured" a patient

with Multiple Personality Disorder (MPD, as it was then called) in four sessions with hypnosis. Those of us in the room who had training in the treatment of Dissociative Identity Disorder (DID, as it is now called) were horrified that he would let her believe she was cured, much less believe it himself. We knew it took years of delicate work to alleviate this disorder. Moreover, we knew that most of our DID patients had been treated by several therapists who were not trained in DID before arriving at our offices, and that they sometimes had been pronounced "cured." This typically leaves patients feeling like hopeless cases with nobody to turn to for help. As one of my own DID patients said after avoiding therapy for years, "Why would I think therapy would work? According to the expert, it already had."

Of all the patients I have seen who have left a therapist who was not sufficiently trained to deal with the problems the patient presented, not a single one has returned to the therapist to point out the problem. And why should they? It is not their responsibility to provide feedback or training to their former therapist; indeed, many of them understandably resent the time, money and hope they feel they wasted. Since former patients don't provide feedback, the therapist who thought he cured DID in four sessions may still think so.

The lack of feedback leads me to wonder about one of my former patients. I began to learn how to diagnose and treat DID in 1988, and realized suddenly during the training that I had treated a patient with the disorder without realizing it. This happens frequently when therapists are learning to diagnose disorders that are typically considered specialized or unusual. But commonality is not a justification for lack of competence. I had consulted with a supervisor concerning this patient, since I was interning at the time, but he also did not have the specialized training. The therapy seemed to be progressing in that the patient and I had developed what seemed to be a strong therapeutic relationship, but her symptoms were not diminishing as my other patients' seemed to do. Hindsight tells me now that I did not do harm, but could have been of more help. One could argue that I was as much help as I could be at the time, and that even my supervisor didn't diagnose correctly; but I wish one of us had considered the possibility of referral to a clinician who could better diagnose this patient. Not referring when it would be in the patient's best interests to do so is an ethical error. I am left hoping that that patient found her way to someone with the special knowledge and skills to be of more help to her than I was.

I have also been in the position of friend to several people who were in treatment but not getting the expertise they needed. These friends typically had a good relationship with their practitioners, which is why they continued treatment in spite of little or no change in symptoms. When friends bring up their therapy with me in conversation, it has at times been difficult for me, as a therapist, to discuss with them the merits of their therapy. They are understandably attached to and defensive of their therapists, and do not want to hear that there may be another type of expertise that may be more useful or efficient. I am thinking now especially of friends who are survivors of abuse, whose therapists have not helped them to identify and validate their symptoms as a normal response to an abnormal and unhealthy situation. There is also a woman I know whose therapist validated the repercussions of abuse, but was unfamiliar with dissociation, so did not recognize or treat it. I have several extended family members who have been told by body-oriented workers (a homeopath, two massage therapists, and a healer of unspecified training) that they don't need psychotherapy, they should continue only with that practitioner and all problems will be solved. Finally, there are several people I know who I believe would have been helped with medication, but their therapists or body workers were opposed to medication for various reasons. All of these people have been left in a therapeutic limbo, unwilling to consider shopping for a professional with more appropriate expertise, but not being helped by the person they consider most helpful to them. They don't struggle with the paradox they live in — that the hope for change is diminishing even as they work to change — because they don't see it. My wish for all of them is that their therapists will recognize that some symptoms seem to be unabated, and arrange a consultation from a clinician with expertise differing from their own.

Dual Relationships

A dual relationship exists when the therapist and patient engage in any relationship in addition to the therapy relationship. Dual relationships are considered unethical in most of the helping professions except in very unusual circumstances. A dual relationship can be initiated either by engaging in therapy with a person known in another context, or by adding another context to the therapeutic relationship.

I have four friends who are struggling with life-threatening illnesses. Two asked me to work with them, since it is an area of expertise for me, and I do energy work. I explained that the friendship precluded us doing therapy together and recommended other avenues. Then the third asked me to work with her, and when I explained why I would not, her response was, "How can you say no to me? You know I have cancer, you know that I know that you specialize in mind-body work, I believe you can help me get well, and you're going to let me die?" What my friend said made me think beyond rules, and I consulted with a colleague. I then called that friend, as well as the two I had previously said "no" to, and arranged to see them with the understanding that we would have to renegotiate the friendships. When the fourth called to see me professionally, I was ready. But the process of ensuring that the therapeutic relationship is not impacted by the previous friendships points up good reasons for not engaging in dual relationships.

One of these friends, for example, has lamented her loss of another friendship in therapy with me. The patient, a therapist herself, and I have put our friendship into suspended animation until we are no longer therapist-patient, and she feels the loss of our friendship, too. The statistical reality of this situation would predict that she is unlikely to survive her illness. Although I believe that what I am doing here is more ethical than not treating her, it hurts her to have given up the friendship with me, although it feels right to both of us that we not be friends while doing this work. Moving deeply into her issues requires that she have the safe cocoon of the therapeutic relationship undisturbed by give-and-take of friendship, which would naturally lead to her knowing many of my issues and needs. People often cannot say to friends what they can say to their therapists.

The above example shows how ongoing friendship can hurt therapy, but it is also possible that the therapy hurts the friendship. One of the four friends-turned-patients was very reluctant to totally suspend the friendship, suggesting instead that we continue both. This friend was not a clinician, and it was difficult to help her see why continuing both could prove hurtful to her. Her illness was demanding, and needed to be attended to quickly, with psychotherapy as an adjunct to physiological intervention. We therefore began the therapy without completely resolving the issue, committing to discuss it. As her issues were clarified in the therapeutic work, I began to see her in a different light, and realized the friendship would be difficult for me to continue for personal reasons. Since I had already resolved to end or suspend the friendship, this discovery was, thankfully, not the basis for the decision. Had I agreed to continue the friendship, however, she would have been hurt to have it end for non-clinical reasons.

We should not know our friends as we do our patients. Therapy is a unilateral relationship: It is for the patient's benefit only. Friendship is bilateral, and requires parity. A patient usually cannot reveal everything to a friend as she needs to reveal to her therapist, and usually should not depend on a friend's unconditional support as she should be able to from a therapist. Any one of these friendships would have been hurt by continuing them while therapy was ongoing. But more importantly, the therapy would have been hurt by the ongoing friendship. The safety of the therapy context is obstructed by parity.

Sex

Perhaps the most reviled dual relationship occurs when a therapist engages a patient sexually. I have treated three patients who were victims of sexual misconduct, as it is called, and one therapist who perpetrated it. All the patients were married women. In two cases the women ultimately quit the affair, informed their husbands, and submitted a complaint to the appropriate professional board. The third patient continued in therapy with the perpetrator following their mutual decision to end the affair.

Sexual misconduct introduces into therapy all the problems inherent in any dual relationship. In addition, the meaning and purpose of the therapy changes. When I think about how patients who terminate well with me describe their relationship with me, I remember them saying things like "It was the first time I felt important without it being for someone's use," "It was the first relationship where I felt really taken care of," "I felt lovable just for being." When a therapist changes therapy into a sexual relationship — or allows a patient to do so — the therapy becomes a vehicle for sex. It isn't only that each session is (potentially) an appointment for sex, but the whole therapy from its beginning changes from something done exclusively for the patient's benefit to something that was being developed to meet the therapist's needs. Benefits the patient derived from this special relationship that exists solely for her benefit disappear, as she realizes (true or not) that the therapy was leading toward the affair, that all along it was really a vehicle to meet the therapist's needs. This is one of the very few ways that history can actually be changed: One of the most beneficial aspects of therapy derives from its meaning to the patient. When the past meaning and purpose of the therapy changes from for-the-patient to for-the-therapist, the positive benefits in the patient that were predicated on that meaning seem to disappear. As one of the patients who complained legally said to me, "I thought I was getting so much better, but now I'm worse off than if I had never been in therapy at all. At least before I started, I could hope for change. Now I know for sure that everyone really is out to use me."

Sexual misconduct tips the power and responsibility within the relationship toward the patient. Although therapy is a collaborative effort between therapist and patient, I acknowledge that because I know more about the process (than most patients), and because I am taking the role of the helper, I carry a bigger burden of responsibility to define what is appropriate and useful in the relationship. It is my job to keep the therapy safe, and to define rules of conduct in the therapy. But once a therapist breaks the sexual boundary, he is vulnerable to the patient. She can cost him his license, or she can protect him (I use the pronouns gendered in this way because the victims seem to be usually female, and the perpetrators seem to be usually male). In fact, during and immediately after the affair, the victims I've known have protected their perpetrators. The protection of the therapist is a role reversal; it is incompatible with the therapeutic relationship, in which the responsibility for safety issues rests with the therapist.

Typically, the patient has been dazzled by positive transference, the idealization of the therapist, and the hints that somehow come to her that she could be more special to the therapist than his other patients. Then, as the affair begins, her hope to be special is rewarded. The therapist is still idealized at this point, seen without weakness or shadow. The patient may feel she has never been loved so well by someone who knows her so deeply. But even as she engages in this heady limerance, she senses a wrongness about the affair. The three women I have treated took from a month to two years to realize that the affair would have to end somehow. Although all three patients and the perpetrator-therapist were quite intelligent, thoughtful people, not one of them considered the consequences of their actions before beginning the affair. Not one of them thought, before beginning, that it would have to end somehow.

When the sexual liaison between patient and therapist ends, the patient typically discovers — if therapy has continued during the affair — that the therapy has lost its significance. The sexual relationship took priority as the most important relationship with the therapist. The therapy suffers for other reasons, too. One patient reported that the therapist said "Therapy just ended," after kissing the patient for the first time. This left the patient abandoned by her therapist, a "therapeutic orphan" (Keith-Spiegel & Koocher, 1985). She could not initiate therapy with another therapist without telling the most important and immediate secret in her life, and would not jeopardize her lover, so she was left without therapeutic support when she most needed it. She came to me a year later, still in the affair, and did tell me of it, using a pseudonym and describing her lover as a colleague. Her therapy proceeded in fits and starts, with me unable to guess why she seemed to be developing a solid therapeutic relationship, then backing away from therapy just as it seemed to strengthen. Her marriage in disarray, racked with guilt, shame and remorse, she finally told me a year after initiating treatment with me that her lover was her former therapist. I reviewed the clinical notes I had received from him, and of course there was no clue. Both she and the other patient who submitted complaints did so years after the affair, when they had shifted their primary loyalty back from lover to husband. Neither marriage was able to benefit from professional counseling, since the husbands understandably did not trust therapists or therapy.

When all four of these patients discussed their reasons for initiating the affairs, they said they were in love. The therapist and two of the patients allowed that perhaps transference was also involved, but they were definitely in love, as if being in love somehow justifies having sex. A former supervisor of mine once said that he thought being in love was always transference, so perhaps it doesn't matter whether it was true love or transference. From the point of view of all the patients long after the affair, it didn't matter. What mattered was that each of them regretted having acted on their feelings.

I was very lucky to have the experience of falling in love — or perhaps only of experiencing strong countertransference — during my first internship, and even luckier to have a supervisor who guided me through these murky waters well. I had told him in a supervision session that I suspected a patient was about to reveal to me that he was in love with me. To my surprise, instead of telling me the rules, this man asked me how I felt about the patient. I was reluctant to acknowledge my feelings, thinking they were wrong, but told him anyway, and he validated the feelings as perhaps quite real and even understandable in light of the patient having shared so much of himself with me. Further discussion led me to respond well to the patient, acknowledging my feelings with him when the time came, validating both of us, and assuring him that I would never let us act on them. Then the issue was dropped and we continued with the therapy. Several months later he remembered having been sexually abused by his mother. We dealt with that, and several months later therapy terminated appropriately. As we were reviewing the course of his therapy, he tearfully realized that it was my reassurance that nothing sexual would occur between us that allowed him to remember and work through his sexual abuse. He said that it was particularly important to him to know that I had the feelings I did, and that I would not act on them, since until then acting on feelings was a matter of course in his family. Had I not acknowledged my own feelings, he would have been afraid to proceed with working deeply with me, since his assumption would be that if I did fall in love with him he would be abused again. Even with my reassurances – which I found I needed to repeat as we worked through this issue — he was not quite trusting of the boundary until the end of therapy.

All the patients I have discussed in this section on sexual misconduct had histories of possible sexual abuse, except the therapist-perpetrator. One, the patient whose therapist said "Therapy just ended," thought she had been abused as a child, but was not sure. I wonder to what extent their sexual abuse by therapists was a recapitulation of this earlier trauma. Certainly none of them had finished working with the issue, which seems to suggest it may have been. The patient who was unsure of her early sexual history terminated with me without knowing whether she had been abused. Her husband, suspicious now of therapy and therapists, discouraged her participation in therapy; and, having been so disloyal to him with her previous therapist, she decided her marriage was more important than her treatment.

Special Problems Arising in the Energy Field

Energy work is felt, by many of its practitioners, to be more powerful than traditional talk therapies, and than traditional body therapies. With more power comes more room for causing harm.

One of the possible sources of harm is toxicity from external sources, whether they be entities, people or situations. I believe I may have allowed this to occur through ignorance, as many may have. But again, commonality is not a justification for this occurrence. The patient was a very energy-sensitive woman who developed severe insomnia for months following the introduction of energy work into her therapy. I had developed a similar insomnia at the same time. Since then, I have worked to learn how to recognize and alleviate energy toxicity, but I would much prefer to have known this well enough to prevent the trouble.

Another, more mundane, source of harm is the mystique that can be allowed to envelop energy work. I notice that when I introduce a procedure and it works quickly and well, patients are typically impressed, and a few regard me in a new light. It is the light of magic; they think I have done this magic myself, that I have some mystical power. I can remember the seductive, heady feeling of this fork in the path of the work: I can choose to go with the patient onto the path of mystical, magical guru, garnering admiration and prestige; or I can demystify the process, show the patient that his work is truly his, and reorganize the therapeutic relationship back to collaboration. I am grateful to my guides and teachers for helping me consistently choose the right path. To date, I have not met a patient who has the experience of therapist-turned-guru due to energy work.

The final source of harm I will discuss here is common to both energy and traditional therapies, the unwitting error of inattention. The harm caused by inattention is harm of omission, rather than commission, and it may seem minor until one remembers the impact of intent (–> Nicosia). Without full attention, intent is insufficiently guided. This is a lapse I commit far less frequently since energy training has heightened my awareness of its importance.

Conclusion

In every situation I have seen in which a therapist caused harm, the situation has arisen from the therapist not having his/her needs met. Clearly, in the sexual arena, the therapists' sexual and/or relational needs were not met in their personal lives. The therapist who claimed to cure DID in four sessions had an unmet need for training, but also unmet desire for status, prestige, admiration. The lapses of my own described here are due to unmet needs for training.

It is incumbent upon us to find ways to identify our unmet needs and deal with them before they arise in the context of our treatment of others. Even then, we may not always be able to stay alert to every possibility, and my own professional and personal history shows me that whatever I am not alert to will pop into a wrong context if I don't catch it first in a right context. For this reason I am a firm believer in ongoing consultation for the practitioner of energy work, as well as daily contemplative practice. (This can be meditation or prayer, but if it is prayer I believe prayer should include at least as much time listening as talking.)

An approach that provides a corollary to identifying and meeting unmet needs is the ethic of restraint. The Dalai Lama notes that lack of inner restraint is the source of all unethical conduct (1999). How we can avoid ethical errors of commission by practicing restraint is easy to see; but we can also avoid ethical errors of omission in this way. If we restrain our sense of omnipotence or compulsion to help everyone, for example, we will be more likely to refer when we are unprepared to help certain patients.

My hope for myself (and for all my patients) is that my ethical lapses will always be minor and unwitting, that my patients will always let me see their effects, and that my heart will be open to seeing them.

Notes

1. The author is grateful to Daphne Greenberg, Ph.D., and Lynn Mary Karjala, Ph.D., for their comments.
2. I use the term "patient" for people who come to me for treatment, reserving the term "client" for those who come to me for consultation. In my discipline, consultation and treatment are legally and ethically distinct.

References

American Psychological Association. (2001). Ethical principles of psychologists and code of conduct: draft for comment. *American Psychologist*, 32(2), 77-89.

His Holiness the Dalai Lama. (1999). *Ethics for the New Millennium.* New York: Riverhead Books.

Keith-Spiegel, P. & Koocher, GP. (1985). *Ethics in Psychology: Professional Standards and Cases.* New York: Random House.

13

Energy Medicine for the Emotional Body

Sharon Cass Toole

Dedicated to my late father, Dr. Isadore Morris Cass who left me the legacy of healing.

Mind-Body Connection

Everything old is new again. Until very recently, physicians would deal only with what the establishment referred to as "real" diseases. Diseases that could be seen – as with a skin lesion, heard – as with a heart murmur, felt – as with a lump, smelled – as is characteristic of certain diseases or documented in a so-called objective blood or urine test, X-ray, EEG or ECG. Complaints that had no measurable or discernable physiological basis were deemed "all in the head." Those patients were regarded as not really being sick and were referred to a psychiatrist. Today, more doctors and patients alike, are convinced of the link between physical disorders and emotional stress. We now realize that serious disease can cause depression and that chronic depression can cause serious illness.

It is not necessary to do double-blind, placebo controlled studies to know that people can literally die of fright, that when one is scared the heart pounds, the blood pressure rises, the mouth becomes dry and we may lose control of bodily functions or break out into a cold sweat. When one is embarrassed or angry, one's face may become flushed, blotchy or red - very much the same as what occurs during an allergic reaction. Put all these observations together and we have a case for the unity of mind and body. The truth is that symptoms resulting from emotional stress are often indistinguishable from symptoms of organic disease. A temporary blush or transient rise in blood pressure, heart rate or cholesterol in response to a short-lived emotional crisis may not be harmful in the long run. However, such reactions do one no good if the stress is ongoing.

The immune system co-ordinates our mental processes and bodily functions. It controls how effectively we ward off infection, cancer, heart attacks, strokes and virtually every other illness that may befall us. It even controls our rate of aging. Many of the chemicals, blood cells, hormones and other components of the immune system have been identified and can be measured. This has lead to the development of psychoneuroimmunology (Benor, 1992, Vol.2, 30–31), which is a new, and important medical discipline devoted to the understanding and documentation of the mind-body relationship. Eastern cultures have been aware of this unity for thousands of years and have evolved techniques to influence it (–> Stoler). In our modern society this has largely been the domain of practitioners of alternative medicine.

Meridian-based Psychotherapy

The first manifestation of an emotion, either positive or negative, is a change in the body's electrical state (Bohm, 1980). Meridian-based psychotherapy a wonderful set of self-care tools is used to balance the electrical disruption caused by negative emotions. These methods that can be learned in minutes because you use only your fingers. Meridian-based psychotherapy, like acupressure, makes use of the same system that is used in acupuncture. Points on the body, known as meridian points, are stimulated to assist healing. The techniques are gentle, quick and painless. They often bring about rapid and lasting relief (Bohm & Hiley, 1993).

Acupressure works by neutralizing disruptions in your body's electrical system, which then stops the chemical chain reaction and frees you from emotional and physical discomforts. As you gently tap or press on a point, neural receptors under the skin convert the pressure to an electrical impulse that is transmitted to the brain (–> Diepold). It is the same as using a VCR remote control or tapping a key on a keyboard to send an electrical signal to the computer (Craig, 1995).

Our thoughts are constantly creating patterns of electrical energy (–> Nicosia) that cause the release of neurotransmitters, hormones and other chemicals in the body that we feel as emotions. When there is a disruption in the body's electrical flow, such as the fight or flight response, we feel it. If the disruption continues, it can lead to emotional distress and eventually physical problems. When the disruption is removed, the distress stops (Craig, 1995). Acupuncture, which has been practiced for over 5000 years in the

Orient, is used today, as is meridian-based psychotherapy, to treat a wide range of issues, including physical pain, stress, anxiety, fears and phobias, trauma, anger, depression, migraines, fibromyalgia, asthma and addictions (–> Friedman, Grudermeyer, Luthke).

Meridian-based psychotherapy is also used to improve personal performance in academics, business and sports by removing anxiety, doubt and negative self-talk (Gallo, 1999). There is now a great deal of research that supports the idea that the body's energy system is primarily electromagnetic and that it can be directly adjusted (Becker, 1961, 1985). Using discoveries from quantum physics, orthopedic surgeon Robert Becker (1961) mapped the entire meridian system in the late 1960s. In 1977, researchers Fritz Popp and Walter Kroy (Gallo, 1999) demonstrated how cells in the body communicate using low energy light photons and microwaves. In 1986, Stanford cellular biologist Bruce Lipton described the interface between the mind and the cells of the body. Around 1979, after studying applied kinesiology, including the work of Dr. George Goodheart (1975) and Dr. John Diamond (1978), psychologist Dr. Roger Callahan combined elements of quantum theory, kinesiology and acupressure to begin curing people with phobias and traumatic stress disorders. Initially, Callahan thought of his method in terms of cognitive therapy but later changed his view and referred to his technique as Thought Field Therapy.

Emotional Freedom Techniques (EFT) evolved from TFT under the guidance of Gary Craig, one of Callahan's first students. Craig has moved EFT away from Callahan's scientific model, where TFT has its own rules and terminology, into a more holistic context. For instance, he teaches the importance of a supportive relationship between therapist and client and he stresses the value of persistence in treating various aspects of a problem in order to resolve all parts of it (–> Shaw, Weil). While Callahan promotes different combinations of tapping points for different issues, Craig uses one, all purpose sequence, which is easier for both client and therapist to learn and remember. Both are extremely effective, however, and the differences between them are simply a matter of personal preference. TFT and EFT bear resemblance to acupressure in that they both address the acupuncture meridian system. Unlike acupressure, these therapies are specifically psychologically oriented.

Many are skeptical when they first hear about the tapping therapies. The alternative health community is especially vulnerable to bogus new discoveries and the claims of TFT and EFT fly in the face of everything we thought we knew about psychology and emotional healing. Despite my own initial skepticism, I have been using meridian-based psychotherapy successfully on clients as well as on myself for the past five years. Although nothing is perfect and even these techniques are not always completely successful, their success rate cannot be ignored. It is estimated that about 85% or more of emotional issues treated with these processes are eliminated within four sessions with the majority of them being resolved even more quickly (Craig, 1995).

Why are not more people are aware of these techniques? First of all, it is difficult to describe them in a way that sounds convincing. There is nothing familiar with which to compare them and the tapping procedure itself can sound rather absurd. There are few clinical studies available to empirically prove the validity of these tapping techniques to traditional professionals. However, there are studies being done and lately there have been some very important research results (–> Narvaez). Most of the evidence of success for these techniques exists in the reports of hundreds of therapists around the world who have successfully treated thousands of patients. It may take some time for this span between energy work and psychology to prove itself solid and reliable enough for the traditionalists.

Energy psychology is still often viewed similarly to penicillin in its early days. That is, for some people, the potential effects of tapping are as suspect as the claimed effects of moldy bread must have seemed. However, like penicillin, it is quite possible to accept the beneficial effects of tapping without understanding their exact physiological basis.

Combined with standard of care, psychotherapy is more effective with the energy therapies. We need to use these methods for the welfare of our patients. We need to combine them with standard of care for obvious good clinical and ethical reasons.

While the energy therapy techniques have lifted the profession to a new level in proficiency, they are just the beginning. We are, indeed, as Dr. William Tiller, the Stanford physicist states "babes crawling on the floor of the Universe" (Tiller, 1997, p. 2) and there is much, much more ahead of us. As the next 10 years unfold, we will undoubtedly be required to question and re-question our paradigms. We are in for some major re-thinking of our sacred belief systems (–> Feinstein, Luthke, Nicosia).

References
Becker, R. O. (1961). *Search for evidence of axial current flow in peripheral nerves of the salamander.* Science, 134, 101.
Becker, R. O. Selden, G. (1985). *The Body Electric.* New York: Morrow.
Benor, D. J. (1992). *Healing Research: Holistic Energy, Medicine & Spirituality, Volumes I and II.* UK: Helix Editions, Ltd.

Bohm, D. (1980). *Wholeness & the Implicate Order.* London: Routledge & Kegan Paul.
Bohm, D. and Hiley, B.J. (1993). *The Undivided Universe: An Ontological Interpretation of Quantum Theory.* London: Routledge and Kegan Paul.
Craig, G. H. (1995). *Emotional Freedom Techniques: The Manual.* Sea Ranch, CA: Author.
Diamond, J. (1978). *Behavioral Kinesiology and the Autonomic Nervous System.* New York: The Institute of Behavioral Kinesiology.
Gallo, F. (1999). *Energy Psychology: Explorations at the Interface of Energy.* Cognition, Behavior and Health. USA/London: CRC Press
Goodheart, G. J. (1975). *Applied Kinesiology.* Workshop Procedure Manual, 11th Edition. Detroit: Author
Tiller, W. (1997). *Science and Human Transformation: Subtle Energies, Intentionality and Consciousness.* Walnut Creek, CA: Pavior Publishing.

14

Four Stages of Trauma Treatment

Mary Sise

Introduction

With the advent of energy therapies, many clinicians have been thrown into the realm of being trauma therapists, without much preparation and clinical grounding in the proper care of multiply traumatized clients. While energy therapies work quickly and without much complication for clients who have single traumas, and have grown up in relatively trauma free environments, the situation with multiply traumatized clients can be rather complex and specialized.

One dilemma with energy therapies, is that because they are often misunderstood by clinicians, referrals can be generated without the prerequisite screening for their appropriateness. These clients are quite frequently the most difficult to treat and therapists who have not been trained in trauma therapies can feel quite inadequate in the face of such suffering. Energy therapists, excited to show their colleagues what these therapies can do, can set themselves up for disaster and potentially cause a client to deteriorate if not careful.

Another dilemma for the clinician is that when clients hear about these fast energy therapies and they have been suffering and struggling for years with their traumas, they understandably want to come in and be "fixed" as fast as possible. While energy therapies will certainly speed up the process, it is not as simple as they hope. A therapist will do well to educate the client in this respect and not set the stage for another disappointment.

The question then becomes, how can we as clinicians serve these clients in a way that minimally is not retraumatizing and maximally eliminates the sequelae of trauma. Since much has been written outlining the stages of trauma treatment, I would like to combine what has been written on trauma therapy with the energy therapies (–> Lane).

I have divided trauma therapy into four distinct, yet overlapping stages. Metaphorically, I have likened it to building a house, with each stage building on the other. The lack of attending to a stage sets the stage for a collapse.

Stage 1 – The Evaluation Stage – Assessing the Foundation

In this stage the primary goal is to help the therapist discover if this is a single adult trauma, or is this a multiply traumatized client. In my opinion, the entire first session or two, (unless the client is in an emergency stage of flashbacks and nightmares), should be spent on assessment. This assessment should especially look for the potential warning signs of previous trauma, specifically asking about previous hospitalizations, past therapy, psychiatric history – past depressions, panic attacks, history of eating disorders, suicidal ideation, drug/alcohol history. In addition, I try to ascertain if the client ever experienced dissociative phenomena such as feeling as though they were "outside" of themselves, or hearing voices either inside or outside of their head? (note: inside of their head is more suggestive of Dissociative Identity Disorder, formerly Multiple Personality Disorder; outside of their head is more suggestive of Schizophrenia). Finally, I ask about PTSD phenomena such as flashbacks, nightmares, numbing, hyperstartle and any self-harm types of behaviors either past or current.

Next, I would begin to access their support system. Are they working, married, have friends, involved in church activities? Do they attend AA or any other support group. Do they exercise, belong to a gym. All of this would provide me with resources when we begin the trauma work. In my intake information, I also gather a phone number of someone that we can use in an emergency

Once a general history has been taken, it is important to gather a formal trauma history. Even if the client has been referred from another clinician, it is still wise not to assume that a trauma history has been taken. I begin by first giving them a rationale for this. I explain that the brain sorts information and puts it in files, that cooking stuff is in their cooking file, and work stuff is in their work file. I tell them that sometimes things that were really frightening end up in the same file, so it is important for me to get a *general* idea of what might be in that file. I tell them that my job is to figure out what might be filed incorrectly, as trauma usually doesn't get put in the "it's over" file.

I talk about the brain being like a computer and that sometimes, things get filed wrong. I explain that when a trauma occurs the brains primary job is to keep you alive, and therefore it doesn't process in the same way as when you are safe. I explain that instead of things being filed in your hard drive under "it's over, I'm safe now" it gets stuck, and metaphorically stays on your "desktop" under the "still current and ready to be opened file". Usually, all someone needs to do is come over and hit the keyboard with anything similar (word, sound, smell) and up comes that old trauma, as frightening as it was years ago.

Once a rationale has been given I begin to ask about anything that might have frightened them in the past. I give examples such as car accidents, house fires, deaths, hospitalizations, broken bones and any types of physical abuse or violence. The objective is to get a brief overview without retraumatizing them or throwing their minds into a flashback. For this reason, it is important to have gathered the above information, as the more indicators you have of previous psychiatric difficulties, the more sensitive you can be to the potential dangers of this line of questioning. The goal is to get a *brief* description of the past difficulties a client has had, whereby the re-experiencing of the trauma is avoided. For some clients the mere thinking about the past is enough to put them into an abreaction. I purposely ask for a general history so as to be non-suggestive regarding past abuse. I ask them not to give me much detail, but just a general idea of what age they were, and what happened. A typical response from a multiply traumatized client might be, dad left when I was 3, I was assaulted by a group of boys age 12, I was in a car accident age 18, raped age 22 etc. If I feel that they are getting overwhelmed I stop this line of questioning. I find it can be sometimes helpful to do a round of tapping without any eyemovents at this stage if you can see that the client is becoming upset. (The main reason I avoid the eye movements is that I don't want to access any additional memory, and it is my experience that the eye movements play a part in this). I might also use the Touch-And Breathe (–> Diepold) here, as I find it to be soothing. If the client has no idea about energy therapies, I would just do deep breathing here, rather than try to do too much and possibly scare them by being "too weird".

Finally, during this stage, I assess the risks involved. If the client has been involved in a crime (i.e. rape, assault) or anything where there might be legal ramifications (car accident), I usually videotape any trauma processing sessions. I discuss this with the client, and if there are lawyers involved I tell them that they must speak to their lawyer prior to us doing any trauma processing. My rationale for this is that I would hate to see a rapist get off because the jury doesn't believe the client, as most people feel that a rape is something you "never get over". I also discuss that there is not much research on these methods (–> Narvaez), so that they have "informed consent" if they choose to proceed. I document as much as possible of the above. In my opinion, clinicians should also be prepared to refer these clients if this is an area outside your licensure, and minimally get good supervision from a clinician who has trauma experience.

Most of these clients are helped by some type of psychotropic medication, as the research has shown that antidepressants, especially SSRIs are helpful. Sound clinical practice would indicate that the client minimally needs to be informed of this. It is my opinion that although these energy therapies are effective with traumas, the risk is too great for suicide or self-injurious behaviors to ignore what research has shown to be effective. I much prefer to combine the energy therapies with "main stream" medicine.

Stage 2 – Beginning Treatment Stage: Stabilization & Safety – Strengthening the Foundation

In the beginning treatment stage, the primary goals are to develop a relationship, and help the client in the here-and-now. The energy therapies can be used here primarily for symptom reduction, i.e. anger management and stress reduction. Targeting events that are currently occurring (conflicts with children, boss, husband, limited finances) the energy therapies can be an effective way to reduce the emotionality of the client, so that they feel more empowered in their day to day interactions.

One caveat for this stage is "Build a life worth living". Focus on job, family etc. By keeping them in the here-and-now, they begin to build ego strength, and experience the therapist as a competent ally. This will serve you well during subsequent stages of the therapy. I teach them mindfulness skills, and encourage them to use energy therapies daily. I use energy therapies to install a imaginary safe place (island, mountain top). If during the evaluation stage it was apparent that the client did not have much support, it would be important to encourage them to join groups, return to church, etc. Therapy groups should be present day focused, and skills based, not survivor groups as they can be especially re-triggering for a multiply traumatized client.

At this stage it is very helpful to teach the client about the effects of trauma on the brain, the limbic system (–> Weil) etc. to demystify their experience, helping them to feel more hopeful regarding their recovery and "less crazy". Any self-injurious behaviors are dealt with in this stage, using energy therapies for calming down the affect. Referrals to psychiatry are important here, especially if there is any suicidality.

During this stage the therapist also needs to establish boundaries and set the stage for therapy (–> Beaudoin). Acknowledge their fantasies that someone can "rescue" them, but also make it clear that they are rescuing themselves, with you as the guide. The goal here is always to empower them. Due to the emotional intensity of this work, there are many rescue traps and illusions, so get good supervision from a therapist who has trauma therapy experience.

As things begin to stabilize, begin to work on the deserving to be well or covenant to be well. (See Matrix Work manual for examples of beliefs that impact or stall treatment). This is a good place to begin once the client is stable. Begin to look at their fears and beliefs, and how they initially served them in the past. E.g. "It was my fault" gets honored for the brilliant illusion it was to help a small child think that if they had some element of control this awful situation might end. They begin to see that if they didn't have their illusions, as a child, they might have been so overwhelmed they would have "cracked". Use trauma therapies now to shift core beliefs (–> Hover-Kramer, Shaw, Weil).

Toward the end of this stage trauma memories may begin to surface. It is here that you begin a tightrope act of accessing traumas, then returning to stabilization and safety strategies.

Stage 3 - Advanced Treatment Stages: Memory Processing – Putting up the Walls

This stage is less discreet, with the client moving back and forth between this stage and the stabilization stage. Usually when working on core beliefs, the client begin to access trauma that helped to create these beliefs.

If you know several energy therapies, the question usually becomes "Which one works best and when?". Due to the newness of many of the therapies, and the lack of any research, it becomes a matter of using intuition or muscle testing. I particularly like to use TFT when I am working on a trauma, as I feel that by tapping on the body it is easier to stay in the "here and now" and there is less chance of abreaction. I also have experienced that the eye movements in TFT have been helpful for processing discreet memories, moving them "farther away".

I prefer to start at the beginning of a trauma and work my way till the end, using TFT at any point where the SUD rating level rises, and continuing until that aspect has dropped to a zero SUD rating. Some clients do not process in that way and as soon as you have finished one round of tapping, the next aspect comes in. Metaphorically, if we were thinking of a forest, the first type of processing would be where we take individual trees down one by one till the forest is cleared. The second type would be where we keep taking the tops off the trees until all of the aspects are low enough that the entire forest clears.

I usually begin by using the TFT algorithm for trauma: (eyebrow, under eye, under arm, and collarbone) then the 9-gamut treatment and repeat the algorithm. I prefer to take the terror of the trauma down first, going through this piece by piece until it is complete. Then I scan to see what related aspects are coming up looking in particular for anger, shame, rage, guilt, grief etc. and treating those aspects. Although affirmations (–> Carrington) are not a part any longer of Callahan's TFT, I find them especially helpful, while tapping, for releasing these aspects (I forgive myself...). Finally, I have them go over the trauma, scanning their body to see if there is any distress. Usually, if the body is clear, with the client reporting a feeling of calm or lightness when they think of the memory, the trauma is processed. I remind them that there can be more aspects to this trauma, and that if anything too distressing comes up, they can use the TFT at home, or any of the other strategies they now have in their possession, to calm themselves down. They are informed to call me if this doesn't seem to help.

With multiply traumatized clients, once one trauma is processed another one will surface. Although I have not experienced the flooding or abreaction that occur with EMDR, I have found that my clients usually have "a few good days" after the work is completed, and then another memory comes in. The goal here is not to become discouraged yourself, to normalize their experience and to encourage the client to stay with this work. They can become suicidal as another usually more painful and horrific experience emerges into consciousness, and feel hopeless that this will never end. If you have used safe place imagery, it is usually helpful to imagine a "vault" that can hold these traumas, with the understanding that we will deal with them one at a time. I usually keep a "Trauma Recovery Plan" (see attached), in which I record their traumas. This acts as a container for the client, and helps me not to forget.

Abreactions can occur, especially with dissociated body memory. Thankfully, they are rare. I have found that if they occur, I try to use all of the senses to keep them in the here-and-now. I speak louder, using words that separate then and now i.e. "It's in the past, you're safe now", I might invite them to hold my arm while I say "know that you're safe" or stomp their feet, knowing that they are safe...". Continuing with the energy therapy I am using, they usually can move through it.

Stage 4 – Consolidation Stage: - Putting on the Roof and Decorating

The goal of this stage is to help the client be in the world, without their traumas. They sometimes now will return to school, start a relationship and have multiple questions about "what's normal". Using energy therapies here to help them to envision a future, asking what they would really love to be doing. Like olympic athletes, visualization along with energy psychology methods is powerful. They need to make new connections as old relationships can sometimes no longer fit. This is an exciting and frightening time for the client, and the support that a therapist offers is invaluable. They are often quite frightened of moving on without the therapist, so it is important not to let them stay stuck here, but to use therapy as a springboard to be the person they came here to be.

References

Courtois, C.A. (1988) *Healing the Incest Wound: Adult survivors in therapy*. New York:Norton.
Herman, J. (1992). *Trauma and Recover*. New York:Basic Books. 1992.
Lenihan, M. (1993). *Cognitive-Behavioral treatment of Borderline Personality Disorder*. New York:Guilford Press.
Van der Kolk, B. (1996). *Traumatic Stress: The Effects of Overwhelming Experiences on Mind, Body and Society*. New York:Guilford Press.

15

Integration of Energy Psychology Meridian Tapping and EMDR

Jim Lane

Innovative psychotherapists are aware that techniques from energy psychology and EMDR provide today's most powerful healing tools for psychological trauma, but struggle with ways to integrate them. These therapeutic methods come from different theoretical backgrounds, have different procedural frameworks, and are taught as individual systems, but can be integrated to provide a rich therapeutic experience for client and practitioner. This article compares the strengths of these methods, and illustrates through a case study, ways that these two powerful methodologies can be integrated. This also provides a way to introduce and motivate practitioners of one of these methods to study the healing power inherent in the other methodology.

It is helpful to start with an understanding of traumatic memories (–> Sise, Weil). The researcher, Bessel A. van der Kolk M.D., notes that accessing traumatic memories leads to an amygdala activated sympathetic nervous system hyperarousal. This arousal generates stress hormones such as adrenaline, coritsol, and epinephrine, which is experienced physiologically as rapid heart rate, shortness of breath, and shakiness. This is known as the fight, flight or freeze response. Traumatic memory may be accompanied by a surge of emotion, memory flashbacks and/or by emotional numbing. Research indicates that traumatic memories are primarily imprinted in sensory and emotional modes, remain stable over time, and may be triggered by reminders of trauma, or by intense stimulation. Van der Kolk concludes that the "extreme emotional arousal leads to a failure of the central nervous system to synthesize the sensations related to the trauma into an integrated whole." In other words, the person is overwhelmed by physiological and emotional activation. This level of activation is so distressing that most people want to escape from it, thereby keeping themselves from the mental and emotional processing necessary to heal from the trauma. Escape can be accomplished by severely restricting activities to avoid confronting cues which trigger traumatic memories. Additionally, trauma survivors often escape into drugs, alcohol, sex addiction, gambling addiction and other high intensity maladaptive patterns.

Energy psychology meridian tapping techniques are particularly suited to working with traumatic memories because they

- reduce self-blame that overlays the trauma by correcting for psychological reversals;
- quickly reduce levels of distress experienced by clients;
- provide a laser like focus for working through aspects of traumatic experiences and provide a tool that can be utilized for self-help.

Meridian-based therapies let the client stimulate acupoints along the Chinese acupuncture meridians to desensitize distress levels. Examples of these therapies include Thought Field Therapy (Callahan), Emotional Freedom Techniques (Craig), Be Set Free Fast (Nims), EdxTm (Gallo), and variations of the above techniques.

The first step in the tapping protocol is clearing unconscious objections to healing known as psychological or psychoenergetic reversals (–> Hover-Kramer). The client taps an acupoint and states "Even though I have this problem, I deeply accept myself". This reduces a level of self-blame, which, when cleared, opens up the traumatic memory to clearing. The acupoints are stimulated by tapping, but can also be stimulated by rubbing or holding as in Touch and Breathe (–> Diepold). The client is asked to "attune to" (think of) the distressing memory and rate the distress level on a subjective zero (low) to 10 (high) scale. The client is instructed to remain focused on the problem to be desensitized, while tapping to bring down the distress level. The protocol may include starting with an energy balancing technique and may also include muscle testing to see that there is nothing interfering with the successful application. Tapping often results in significantly lowering the distress level within minutes. Several rounds of tapping can be used to treat different aspects of the problem. Meridian tapping therapies are easy to learn and apply and are growing in popularity among therapists.

Eye Movement Desensitization and Reprocessing (EMDR), is a system of psychotherapy developed by Francine Shapiro PhD., which uses alternating bilateral brain stimulation to process and desensitize traumatic materials and to install positive mental states. EMDR is particularly suited for working with traumatic memories because: it has a highly effective set up which targets affective, cognitive, imaginal and kinesthetic aspects of traumatic memories; it access a broad network of inner experiences and resources, it seems to flow from the client's own inner experience; it seems more like psychotherapy than energy psychology, and it has resource installation procedures in its standard protocol.

In trauma reprocessing, the client targets the trauma by focusing on the internal awareness while he or she experiences sets of bilateral brain stimulation. The alternating bilateral brain stimulation can be accomplished through eye movement, kinesthetic stimulation and/or auditory stimulation. EMDR is based on an information processing model which assumes alternating bilateral brain stimulation activates both cerebral hemispheres to process "stuck" traumatic materials and bring full brain resources to the installation of positive mental states. In this way, the verbal, logical, sequential capabilities of the one hemisphere (usually the left) and the kinesthetic, intuitive and imaginative qualities of the other (usually the right) hemisphere are brought into play. Resources which have been developed by the individual after the trauma (e.g. an ability to protect oneself), become available in the processing. These positive resources can then be installed, so that the client can utilize them. The key concept is that both hemispheres must be activated in a focused way in order to process cognitive and affective information and move towards integration and resolution of the traumatic memory. EMDR's success is highly researched and studies are underway to validate some of the underlying assumptions.

The EMDR setup has the client focus on inner images, body sensations, definable emotions, and cognitive self-statements (e.g. "I am a weak person") in the reprocessing. EMDR, like many Energy Psychology techniques, uses a SUDS (subjective units of distress scale) to assess and measure changes in the client. Additionally, EMDR uses a VoC (validity of cognition scale) to assess the client's belief in a positive self-statement (e.g. "I am a strong person"). The positive cognition and associated resource state are installed after the trauma and negative cognition are cleared. I have found that utilizing the EMDR setup (image, body sensation, emotion, negative self-statement), when doing Energy Psychology work, helps the client access and focus on the trauma to be desensitized. This is especially helpful for clients who have symptoms of Attention Deficit Disorder. The ability to remain focused is necessary, in order to desensitize a traumatic memory.

As a client experiences EMDR bilateral stimulation in the processing of traumatic material, associational networks are accessed. The associational networks may contain other related traumas. The client's SUDS level often starts at high levels and may even get higher at the onset of EMDR processing. There is a danger of flooding the client with overwhelming feelings of distress, and the possibility of retraumatization exists. For this reason, EMDR has a set of procedures for reducing distress such as: establishing an imaginary safe place , deep breathing, body centering (grounding) and containment procedures. These procedures are taught to clients before traumatic reprocessing is attempted.

Energy psychology tapping techniques have the ability to rapidly reduce the SUDS levels. I find that this is an especially helpful way to reduce the high levels of distress encountered when a traumatic memory is first accessed. If a client is getting overwhelmed by emotional intensity, tapping often provides permanent relief more effectively than the standard EMDR technique of going to the safe place , deep breathing, centering or containment. This creates safety for the client and speeds up the overall processing of a trauma. Yet, EMDR has definite advantages which should not be overlooked.

EMDR has the ability to access broad associational affective/cognitive networks within the client. EMDR is especially helpful when a client has a vague body feeling rather than a clear traumatic memory to heal, because EMDR can access associated material to resolve it. Since the material flows out of the processing of the client, it is easier for the client to own. In the processing, the therapist can ascertain, by the clients verbalizations, the relevance of other traumatic experiences which also need to be targeted and cleared. Traumatic material generated from EMDR reprocessing may resolve in the processing of the initial target, or may be separately targeted as the focus for further desensitization. Additionally, client resources and understandings, not previously applied, become integrated into EMDR processing. For example, a client may become aware that he or she really was a resourceful kid, given the circumstances. As a result of EMDR reprocessing, the client can develop an understanding of the traumas, their effects, their own strengths and the internal ability to process and resolve these issues.

Correction of psychological reversal can be a very helpful intervention, when EMDR processing gets temporarily stopped ("looping"). Psychological reversal can take many forms such as: "I don't deserve to get over this problem", or "It would be unsafe for me to get over this problem". Treatment for psychological reversal (–> Hover-Kramer) applied with other tapping techniques can relieve the client of the self-limiting beliefs which has stopped the processing of traumatic material. Clearing the reversal helps the client to continue EMDR reprocessing.

Mental and emotional processing of traumatic material often continues after an EMDR session. Energy psychology tapping techniques can be very helpful coping/desensitizing tools. I often teach clients techniques to correct psychological reversal to deal with feelings of guilt and self-blame. I also teach at least one energy psychology tapping sequence to reduce distress associated with traumatic memories. This helps the clients feel more empowered and better able to cope.

EMDR is also used to strengthen and install positive emotional/mental states (resources) in the client. This is helpful as a way to improve the client's self-concept and as a behavioral rehearsal for utilizing resources in upcoming events. This can be used in situations which used to trigger anxiety or PTSD (Post Traumatic Stress Disorder) responses in the client. These installations and positive mental rehearsals prepare the client to be successful in real world situations. This success, once experienced in the real world, can later be reinstalled and reinforced in subsequent counseling sessions using EMDR.

EMDR looks and feels more like psychotherapy to clients. This has very specific advantages to the client. It feels like the client is doing the work rather than something is being done to the client. The internal mental emotional processing associated with EMDR helps clients attribute the healing to themselves and therefore builds a richer sense of self-esteem.

I have outlined how the strengths of energy psychology meridian tapping techniques and EMDR can support each other in an integrated therapy (–> Benor). I would like to present a general outline or flow chart for integrating these two therapies below:

One Method of Integrating Tapping and EMDR
1. Use EMDR setup: image, body sensation, emotion, negative cognition and then get a SUD rating.
2. Use tapping to reduce high SUD ratings to get to a SUD rating of 6 or lower, before using EMDR.
3. Use EMDR to access broad associational networks and reprocess.
4. Use psychological reversal correction procedure if EMDR processing "loops".
5. Use tapping to reduce high SUD ratings, if distress levels get too high during EMDR.
6. Use EMDR to install positive resource states and cognitions.
7. Use EMDR to create cognitive behavioral rehearsal ("future template").

Please note that this procedural outline needs to occur in the context of sound therapy practices (–> Beaudoin): history taking and accurate diagnosis, assessment of risk factors (harm to self and/or others, potential for drug/alcohol abuse), informed consent, ability to function in daily life, client readiness, assessment of client strengths and outside social support network, etc. (– Sise). I would like to highlight the therapist's responsibility in using good judgment as to when the client is ready to reprocess traumatic memories. Accessing traumatic memories, even using these effective techniques, can destabilize the client's emotional state. Timing these interventions is important. If the client is having difficulty dealing with a lot of present day stress, it is better to focus on coping techniques for the client's current situation. The priority needs to be placed on the client's ability to function.

The following case study gives you a sense of the how energy psychology and EMDR support each other and work well together. Emotional Freedom Techniques (EFT) was the meridian-based therapy utilized in this case. The notation – indicates the number of cycles of eye movements used in EMDR reprocessing. In this particular example, two EFT treatments were used and the distress level came down to a low SUDS level of 2, before EMDR was employed.

Case Overview

Client:
50 year old female, whose partner of fourteen years ended the relationship precipitously to go live with another person. The client is still experiencing significant distress after eight years of separation including depression, weight gain, poor self-image, fear of entering other relationships, flashbacks stimulated by anniversaries and other triggers, sleep disturbances and a felt sense that life is not worth living. The client's personal family history includes parents whose marital relationship was fraught with conflict, which culminated in divorce, when the client was age thirteen. It included incidents of her alcoholic father stalking and threatening her mother. The client had only one prior session which utilized EFT and EMDR and was still skeptical of its effectiveness.

Problem:
Traumatic memory of being alone in empty family house at age thirteen. Her mother and brother had just moved the furniture out. The client had been left behind. Her father was banging on the door and yelling. Client did not answer door and hid in a closet.

Target:
Alone in dark closet, grandma's fox stole against her face, father banging and yelling outside house. Client feels an "electric charge" in her chest, feels her stomach unsettled and notices her right hand holding on to her body as she accesses memory.

Pre-treatment SUD rating of between 8 and 9.

Treatment:
Psychological reversal:
>Even though I feel scared, confused and uncertain, I deeply and completely accept myself.

EFT Tx: I don't feel electric charge in chest...
I feel some heat in chest, but I feel calm...
SUD rating=5. Client aware of sound of father's voice.

Psychological reversal:
>Even though I still feel scared, confused and uncertain, I deeply and completely accept myself.

EFT Tx: It's like being there with more skills... I never thought of turning off the intercom (in the house)...The volume and words were scary. SUDS=2.

EMDR
- 23– have appreciation to pick that closet... comforting to be with grandma's clothes.
- 15– more appreciation to be in my room... a long closet... recesses of long narrow closet... some security... and least likely to be found by him... he would not have looked there.
- 8– I feel more cherishing of that kid... of me.
- 15– I sucked my thumb for years...I used to wrap hair around my nose... the feel of fur... I like my dog there (this alludes to prior Tx, where hypnosis was used to bring her dog to her younger self for nurturance and security).
- 12– my father is afraid of dogs...my dog has a wolf voice... nurturing to me. SUDS=0-1
- 12– a warmth still in chest...feels comforting...something about me and my dog...see my father being little...If he had a gun, my dog could eat it (laugh)...I feel much better...It's hard to believe...this stuff really works.

This case illustrates the processing that went on with EMDR. I'd like to point out that the processing was psychologically significant, as the client was generally critical of herself for the way that she handled problems and she often doubted her own perceptions and choices. She was also fearful of others' judgments of her, especially family members. The EMDR naturally brought up the resource of protection and comfort associated with her dog. As a result of this session, the client became more confident in her own perceptions. She was subsequently able to verbally confront her father over the telephone on an unrelated manner. She did this in a way that she had not been able to in the past.

I hope that this article helps other therapists to see the strength, flexibility, effectiveness and advantages of integrating energy psychology meridian-based therapies and EMDR. There are other ways that I have integrated energy psychology and EMDR, but have limited the scope of this article in my attempt to give a clear overview.

References

Callahan, R.J. (1985). *Five Minute Phobia Cure.* Wilmington, DE: Enterprise Publishing.
Callahan, R.J.& Callahan J.(1996). *Thought Field Therapy and Trauma: Treatment and Theory.* Indian Wells: Author
Craig, G.& Fowlie, A. (1995). *Emotional Freedom Techniques: The Manual.* The Sea Ranch CA: Author
Diamond, J. (1979). *Your Body Doesn't Lie.* New York: Warner Books.
Diepold, J.H. Jr. (2000). *Touch and Breathe.* Invited Presentation. Energy Psychology Conference, Toronto, November.
Durlacher, J.V. (1995). *Freedom From Fear Forever.* Tempe AZ: Van Ness Publishing.
Gallo, F.P.(1999). *Energy Psychology.* Boca Raton FL: CRC press LLC.
Gallo, F.P. & Vincenzi H. (2000). *Energy Tapping.* Oakland: New Harbinger
Nims, L.P.(2000). *Be Set Free Fast.* Invited Presentation. Energy Psychology Conference, Toronto, November.
Manfield, P. (1998). *Extending EMDR.* New York: W.W.Norton & Co.
Parnell, L. (1999). *EMDR in the Treatment of Adults Abused as Children.* New York: W.W.Norton & Co.
Parnell, L. (1997). *Transforming Trauma: EMDR.* New York: W.W.Norton & Co.
Shapiro, F.(1995). *Eye Movement Desensitization and Reprocessing.* New York: Guilford Press.
Shapiro, F.& Forrest. M.S.(1997). *EMDR: The breakthrough therapy for overcoming anxiety, stress, and trauma.* New York: HarperCollins.
Van der Kolk, B.A. (2000). *The assessment and treatment of Complex PTSD.* Invited presentation.

16

Self-Healing: Meridian-based Therapies and EMDR

Dan Benor

Clinical Explorations

When I learned about psychotherapy as a teenager, I knew that was what I wanted to do. I couldn't imagine anyone actually getting paid to do something so fascinating. I trained as a psychiatrist 1967–1973 (with two intervening years in the Air Force during the Vietnam War), when psychiatry was mostly psychotherapy. Over the years, managed care has squeezed psychiatrists towards medication management. While I've resisted prescribing medications exclusively, it is pretty difficult to do much psychotherapy in a 15–20 minute medication visit – the amount of time allowed under managed care.

Fortunately, I work mostly with children (in a clinic and a day hospital), and am allowed the "luxury" of 30-minute sessions because I have to speak with parents, teachers, school counselors, and pediatricians, in addition to pharmacists and managed care companies – all in addition to speaking with the children.

I constantly sought to develop ways of providing psychotherapy along with the medications, but was unable within my limited timeframe to use the psychodynamic approaches I was taught as a psychiatric resident. EMDR was a blessing to me, as well as to my clients. I was able to use EMDR with children who had post-traumatic stress disorders, as children respond very quickly to this approach – not having barnacles on their problems like adults do. I also used EMDR to de-stress myself. With adults, it is recommended that EMDR should be done only during sessions with the therapist. This is to prevent being overwhelmed by intense emotional releases that can occur during treatment. I found that children rarely had such intense releases, perhaps because they had not kept their hurt feelings bottled up for as long a time, or perhaps because their emotional defenses are not a strongly developed. Another factor may be that I am comfortable doing this, having used EMDR for myself without the constant guidance of a therapist.

As I usually see children with their parents, I also taught the more stable parents to guide their children in doing the EMDR. If the children were mature and responsible, I encouraged them to practice the eye movements on their own, at home or at school, whenever they were upset. This was very helpful, for instance, with nightmares, when traumatic memories were stimulated by current stresses, or where excessive angers erupted. I still worried, however, that there might be intense emotional releases which could be traumatic.

I then learned to use Gary Craig's Emotional Freedom Techniques (EFT). This worked more quickly than EMDR and had extra advantages. Because it works rapidly and does not evoke intense emotional releases, I started offering "two (or three) for the price of one" introductions to EFT to children together with their mothers, including their fathers as well when they are present. This way, the children more often accept the therapy and comply with the recommendation to use it at home to deal with stresses. Parents are more confident of its therapeutic efficacy because they have experienced its benefits themselves, and therefore encourage their children to use it more often.

I had difficulty introducing EFT in my work settings. EMDR has an extensive research base to confirm its efficacy in treating post-traumatic stress disorders (PTSD). On the basis of my certification in EMDR, I was able to obtain official permission (from the administrators of the child and adolescent clinic where I work) to use this with their clients. Because EFT's research base is limited (–> Narvaez), they would not grant me permission to use it. Giving this a hard think, I turned it around and now call it an "affirmation technique." No one has faulted me for using affirmations in therapy, and never mind what clients do with their hands on their own bodies while they recite these.

In an introductory workshop by Asha Nahoma Clinton on Matrix Work, Asha observed that alternating tapping the eyebrow points while reciting the affirmation works just as well as the entire series of EFT points. Ever conscious of my time limitations, I immediately started exploring this hybrid approach, that combines aspects of EMDR and EFT (–> Lane).

It has been hugely successful for several reasons.

- It takes a fraction of the time that EFT requires.
- It allows for much greater flexibility in working on target problems within the session because it is so rapid. If the child is successful but the parent is not, or vice versa, there is plenty of time to explore alternative target symptoms or alternative methods of addressing these.
- It is better accepted and the compliance outside the therapy room is much higher because of this simplicity.
- It works marvelously well and rapidly on pains, and is excellent for allergies, though it may take several days to be effective for the latter (–> Radomski).
- It is tremendously empowering, as it is so simple and so rapidly effective in self-healing.

EMDR suggests the use of a "butterfly hug" as one of its self-treatment interventions, particularly for children: Your arms are crossed so that your hands rest on your biceps muscles, and you alternate tapping on each arm with your hands. Instead of tapping at the eyebrows, I often have children and parents use the butterfly hug with the affirmation. Many find the self-hug comforting, in addition to being highly effective in combination with the affirmation (–> Carrington).

Teenagers would often refuse to use either of these EMDR approaches outside of the therapy room. Their typical comment was, "Sure, dad! Like I'm going to tap my forehead or pat my arms in front of my friends! They'll think I'm some sort of nut case!" I speculated to myself that if they alternated tapping with their tongue on their teeth on the left and then on the teeth on the right this should work just as well, and found that indeed it does. This has been received much better by those who are shy or uncomfortable with tapping in public.

A deep breath (–> Diepold) following the affirmation facilitates releases. Holding your other hand over your heart center (chakra) while you tap or touch your eyebrow points deepens the effects. Reversals and blocks are effectively managed by massaging the sore-spot/releasing point below the collar bone (K-27).

With adult clients I find the Sedona Method is an even faster approach. This involves simply asking clients whether they are prepared to let go of their problems and then inviting them to do so (with a structured series of questions that are trademarked by the Sedona teachers). In my experience, younger children don't respond as well to this approach.

Clinical example (assumed name, composite case): Six-year old Joe had been seriously abused emotionally, physically and sexually by his mother from at least the age of two and probably earlier. He was removed from her home at age four, and had nine foster home placements before his latest foster mother suggested to the welfare worker that counseling might be helpful to him for his temper outbursts, fighting children in his first grade class and after school, inability to fall asleep till past midnight, frequent nightmares and night terrors, and bedwetting — his more serious problems. In addition, he was unable to sit still, was impulsive, distractible, constantly forgetting and losing things, and had no friends.

I diagnosed PTSD (moderately severe) and possible attention deficit hyperactivity disorder (ADHD). I prescribed small doses of Ritalin (–> Tenpenny), as this acts within minutes and, if effective, could provide rapid relief for some of his problems. He responded well to the medication and was much better able to sit and attend in class, less impulsive, and less forgetful. His other symptoms remained. He also had counseling sessions weekly with a social worker at the clinic where I work, focused on issues of relating to his new family, multiple losses, and PTSD issues.

At the initial interview, I taught Joe and his mother to use the butterfly hug. Joe chose an affirmation about one of the bad memories he had of being left in the dark cellar by his mother. He was unable to count, so I had him show me a Visual Analog Scale (VAS – equivalent of a SUD rating) with the gap between his hands representing how big his bad feeling was when he thought about being in the dark cellar. He opened his arms wide and said, "I can't reach to show you how big the bad feeling is." Within minutes of using the butterfly hug, his hands were touching in the VAS. He had reduced the bad feelings to zero.

Over the next several weeks, Joe (with the help of his mother) used the butterfly hug daily on various fears, difficulty falling asleep, and nightmares, as well as to calm down after he had temper outbursts.

Within two months, Joe was functioning at near-normal levels of behavior in school and at home. Counseling continued for another four months and was discontinued. I have followed him for Ritalin prescriptions for two years and we have all been pleased with his excellent academic progress in school, and with his good behavioral and improved social adjustments in school and at home.

I have also had excellent results with proxy use of the EMDR and affirmation hybrid. In proxy treatments, the person receiving the treatment focuses her or his awareness on another person who is intended to receive the treatment. Therapists may do this on themselves as proxies for their clients. (While this may seem far-fetched, it has an excellent basis in research as distant healing (Benor 2001).

Clinical example: I visited a healer who was baby-sitting a six-year old boy who has developmental delays and may have mild autism. He was severely frightened by the healer's two dogs, who were lively and playful, and nearly as frightened of her two cats. He had been in the healer's home several times previously, and was constantly on the alert, if not alarmed, by any approach of the animals to within several feet. Within minutes of surrogate tapping for his fears of the animals, he was markedly less fearful, and within a few more minutes he was even able to pet the quieter dog. He had never been that calm before in the animals' presence, and certainly would not have petted them..

Clinical Efficacy

I find that 85–90 percent of clients obtain immediate benefits from the EMDR/EFT-affirmation hybrid. When they practice this for their problems at home, there is almost universal success. (The last observation may be a matter of self-selection.) Where it doesn't work, the most frequent problem are:

1. The client has not targeted the problem accurately in the affirmation.
2. They are reporting that the memory has not faded. This is an incorrect expectation, as it is the negative feelings about the memory that fade, not the factual memory.
3. They have forgotten to massage the releasing point when there is a block in the process.

If the above do not apply, the few remaining clients usually respond to the full EFT routine.

Theoretical considerations and conclusions

I see a progression in meridian based therapies (MBTs) towards greater and greater simplicity. Gary Craig, with EFT, has simplified the procedures of Thought Field Therapy (TFT). The EMDR/EFT hybrid provides a further abbreviated tapping procedure with affirmation. The Sedona method is simpler yet, requiring only the decision to release whatever the problem is. There has been controversy and extensive discussion in MBT circles on whether the specific protocols of TFT are necessary, or whether the generic EFT protocol is adequate, with strongly held opinions on both sides. We can anticipate further discussion on the benefits and limitations of the hybrid and Sedona approaches.

Having advocated for the abbreviated procedure of the hybrid, let me step back and add that I do not see this as a "cure-all." I find that the meridian-based therapies are outstanding for addressing focal traumas, fears, pains, allergies, and beliefs. For many people, relief of these focal problems is all that they want to achieve. For others, deeper levels of work may require more elaborate approaches. I have found Clinton's Matrix Work (chakra based) enormously helpful to me personally and to selected clients who want or need deeper levels of work, particularly when there is an openness to including spiritual dimensions in the focus of therapy. I truly value the stimulating discussions within the Association for Comprehensive Energy Psychotherapy (ACEP) that will continue to innovate and clarify the best ways to help people deal effectively with their problems.

References

Benor, D.J. (2001). *Healing Research,* Volume I, Southfield, MI: Vision Publications.
Further references on the therapies mentioned are listed in the resource section (Appendix C).

17

Relationship-Oriented Meridian-based Psychotherapy and Counseling[1]

Thomas Weil

Meridian-based Psychotherapy and Counseling (MPC)

Negative emotions originate in disturbances of the energy system within the body. Unresolved conflicts and traumatic experiences impede the natural flow of life energy and influence the emotional state of a person – often in spite of her/his better understanding.

Meridian-based Psychotherapy and Counseling (MPC) facilitates the release of body blocks by tapping specific points on the acupuncture meridians, age old knowledge from Traditional Chinese Medicine.

Recent findings in brain research are considered insofar, as MPC focuses primarily on stimulation of those data-processing functions within the brain's limbic system, that were disturbed by traumatization, and help the client, to gain emotional distance to historical traumas, in order to eventually be free to deal with the challenges of the present.

MPC goes beyond primarily frontal lobe oriented methods of traditional psychotherapy and contribute to a fast resolution of severe emotional blocks by the client.

Integrative Therapy

Multiple traumatizing experiences are responsible for the development of a set of *basic beliefs,* that are in Transactional Analytic terms, elements of the so called "life-script" (Erskine & Zalcman, 1979). These basic convictions, once developed during the developmental course of a persons life, endure and persevere beyond childhood, as unconscious and private truths, and can severely impede the cognitive, emotional, behavioral, physiological and spiritual flexibility of a person (–> Eden & Feinstein, Feinstein, Shaw). Specifically these basic beliefs can be directed against the self, like "I am not important", against others, like "Others resent me" or against life in general: "Life is hard".

Basic beliefs are an important key to the roots of clients' disturbed sense of being. They underlie the level of obvious symptoms: Clients may suffer under acute symptoms, that they can identify and describe, but the origin of their disturbances is to be detected in "distorting eye-glasses", clients unconsciously wear, through which they look at life and which limit them in choosing and forming relationships. When we succeed to identify these basic beliefs, as clients sometimes verbally state them in generalizations or imply them non-verbally, we gain multiple therapeutic possibilities to facilitate a resolution of the blocks that go hand in hand with these basic beliefs (–> Carrington, Eden & Feinstein, Hover-Kramer).

Many therapeutic approaches are familiar with the phenomenon of basic beliefs. They use different terms to describe them and different therapeutic approaches to treat them. To connect these different approaches creatively is a significant element of integrative therapy. In order to be able to place them in a consistent context we require theoretical metamodels (Christoph-Lemke, 1999). The following considerations are to be understood as a metaperspective that allows us to describe basic beliefs from the perspectives of different theoretical schools. They're represented in the table below:

Transactional Analysis	The results of double contaminations
	Course of action: ego state diagnosis by four criteria, decontamination, deconfusion, therapy with Parent ego states
Psychoanalysis	Early rationalizations
	Course of action: analysis of the defensive functions: control demands from the superego and drive demands from the id

Cognitive-Behavioral Therapy	Stereotypical thinking-patterns
	Course of action: Exploration of historical learning experiences, Confrontation of irrationality, Construction of a reality-oriented, positive self image
Gestalt Therapy	Forming a secondary gestalt closure (Perls)
	Course of action: Analysis of strategies to avoid contact, Identification of the "missing part"
Relationship-oriented Therapy	Reflective results of incomplete relational experiences (Weil)
	Course of action: Analysis of relationships, Decoding the "unheard" story, Offering antithetical relationships
Body Therapy	Psychological expression of the character/body armor (Reich)
	Course of action: Character analysis, diagnosis of the body script, identification of blocks, energy management
Hypnotherapy	Forms of destructive self-hypnosis
	Course of action: Giving affirmations, Reframing
Spiritual Approaches	The attempt to ward off the experience of meaninglessness, by creating a construct of reality experienced as having and giving meaning

	Course of action: meditation, dream-work, work with imaginative procedures, like Tarot
Psychotraumatology	Cognitive deductions, arrived at on the basis of developmental and/or present complex psychotraumatization – in terms of "small T traumas" and/or "big T traumas" (Shapiro)
	Course of action: stabilization techniques, screening-techniques, MPC, EMDR
Energy psychology	Frontal-lobe-directed avoidance attitudes of corresponding to energy blocks within the limbic system
	Course of action: MPC.

Integrating Therapeutic Work into the Area of the Frontal Lobes and the Limbic System

Traumatic experiences are stored in different areas of the brain at the same time. Within the limbic system, traumas persist as unresolved fragments of experiences, as "mirror splinters" (Besser, 2000). Their pathogenic attraction continues because of blocked pathways between amygdala and hippocampus, caused by the traumatic overflow of information. The person is captivated by the trauma. The amygdala stays extremely sensitized and induces, as a reaction to seemingly irrational events, neurovegetative reactions, which are experienced as discomfort in the broadest sense and impede significant life functions of the individual.

In the area of the neocortex (frontal brain) coping strategies are developed, in an attempt to overcome the traumatization by unconsciously re-enacting measures, in terms of the "desiring and proud side of the repetition compulsion" (Weil, 1985). Those script patterns, that were developed in an attempt to cope with conflicts, are experienced as cognitive, emotional, behavioral and physiological limitations.

Beneath every basic belief of the life script lies a specific set of trauma blocks within the limbic system. Every trauma block in turn provokes processes of script formation and script maintenance within the frontal area of the brain. In this manner the basic beliefs of the life script can be understood as "avoidance-attitudes" – motivated by the illusionary intent to avoid retraumatizing experiences in the future.

To cure the script, integrative therapy must address both areas of the brain, where traumatizations are stored: While therapeutic work within the limbic system deals with facilitation of the information processing, therapeutic work in the frontal areas of the brain deals with accessing of information already acquired, introduction of new information and inhibition of accessing information (Lipke, 1996).

MPC procedures allow to directly address the limbic system. They resolve blocks between amygdala and hippocampus and withdraw the energetic basis of the script. The individual can put a distance between him/herself and the burdening trauma and experiences, and so the trauma moves to a far distance, that is: finds an adequate place in the person's history.

Relationship orientation
When their basic beliefs are questioned, clients usually resist, because these beliefs have a homeostatic function. On the frontal lobe level, defense mechanisms (Freud, 1936) apply, whereas on the level of the limbic system, psychological reversal (Callahan, 1985, 1989) applies.

The analysis of a client's resistance – resistance against growth and change – is a key to the clients' unfinished experiences in relationships, the "unheard story". Because the traumas, suffered by the client – with the exception of some severe traumas – as a rule have their place within the developmental context of so-called "unfulfilled experiences in relationships", "offers of an antithetical relationship" are mandatory in the therapeutic work with frontal-lobe areas, in order to stimulate script changing "re-reactions": The antithetical, that is, modeling behavior of the therapist, initiates an "antithetical parallel process", which interrupts the compulsion to re-enact, stimulates the confrontation with the own history and facilitates corrective experiences for the client. The client can now choose from alternative cognitive, emotional, behavioral, physiological and spiritual options.

In applying MPC procedures, as well as by doing traditional therapy, the therapist significantly forms the relationship with the client. If, in choosing from the various MPC procedures, the therapist considers their impact on the forming of relationships, this relationship can continually be formed in an antithetical way, as long as these procedures are applied in a consistent and integrative way and the impact of the entire therapeutic involvement on frontal-lobe brain *and* limbic system can be optimized. Re-reactions will be all the more efficient, if they cause the resolution of basic beliefs in the frontal lobe area *and* simultaneously withdraw their energy base within the limbic system.

ROMPC

Relationship-oriented MPC (ROMPC) uses a diagnostic window, inspired by Riemann (1984), to recognize the client's relationship status in terms of the problem at hand. In doing so, it has to be determined, to which degree the client's basic attitude is oriented toward change or perseverance, to which degree the client is "I"- or "YOU"- related, and how this influences his/her attempts to deal with the problems and to find solutions.

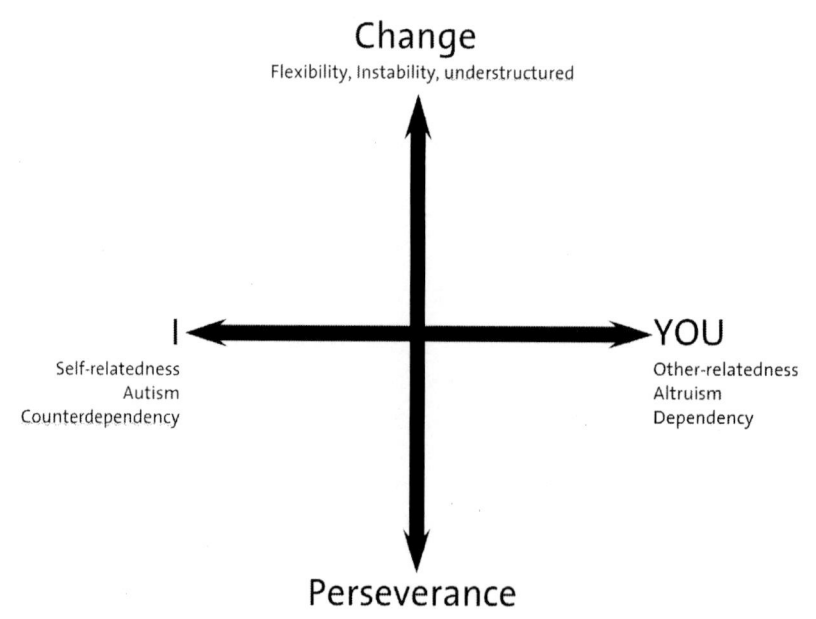

Change
Flexibility, Instability, understructured

I ←——————————→ YOU
Self-relatedness   Other-relatedness
Autism   Altruism
Counterdependency   Dependency

Perseverance
Rigidity, Compulsiveness, overstructured

In the light of this diagnosis, adequate antithetical MPC procedures are chosen. They must introduce the missing part, in order to facilitate the balancing of the client. The diagnosis has to be repeated for each new *holon* and for each new aspect to be treated. The chosen, antithetical MPC procedures can thus vary during treatment, depending on specific diagnostic findings.

Relationship-Oriented Meridian-based Psychotherapy and Counseling

ROMPC uses various relationship-forming effects of self-tapping by the client or tapping by the therapist, according to the specific *relational needs* of the client (Erskine & Trautmann, 1996), as well as the various MPC-procedures, Thought Field Therapy (TFT; Callahan, 1985, 1989), Emotional Freedom Techniques (EFT; Craig, 1995, 1997), Be Set Free Fast (BSFF; Nims, 1999) and the Successive Point Process (SPP, Lammers, 1999), to form antithetical relationships. The following treatment window illustrates this:

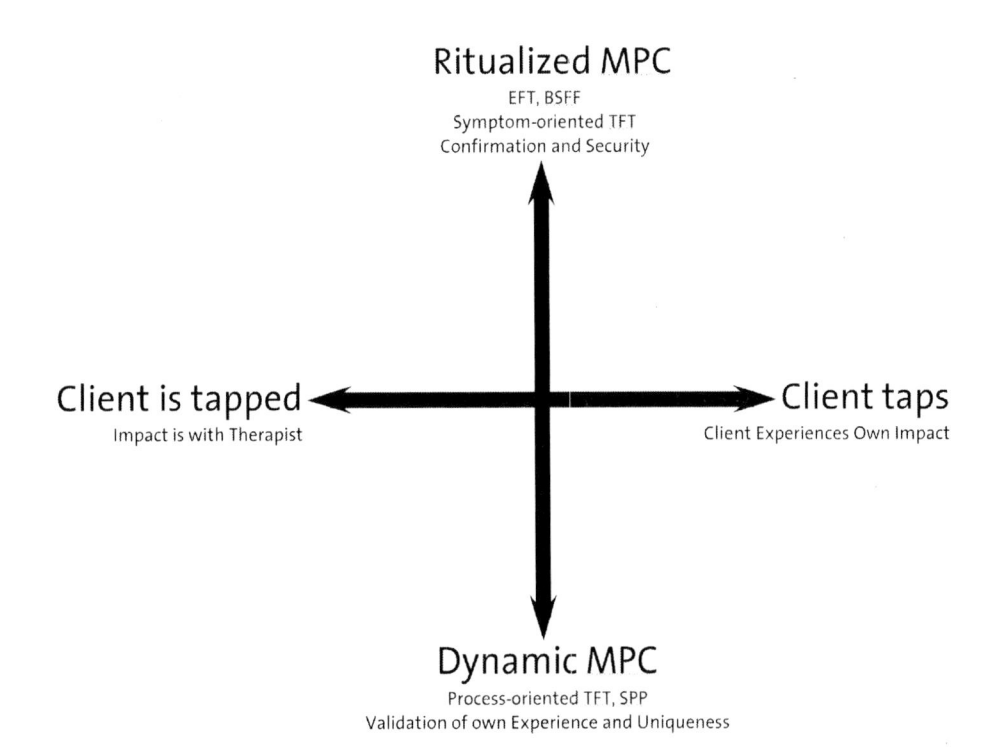

Ritualized MPC
EFT, BSFF
Symptom-oriented TFT
Confirmation and Security

Client is tapped ←――――→ **Client taps**
Impact is with Therapist   Client Experiences Own Impact

Dynamic MPC
Process-oriented TFT, SPP
Validation of own Experience and Uniqueness

Before the therapist offers an antithesis, the client has to feel secure. To achieve this sense of security it may be necessary to work with those MPC procedures, even for a longer period of time, that fit better into the client's frame of reference before the antithetical procedure can be chosen. The principle of pacing and leading (Grinder & Bandler, 1981) applies here as well. In practice, this can mean that an overstructured, compulsive client will at first be treated with structured MPC, e.g. BSFF, before offering him SPP. It is however essential, that the therapist keeps the antithetical *leading point* in mind and plans the treatment accordingly.

In approaching the antithesis, the client's defense against self-orientation or against other-orientation, as well as against perseverance or against change can be directly addressed with MPC. In doing so my method for *troubleshooting* has proven highly effective: Muscle test and treat for example:

- "I have the right to change."
- "I have the right to change now."
- "I want to change."
- "I want to change now."
- "I will enjoy change."
- "I will enjoy change now".

Defragmentation of the Personality

The roots of the basic beliefs of the life script can stem from own recent traumatizations, from developmental traumatizations as well as from internalized traumatizations of others. Because multiple trauma-experiences, in terms of complex traumatizations, are most of the time concentrated within a single basic belief, it may prove necessary, to address and treat the involved sub-personalities separately (–> Shaw).

For this endeavour transactional analysis offers the concept of ego states (Federn, 1978; Berne, 1972, 1977), that can be classified as *historical* or *Child ego states*, as *present* or *Adult ego states*, or as *introjected* or *Parent ego states*. These are subsystems of the psyche, held together by an *ego skin*, thus allowing the individual the experience of an I-feeling and of I-continuity. Every subsystem is a coherent system of thinking and feeling with corresponding behavioral and body patterns, as well as associated constructs of meaning. Each separate subsystem has its own history of traumatization and can be treated separately.

Through traumatization, additional personalities or "life states" can be formed, each with their own set of ego states. These are experienced as independent of the biological personality, or biological Life State. They sometimes – often against the intentional will of the client – control his/her thinking, feeling and acting. In addition to the biological Life State, we discern Dissociative Life States, Past Life States and Intrusive Life States, which in turn have their own separate history of traumatization and can be treated separately. This concept can be illustrated in an ego state model of transactional analysis, with the addition of Life States – as shown below:

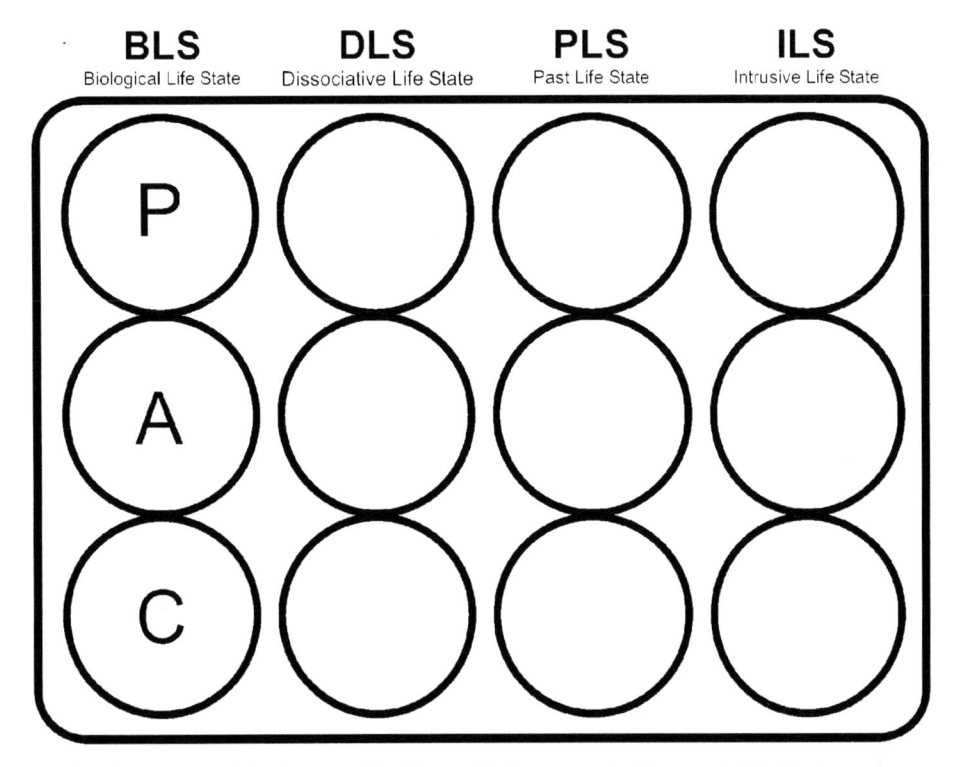

BLS	DLS	PLS	ILS
Biological Life State	Dissociative Life State	Past Life State	Intrusive Life State

P
A
C

Fixations caused by traumatization within separate Ego and Life States are accompanied by schizoid processes. This means: The individual looses contact to certain aspect of his/her personality. We talk of a fragmented personality. These split off personality parts can remain as "undercover agents" and sometimes surprisingly and unexpectedly take control of a given situation as the "boss". Clients often report, that they felt unable to act, while watching themselves do things they had no intention to. Sometimes they also report the experience of having no access to capabilities they usually own. The following schizoid processes can be diagnosed by muscle tests and consequently be treated:

Horizontal schizoid process (Biological Life State – BLS)
Symptoms: Regression to an early developmental stage or identification with an introjected parental figure.
Treatment: Dissociation from Parent- and/or Child ego state contaminations through deconfusion work or through work with the Parent ego states.

Vertical schizoid process (Dissociative Life State – DLS)
Symptoms: Dissociation of a personality part, which is not being experienced as belonging, and which leads a shadow life.
Treatment: Association through befriending and teamwork, establishment of a feeling of togetherness between biological and dissociative Life State.

Spiritual schizoid process (Past Life State – PLS)
Symptoms: Influence of the unfinished life concept of one's own identity, that is being experienced as stemming from an earlier life.
Treatment: Treatment of the unfinished death scene in the past life, finding orientation with new meaning by letting go of the Past Life States.

Intrusive schizoid process (Intrusive Life State – ILS)
Symptoms: The client feels influenced by energies of a foreign identity, which is experienced as possession by someone deceased.
Treatment: Elimination of the intrusions through light or angel rituals.

Conclusion

Without treatment of the limbic system aspects of the trauma, the *energetic attraction to the trauma* persists: Those neurovegetative reactions that are associated with the trauma will continue to be triggered.

Without treatment of the frontal brain aspects of the trauma the *attraction to the content of the trauma* persists: There is no conscious knowledge of those resources that have been gained by dealing with the conflict, nor of possible alternatives to the script.

Without treatment of the relational aspects of the trauma, the *attraction to the traumatic process* persists: There is a risk that the therapeutic relationship becomes the stage for a re-enactment of the experience of the traumatic relationship. The therapy process, experienced as re-traumatizing, will finally have a counterproductive effect.

Without treatment of the schizoid aspects of the trauma, the *attraction to the fragmentation of the trauma* persists: Since a fragmented personality persists, unrecognized *ego and life states* sometimes can take control as "undercover agents" and reduce long term success of the clients therapy. In this sense relationship-oriented MPC (ROMPC) is relationship-oriented as well as integrative.

Note
1.   Translated by Elisabeth Feuersenger.

References
Berne, E. (1961). *Transactional Analysis in Psychotherapy.* New York: Ballantine Books.
Berne, E. (1972). *What Do You Say After You Say Hello?* New York: Grove Press.
Berne, E. (1977). *Intuition and Ego States. The Origins of Transactional Analysis.* San Francisco: TA Press.
Besser, L. (2000). *Psychotrauma.* Kassel: Workshop Presentation.
Callahan R. (1985). *Five Minute Phobia Cure.* Indian Wells, Ca.
Callahan R. (1989). *The Anxiety-Addiction Connection: Eliminate Your Addictive Urges.* Indian Wells,Ca.
Christoph-Lemke, Ch. (1999). The Contributions of Transactional Analysis to Integrative Psychotherapy. *Transactional Analysis Journal*, 29, 198–214.
Craig, G. & Fowlie, A. (1995, 1997). *Emotional Freedom Techniques. The Manual.* The Sea Ranch, Ca.
Ellis, A. (1975). *Reason and Emotion in Psychotherapy.* New Jersey: Lyle Stuart, Secausus.
Erickson, M. & Rossi, E. (1979) H*ypnotherapy.* New York: Irvington Publishers.
Erskine, R. & Trautmann, R. (1996). Theories and Methods of an Integrative Transactional Analysis.*Transactional Analysis Journal*, 26, 316–328
Erskine, R. & Zalcman, M. (1979). The Racket System. *Transactional Analysis Journal,* 9, 51–5.
Federn, P. (1978). *Ich-Psychologie und die Psychosen.* Frankfurt am Main: Suhrkamp Verlag.
Freud, A. (1936). *Ego and the Mechanisms of Defense.* New York: International Universities Press.
Gallo, F. (1999). *Energy Psychology. Explorations at the Interface of Energy, Cognition, Behavior, and Health.* Boca Raton / Boston / London / New York / Washington: CRC Press.
Goleman, D. (1995). *Emotional Intelligence. Why it can matter more than IQ.* New York: Bantam Books
Grinder, & J. Bandler, R. (1981). *Trance-Formations. Neuro-Linguistic Programming and the Structure of Hypnosis.* Moab, Utah: Real People Press
Klinghardt, D. (1996). *Lehrbuch der Psycho-Kinesiologie.* Freiburg: Hermann Bauer Verlag.
Lambrou, P. & Pratt, G. (2000). *Instant Emotional Healing. Acupressure for the Emotions.* New York: Broadway Books.
Lammers, W. (1999). *Successive Point Protocol.* Maienfeld, Switzerland: Unpublished workshop manuscript.

Lipke, H. (1996). *A Four Activity Model of Psychotherapy and Its Relationship to Eye Movement Desensitization and Reprocessing (EMDR) and Other Methods of Psychotherapy* (The International Electronic Journal of Innovations in the Study of the Traumatization Process and Methods for Reducing or Eliminating Related Human Suffering). Tallahassee, Fla.
Nims, L. (1999). *Be Set Free Fast. Behavioral and Emotional Symptom Elimination Training For Resolving Excess Emotion: Fear, Anger, Sadness and Trauma.* Training Manual. Orange, Ca.
Perls, F. (1969). *Gestalt Therapy Verbatim.* Lafayette: Real People Press.
Polster, E. & Polster M. (1973). *Gestalt Therapy Integrated. Contours of Theory and Practice.* New York: Brunner/Mazel..
Reich, W. (1945). *Character Analysis.* New York.
Riemann, F. (1984). *Grundformen der Angst. Eine tiefenpsychologische Studie.* München/Basel: Ernst Reinhardt Verlag.
Shapiro, F. (1995). *Eye Movement Desensitization and Reprocessing. Basic Principles, Protocols and Procedures.* New York: The Guilford Press.
Weil, Th. (1985). How to Deal with Resistance in Psychotherapy. *Transactional Analysis Journal*, 15, 159-163.

ζ

Mastery

Willem Lammers

Odysseus is a smart man, a master. He manages to win a war, not by force, but by intelligence and wit. He's the inventor of the wooden horse, through which in the end Troy is conquered. Let's have a look at how he builds his raft, after the gods have finally allowed him to sail home from the island home of the powerful goddess Calypso, who kept him –conveniently– trapped for seven years.

> "... Odysseus began to cut down the trees. He worked fast and felled twenty in all, and lopped their branches with his axe, then trimmed them in a workmanlike manner and with a line made their edges straight. Calypso brought him boring-tools. With these he drilled through all his planks, cut them to fit each other, and fixed this flooring together by means of dowels driven through the interlocking joints, giving the same width to his raft as a skilled shipwright would choose in rounding out the hull for a broad-bottomed trading vessel. He put up the decking, which he fitted to ribs at short intervals, finishing with long gunwales down the sides. He made a mast to go in the raft, and constructed a half-deck and a rudder to keep it on its course. And from stem to stern he fenced its sides with plaited osier twigs and a plentiful backing of brushwood, as some protection against the heavy seas. Meanwhile the goddess Calypso brought him cloth with which to make the sail. This too he skillfully made; then lashed the braces, halyards and sheets in their places on board. Finally he dragged it down on rollers into the bright sea..." (5,242)

Reading this fragment, we're impressed by the knowledge and the skills demonstrated by Odysseus. Our age of specialist knowledge has lost contact to many of these methods to come to grips with nature.

If we want to learn to use the wind and the streams, and to avoid the Scylla and Charybdis on our own odyssey, we have to learn everything needed to sail.

We have to listen to energies of the world, let it act upon us without either-or judgments and ideas, and in the pacing of the interaction we learn to take the lead and set our sails home.

If we worship all the gods, they all will see upon us with benevolence.

18

Touch And Breathe: an Alternative Treatment Approach with Meridian-based Psychotherapies

John Diepold

Tapping on acupuncture meridian points for the treatment of psychological problems has persisted over the 19-year period since psychologist Roger J. Callahan, Ph.D. introduced his Callahan Techniques. The Callahan Techniques, also known in a generic way as Thought Field Therapy (TFT), has explored a revolutionary conceptualization of the nature of psychological problems and the rapid alleviation of emotional distress.

Callahan developed a causal diagnostic procedure gleaned in part from the insights and discoveries of chiropractor George Goodheart, D.C., who related neuromuscular function and organ system health to the acupuncture meridian system. Callahan (1985) utilized muscle testing methods found in Goodheart's Applied Kinesiology and John Diamond's Behavioral Kinesiology (Diamond, 1979) to therapy localize (identify) which acupuncture meridians were involved in psychological issues. Once the meridians are identified, Callahan has the patient repeatedly tap fingers on a designated treatment point along that acupuncture meridian to effect change or restore balance in that meridian. Frequently the causal diagnostic methods produce a sequence of acupuncture meridian points to be tapped.

As an outgrowth of the success of the Callahan Techniques, tapping on the acupuncture meridians has continued as a treatment and has been incorporated into other acupuncture meridian based psychotherapies (e.g., James Durlacher's Acu-POWER, Gary Craig's EFT, Fred Gallo's EDxTM, etc.). Accordingly, tapping appears to have been established, without critical review, as the "Gold Standard" in the treatment of psychological and psychosomatic disorders.

Why Tapping?

In *The Rapid Treatment Of Panic, Agoraphobia*, and Anxiety, Callahan (1990) wrote:

> ... the tapping provides an external source of energy which, when done correctly, at the right spot, with the mind tuned to the problem being treated, balances the energy in a particular energy system in the body which is suffering from a deficiency or imbalance. We hypothesize that the energy from tapping is transduced into the system into usable energy as needed. (p. 7)

A couple of years later Callahan (1992) commented on his practical and theoretical ideas related to tapping.

> The points we tap are related to the ancient meridians of acupuncture. Tapping the *proper* point when the person is thinking of the problem is quite effective. . . . It appears to me that these points are transducers of energy; where the physical energy of tapping can be transduced into the appropriate (probably electromagnetic) energy of the body so that the person with a problem can be put into proper balance by a knowledgeable person. (p. 11)

Callahan's decision to tap acupoints originated in a procedure introduced by Goodheart in Applied Kinesiology (Callahan, 1985; Gallo, 1999). In *The Five Minute Phobia Cure*, Callahan wrote:

> Rhythmic tapping at a specific point on a meridian will improve the condition of the associated vital organ. This, they say, occurs because the "energy flow" within that meridian is freed to move again. (p. 32)

The "they" in the above quote is most likely a reference to Goodheart, and to Walther and Blaich from whom Callahan studied Applied Kinesiology (AK). Walther (1988) described a meridian technique in AK called the "Beginning and Ending Technique" (B and E), which involves tapping the beginning or ending acupoints of the yang meridians. Nearly all the treatment points in the Callahan Techniques are at or close to the beginning or end points of the involved meridians.

While describing the AK Melzack-Wall pain treatment, Walther stated, "The most productive tapping is when there is a bony backup to the tonification point. If possible, direct the tapping to obtain a bony backup" (Walther, 1988, 263). Accordingly, it is speculated that tapping may cause a piezoelectric effect (–> Narvaez) due to bone stimulation at the acupuncture points. The piezoelectric effect occurs when tiny amounts of generated electrical current result from stimulating the crystallized calcium in the bone, and thus impacts the meridian system (Gallo, 1999). Use of cold lasers, rubbing, imaging of tapping, and pressure holding of the acupuncture points, in meridian based psychotherapy, were also reported by Gallo to be "effective at times". Gallo, however, provided no further explanation about the effective times or related circumstances but opined that "in most instances, percussing appears to more profoundly stimulate the acupoint and produce more rapid results" (Gallo,1999, 150). Walther, however, writes an interesting hypothesis about when tapping fails to yield results (in pain reduction):

> Another factor that may cause less than adequate results with the Melzack-Wall technique is *tapping at an improper frequency*. It is often necessary to reduce the tapping rate. Two to four Hz appear to be the most productive (p. 263). [Italics are mine]

As Callahan followed Goodheart, Walther and Blaich, other interested energy therapists now follow Callahan in the continuation of the tapping treatment to effect change via the acupuncture meridians. Nevertheless, there is no empirical evidence from experimental studies to establish that it is the tapping that works in the treatment of psychological problems. This author has studied with both Callahan and Gallo and has exposure to the other similar meridian based psychotherapies. Like many others who have studied Thought Field Therapy, this author has tapped his way to psychotherapeutic success hundreds and hundreds of times. Tapping does work, as evidenced in clinical treatment and the multitude of anecdotal reports and patient testimonials. While it is true that nothing succeeds like success, this author believes that the time has come to empirically validate the tapping approach to treatment and to explore and evaluate alternate treatment approaches. We, as practitioners, have reached the point in the development of meridian-based psychotherapies where we need to re-examine what works and why. This ought to be done in the context of the patient and the increasing information about subtle energy fields (–> Eden & Feinstein, Hover-Kramer. Luthke, Nicosia).

It is this author's intention to introduce an alternative treatment approach that also works (according to both therapist and patient reports) and appears more congruent with the current information about our bioenergy system. This alternative treatment for use with meridian-based psychotherapies is called Touch And Breathe (TAB).

Touch And Breathe (TAB)

The TAB approach is a gentle, mindful, and natural treatment, used in lieu of tapping, to facilitate Qi influence along the acupuncture meridians. Traditional acupuncture meridian theory holds that Qi is a form of bodily energy which is , in part, generated in internal organs and systems (Tsuei, 1996). Further, it is believed that Qi enters the body from the outside through breathing and the numerous acupuncture points. Qi, often called the Life Force, combines with breath to circulate throughout the body along complex pathways called meridians and vessels. In essence, breath facilitates the flow of Qi in its most natural state. Imbalance of flow or distribution of Qi throughout the body is the blueprint for physical and/or psychological problems. Such imbalances become evident at the acupuncture points through definite changes in electrical activity and possibly tenderness.

The TAB approach is consistent with traditional and contemporary Chinese thinking related to the flow of Qi and with emerging evidence of the complexity of bioelectric currents throughout the body. With TAB, the patient is invited to touch lightly the diagnosed treatment sites along the acupuncture meridians with 2 fingers and to take one complete respiration (at their own pace, usually through the nose) while maintaining contact at each treatment site. The TAB approach is an effective replacement for tapping in all TFT, EFT, EDxTM and other meridian based psychotherapy procedures. [Note: TAB does *not* replace rubbing at the Neurolymphatic Reflex Area, the "sore spot" in the upper left chest.

The pioneering work of Reinhold Voll, M.D. (–> Narvaez) revealed that acupuncture points show a dramatic decrease in electrical resistance on the skin compared to non-acupuncture points on the body. In addition, Voll and his colleagues found that each acu-points seemed to have a standard measurement for individuals in good health and notable changes when health deteriorated (Voll, 1975). Becker (1990, 1985) reasoned from his research not only that an electrical current flows along the meridians but also that the acupoints functions as amplifiers, which boost the electrical signals as they move across the body.

More recently, the research and theories of Stanford University's Professor Emeritus in Physics, William A. Tiller (1997), have shed more light on the interplay among mind, body, spirit and subtle energies. His work is particularly relevant to the applicability of Touch And Breathe for use with meridian based psychotherapies. Considering the complex array of electrical and electromagnetic circuitry in and around the body, Tiller theorizes that "the body can be thought of as a type of transmitting/receiving antenna" (p. 107; –> Nicosia).

Tiller cites the autonomic nervous system (ANS) as a signal carrier, waveguide, and signal conductor utilizing both sympathetic and parasympathetic branches. He describes the acupuncture points as a set of antenna elements that "provide an exquisitely rich array with capabilities exceeding the most advanced radar system available today. These sensitive points are coupled to the ANS via the fourteen known acupuncture meridians" (p. 117). Walther (1988) also reported that Goodheart observed "an antenna effect" regarding the acupoints that he believed could be easily demonstrated.

From the above, it could be argued that the body's acupoints have the potential to transmit and receive Qi, in accordance with the meridian system's need to restore balance. This author hypothesizes that the inserted acupuncture needles serve as a literal antenna / transmitter extensions of the acupoints. When we touch an acupoint we perturb it and stimulate ion flow, "which reacts at the etheric level to unclog the meridian flow channel"(Tiller, 1997, 121). In maintaining the contact by touch, we extend the antenna / transmitter capacity of the body system with a direct feed to the held acupoint. In contrast, while tapping perturbs, it also connects then disconnects the circuits and thereby creates an inconsistent and disrupted signal to the body. Empirical study is warranted to evaluate this hypothesis. While anecdotal reports indicate that tapping and TAB are effective treatment approaches, research is needed to discern quantitative energetic differences between the two approaches as well as qualitative differences experienced by individual's utilizing tapping and TAB.

In TAB, the use of one complete respiration (one easy inhalation and exhalation) is the natural vehicle of Qi circulation, which also creates a piezoelectric effect via vibration and sound (sonic resonance). In this regard Tiller writes:

> An additional indirect mechanism exists for emissions from the body. Here, the primary stimulus comes from the sound spectrum (also called the phonon spectrum) of the body's cells, muscles and organs associated with their relative motion. The sonic resonances for a particular body part occur in a significantly lower frequency range (by a factor of ~1 million to ~10 million) than its EM [Electro Magnetic] resonances. This is so because the sound wave velocity through tissues is about 1 million times slower than the EM wave velocity.
>
> Because collagen, tissue and bone are all piezoelectric materials, the small stresses produced by the sound wave patterns generate associated electric field patterns and thus emit EM wave patterns. Thus movements of a particular body part give rise to two emitted EM wave pattern signatures. One signature occurs at a very high frequency due to direct ion movement while the

other occurs at low to intermediate frequencies via electrically neutral mass movement coupled to the piezoelectric response mechanism. (106–107).

It appears that the natural motion and sound of the breathing process creates a powerful energetic influence involving the piezoelectric response mechanism. The radiation of this energy conceivably enhances the antenna/transmitter function of the body as it is directed to the specific acupuncture points by way of sustained touch. Perhaps this connection explains why various types of breathing and movements have been such an integral aspect of many Eastern practices (e.g., Yoga, Qigong, Shiatsu, etc.) used to facilitate a balanced flow of Qi (–> Stoler). Additionally, Goodheart recommends that when there is difficulty therapy localizing (diagnosing meridian involvement), "*have the patient quit breathing for ten seconds prior to testing*; this slows down meridian activity" (Walther, 1988, 262). [Italics are mine.]

In 1972, Tiller observed and reported that variations in mental alertness caused significant changes in the electrical characteristics of the acupuncture skin points. This author suspects that this reflects the influence and impact of intentional thought attunement (–> Nicosia), which is paramount in TFT and the other meridian based psychotherapies. Tiller's experiments from 1977-1979 (several thousand) revealed that mind direction or intentionality is evident and measurable and is not indicative of a "classical electromagnetic energy" (p. 10). Accordingly, this author hypothesizes that treatment of therapy localized acupuncture meridians, which are diagnosed while attuned to the specific problem, will be more profound using the TAB approach rather than tapping or pressure alone. Empirical and clinical study is also recommended regarding the effectiveness of imagined-Touch And Breathe (where the patient only imagines touqing the treatment point while also taking one full respiration).

While the aforementioned information and hypotheses appear reasonable to explain the development and use of TAB in treatment, the origin of this discovery and subsequent application was derived from listening to and watqing patients. It has been this author's understanding that many therapists employing the tapping treatment have heard various patient criticisms and reports of discomfort regarding the tapping (–> Benor, Carrington). It was common to hear comments like: "This looks/feels stupid. This is silly. I can't do this in public. It hurts if I do tapping too much. Tapping distracts me. I couldn't remember how many times I was suppose to tap. How hard do I tap?" Compliance with "homework" as follow up self care also suffered because of concerns like those voiced above. In addition, there have been therapist reports to this author that tapping was completely out of the question for some victims of abuse who refused to tap on themselves.

Nevertheless, the vast majority of patients do perform the tapping, as it is a requirement of successful treatment. The use of TAB extends meridian-based psychotherapies to these reluctant and/or sensitive populations.

Watching patients while they tapped proved most interesting. Often it was observed that a full breath or sigh accompanied the tapping procedures. Additionally, when patients were not reminded about the number of taps to do, it was observed that they would tap as many times as matched a full respiration before inquiring or looking for guidance. In response to these observations, the author began to experiment and develop the Touch And Breathe approach to treatment. Much to this author's surprise, every single patient preferred the TAB approach to the tapping, and they reported more profound, comfortable, and relaxing effects. Consequently, this author has exclusively employed TAB over the last 15 months while working within the TFT framework in doing psychotherapy. In addition, this author has demonstrated and shared the TAB approach over the past year with over a hundred therapists for use with their patients. Again, the patients were reported to respond positively, as did the therapists when they were treated using TAB.

Incorporating The TAB Procedure

The TAB procedure is easily inserted into any meridian-based psychotherapy in place of tapping. This includes treatment of all acupoints in a Major treatment sequence, the 9 gamut treatment, the eye roll treatment, and all treatments for psychological reversal and neurological organization that do not use the NLR area. All treatments are done while the patient is attuned to their problem:

> For treatment of any given acupoint, the patient is directed to lightly touch the acupoint (usually with one to four fingers depending on the location), *and* take one full respiration, while maintaining contact at the treatment site. Afterwards, simply move to the next treatment point or procedure.
>
> For treatment with the 9 gamut sequence, have the patient lightly touch the gamut spot, *and* take one full respiration while maintaining contact at the gamut spot. Then have patient proceed through the 9 gamut sequence while maintaining contactat the gamut spot and breathing normally.
>
> The reader unfamiliar with the 9 gamut treatment is referred to Durlacher (1994), Callahan & Callahan (1996), and Gallo (1999), for a detailed description of the procedure. For the eye roll treatment, have the patient lightly touch the gamut spot, *and*

take one full respiration, while maintaining contact at the gamut spot. Then have patient proceed through the eye roll treatment while maintaining contact at the gamut spot and breathing normally. In the eye roll treatment, the patients first close then open their eyes, then they look directly down at the floor. They are then instructed to take 5 to 7 seconds to roll their eyes slowly upward to the ceiling.

For the treatment of all Psychological Reversals *not* corrected at the NLR area, have the patient lightly touch the appropriate treatment site (e.g., side of hand, under the nose, etc.), *and* take one full respiration, while maintaining contact at the treatment site. Have patient proceed through the appropriate corrective affirmation statements (when they are used) while maintaining contact at the treatment site and breathing normally. The reader unfamiliar with the treatment of psychological reversal is referred to Callahan & Callahan (1996), Gallo (1999), and Durlacher (1994) for a detailed description of the procedures.

For treatment at the gamut spot for depression, sadness and pain, have the patient lightly touch the gamut spot, *and* take one full respiration (pause), and continue the respirations for as long as you feel change continuing, or as long as you might need" while maintaining contact at the gamut spot. Often a patient will continue for 5 to 8 respirations before spontaneously releasing the touch. The gamut spot – the 3rd point on the Triple Heater meridian on the back of the hand between the little finger and ring finger knuckles – is often used in algorithmic and diagnostically determined treatment sequences involving pain and depression related issues.

For the collarbone breathing treatment (CB2), have the patient touch the collarbone spot (K-27) with 2 fingers of one hand and lightly touch the gamut spot with two fingers of the other hand. Begin each sequence of breathing positions (for fingers and knuckles) with "Breathe normally, one full respiration". In lieu of making five taps on the gamut spot for each breathing position, have the patient gently maintain touch at the Gamut spot for two seconds at each breathing position.

The reader unfamiliar with CB2 is referred to Callahan (1990) and Gallo (1999) for a detailed description of the procedures. This author uses a modified breathing pattern when using CB2 which incorporates forced-in and forced-out breath positions based on the original procedures used by Blaich (1988).

In Conclusion: Benefits Of The TAB Approach

The TAB approach permits energy treatments within meridian-based psychotherapy to become more versatile and user friendly. Gone are patients' critical comments and resistance previously related to tapping. Instead patients enjoy a pleasant, mindful, and comforting procedure which appears to intensify the energy activity that the treatment purports to create. Patient comments are now of amazement, relief at not having to tap, relaxation, and "Wow, I like that so much better". Follow up self-care at home is more palatable and less conspicuous to others with TAB and, therefore, more likely to enhance compliance. Therapists who have employed TAB with their patients have described this treatment refinement as "natural, ...powerful, ...elegant" and "a major contribution" when using meridian-based psychotherapy.

The TAB approach is consistent with traditional and contemporary Chinese thinking related to the flow of Qi via breath and with the emerging evidence of the complexity of bioelectric currents and circuits throughout the body.

When using TAB, the treatment site for the Bladder Meridian is now restored to the Bladder 1 acupoint (inner eye/medial canthus at the bridge of the nose) without risk of injury to the eye. Walther (1988) cautioned about the possibility of an eye injury when tapping the Bladder 1 acupoint. The Bladder 1 acupoint is the preferred acupoint given the Beginning and Ending Technique used in Applied Kinesiology with Yang meridians.

This author has found only one relative disadvantage in using TAB. One full respiration takes a few seconds longer at each treatment site compared to five quick taps. However, it is believed that the few extra seconds in total treatment time is well worth the investment given the energetic connection and patient satisfaction.

References

Becker, R.O. (1990). *Cross currents: the promise of electromedicine, the perils of electropollution.* Penguin Putnam, NY.

Becker, R.O. & Shelden, G. (1995). *The body electric: electromagnetism and the foundation of life.* William Morrow, NY.

Blaich, R.M. (1988). *Applied kinesiology and human performance.* In Selected papers of the college of applied kinesiology (Winter), 7-15.

Callahan, R.J. (1985). *Five Minute Phobia Cure.* Wilmington, DE: Enterprise.

Callahan, R.J. (1990). *The rapid treatment of panic, agoraphobia, and anxiety.* The Callahan Techniques ™, Indian Wells, CA.

Callahan, R.J. (1992). *Special report #1: The cause of psychological problems.* Introduction to theory, second ed. Indian Wells, CA.

Callahan, R.J. & Callahan, J. (1996). *Thought field therapy and trauma: Treatment and theory.* Indiana Wells, CA.

Diamond, J. B.K (1979). *Behavioral Kinesiology.* New York: Harper Row.

Durlacher, J.V. (1994). *Freedom From Fear Forever.* Tempe, AZ: Van Ness.

Gallo, F.P. (1999). *Energy Psychology: Explorations at the interface of energy, cognition, behaviors, and health.* Innovations in Psychology, CRC Press, Boca Raton. .

Tiller, W.A. (1997). *Science and human transformation: subtle energies, intentionality and consciousness.* Pavior Publishing, Walnut Creek, CA.

Tsuei, J.J. (1996). Scientific evidence in support of acupuncture and meridian theory: I Introduction. Institute of electrical and electronic engineers. (with permission from IEEE, *Engineering in Medicine and Biology Magazine*, Vol. 15 (3).

Voll, R. (1975). *Twenty years of electroacupuncture diagnoses in Germany.* A progress report. Am. J. Acupuncture, Special EAV issue, Vol. 3, 7-17.

Walther, D.S. (1988). *Applied Kinesiology: Synopsis.* Pueblo, CO: Systems DC.

19

The Power of Using Affirmations with Energy Therapy

Pat Carrington

Energy therapy is making tremendous strides, with practitioners worldwide reporting impressive, often astonishing results from its use. Like any other rapidly developing field, however, some areas which may hold a promise of extending the usefulness of these techniques even more are being given relatively little attention, while others take the center of attention both on the professional internet lists and in clinical practice. While this is to be expected at this stage of development, I would like to devote this chapter to describing an approach I have found useful in compensating for a deficit in two important areas of concern for therapists.

The two challenges which have in my opinion not yet received enough attention from those of us in the energy field are the problem of generalization – how can we ensure that the gains a client may make in our office are carried over in a permanent way into his or her everyday life? – and how positive attitudes and true pesonal growth can be encouraged in our energy work.

These issues are important because while frequently, if a client has been cleared of a block by using an energy therapy, the problem may be gone forever, or only require a few "booster" tapping or Tabbing (–> Diepold) sessions for EFT or TFT, or the use of TAT or BSFF at home before the treatment 'takes', this is by no means always the case. What of those issues which, having been successfully cleared in our office, still need to be assimilated into a client's life pattern (–> Eden & Feinstein, Hover-Kramer) to have their greatest effect?

The way a person has lived their life up until now – their self-image and habitual ways of being – can work against even the most beneficial changes brought about by our therapies (–> Feinstein, Weil), and although it may not wipe out the gains made, it can make these gains less pervasive and influential in that person's life than they could be. In this event we will not have gotten everything we could out of that stunning switch in perspective that can occur with these new therapies. We may be settling for fewer benefits than we should in our excitement about the almost magical "cures" we so frequently see.

Here is where the use of "Choices" (a form of affirmation which I find more effective in many instances than the straight declarative form of affirmation for reasons I will discuss later) comes in. I have found that the Choices method can assist a client (or anyone else) to consolidate and make permanent the beneficial changes brought about by energy therapy, helping these changes to generalize to many aspects of the client's life. When that happens, we see true transformation.

Let me give you an example of Choices as I have used them in therapy.

Tara (name changed) came into treatment for help with an intermittent depression and marital problems. She is an accomplished singer who grew up in a world of theatre people. Her mother played a regular bit part on a TV series, her father was a well-known TV director. Their friends were all showbiz people.

An only child, Tara recalls that she was always dressed up in adorable clothes with an ever-different colored bow in her soft blonde curls. She would often recite Longfellow poems and do a little tap dance at age three to excited rounds of applause from their guests, which of course is the highest form of compliment from show people. At superficial glance one might conclude that she was "over-valued" since her every move was subjected to exaggerated attention (either praise or criticism), and her mother professed incredible pride in her and seemed to glory in her daughter's achievements, never missing a detail of one of her recitals. In fact, the mother seemed almost to have lived vicariously through her daughter, enjoying a triumph that she had never achieved in her own modest career.

When Tara came into therapy she acted as though she had no identity of her own, and this became a main focus for her treatment. In her year and a half of therapy we have made heavy use of EFT (the energy therapy I use most for my clients), with many sessions of tapping on her original family situation, on her fear of being more successful than her pretty actress mother, on her fear of failing to please her highly directive director father, and on the depression she feels today when she isn't getting what she considers enough attention (no applause in other words) from others.

During this time, Tara has changed remarkably. She now walks with dignity where before she seemed to flutter into a room. She now speaks more slowly and with a new sincerity and directness that make her come across as a real person to others for the first time. Her life in general, and her relationships have become much more compelling and very much richer. It often seems as though I am greeting a new person when she walks into the office. Despite all these gains, however, she still had a residual sadness in her face until recently, the look of a person gazing at some far away painful scene.

When she came for a session recently, her sadness had come to the surface (which was good because now we could deal with it directly), and as we tapped on the sadness, it became evident that it was not due to anything in the present, nor was it about her being forced in childhood to uphold a facade for their guests – none of that. In fact, it was not about attention per se – rather it was about being in people's awareness, having them *aware* of her.

In the middle of this session, Tara's eyes lowered, and she became silent. Then she said in a low voice: "It's not about my worry about pleasing people anymore – that's doesn't bother me the way it did. It's just that, attention or no attention, and no matter how much she *said* she loved me, and no matter how much she boasted about me – my mother wasn't really *aware* of *me*." Her eyes welled up with tears as she spoke about this, and she explained that even when she had performed beautifully, and tap-danced and sung and recited the way her parents wanted her to, that she now realized that her mother never really saw the real "her".

"She saw the little puppet she'd created, she was so proud of that puppet, but she never saw *me*...." She said. Here was a source of some of the deepest sadness within Tara – and we were able, gently and with respect for the difficulty it was for her to articulate this, to dissipate this painful memory through quietly tapping on it:

"Even though Mommy never really saw me..."
"Even though Mommy didn't know I was there..."
"Even though her eyes didn't really look at me..."

As she tapped away, a quiet came over Tara, a peace I hadn't seen there before. At the end of the session when she looked up at me there was a new clarity in her eyes as she said very slowly, "I never – really – realized this before. She saw the performer. She loved her. She never saw me...". She then said that she had a peaceful feeling about this and that it was a tremendous relief to have faced it and been able to tap right on it, not on issues "around it". It was clear that this was a turning point for Tara.

I knew how fundamental the session had been and I wanted to help her consolidate her gain, to allow this insight and understanding to become a basis for her life from now on. To help this along, I suggested that we make a few Choices relating to what she had discovered. She was familiar with making Choices since we'd used them a number of times during her therapy, so she worked with me to create several to take home with her.

These Choices evolved from a discussion which she and I then had about how we can "see" and respect ourselves even though someone as vital in our life as a parent may not have been truly aware of us as a child, because, of course, of problems of their own. Our discussion led to Tara realizing that her mother had not seen "her" (but only the little budding stage star) because the mother had never seen herself as real, but only as a would-be "star" – not because she didn't love Tara. Love had nothing to do with it one way or the other, her mother's sense of insignificance was the factor operating here.

This was a time of deep understanding for Tara, a melting of a resentment she had carried around against her mother for years. She realized now that the two of them had both been caught in the same dilemma, both had felt they were non-entities, only Tara had the advantage of beginning to be genuine and significant in her own eyes due to her work in therapy.

Several Choices (which Tara took home with her to work on) came out of this session, each dealing with a slightly different aspect of the problem and stating her preferred solution for it. These were worded as follows:

"I choose to know and love the 'real' me, even if Mommy couldn't."
"I choose to understand why Mommy could never 'see' me."
"I choose to feel close to Mommy because we both had the same problem."

And finally, "I choose to allow my real self to be seen."

This last one was probably the most important Choice of all for Tara because she had been terribly afraid to take this chance before. She took home the little blue cards with her Choices written on them (I'll explain the process in a moment) and has used them ever since. The feeling that she could know her real self has grown in her as a result of this to a point where she has been largely able to dispense with the façade she had had all her life.

She is still a fine and studied performer on stage (in fact she claims to be an even better one now) but unlike before, she is now able to be a "real" person off stage, one whom she herself genuinely likes and respects, as do many others. Her Choices have strongly reinforced the insights she gained during the EFT process.

If you would like to make use of Choices to consolidate gains made with an energy therapy, here is the procedure I use:

At the end of a session where we have used such a therapy, when we have cleared, or partly cleared, important emotional blocks, I will suggest that the client formulate, along with me, a meaningful Choice or series of Choices (the latter covers more than one aspect) relating to the issue they have just been tapping on.

I then write down each Choice for them, using their exact words, on a 3 x 5 inch card (usually light blue colored), a separate card for each Choice, and hand these to the client at the end of the session. This little ritual has the effect of serving as a symbolic gift from me and is almost always treated with respect and seriousness because of this.

I then instruct the client to read over their Choices at home, out loud, twice a day (at a minimum) – when first waking in the morning, and before going to sleep at night. They may if they wish carry the cards with them and read aloud the choices when they find themselves with spare moments during the day too – say in the car waiting for a traffic light to change. Many people do this and some have even recorded their choices and listened to them on tape as they drive.

I tell the client not to bother to think about what is on the card between times, rather to just read aloud each Choice once and then let it slip out of their mind, to enter their "subconscious" mind, which will do the work *for* them. That is, in fact, exactly what happens.

After that, from time to time during therapy, I will inquire about how a particular Choice is progressing (is it manifesting in their life? If so, how?) since I keep a record of their Choices in the patient records.

The formulating of the Choice (or affirmation) is in itself a part of the therapy, serving to clarify the positive goals of the client. I use Choices regularly hand in hand with EFT to achieve profound therapeutic change. To make the distinction between Choices and conventional affirmations, a way of wording a Choice for a person with a fear of public speaking, for example, would be, "I choose to feel confident and at ease when speaking before groups". This is different from the wording of a traditional form of affirmation used for the same issue which would be, "I am confident and at ease when speaking before groups." Both are productive ways of using affirmations, but they differ somewhat in their effects, and in my experience are different in terms of their likelihood of being accepted by the average client.

There are of course times when I find traditional affirmations to be more suitable with EFT or other forms of energy therapy, I'll speak about this later, but for the most part I use Choices to help carry over the effects of an energy session into a client's everyday life. I have found this extremely helpful in solidifying changes outside of treatment sessions.

Choices seem to be more acceptable to many people because the conventional affirmation, which asserts that something is "so" in present time which another part of the same person perceives as *not* being so, tends to invite unspoken thoughts and reservations about the affirmation which can rob it of its effectiveness. Of course this isn't the only reason or even the primary reason that people have such limiting thoughts (what Gary Craig has called "tail-enders"), but my thinking goes like this – Why invite trouble? If we can make an affirmation more comfortable and inviting by casting it in the form of a Choice - why not do so?

Familiarity and positive associations play a big role here. Choices are not perceived as "far out" because we all make choices every day and "having a choice" in a situation versus "having no choice" is clearly preferable. This is important because when we use EFT or any other form of energy therapy we are asking the average person to do a pretty unorthodox thing – tapping on acupoints, holding points on their head, saying unfamiliar types of phrases, etc. (–> Benor, Diepold). And I find it helpful not to stretch their acceptance of new and unusual things too far by following an energy therapy with the suggestion that they use a traditional affirmation that may challenge their credulity – unless the person is very used to and comfortable with these.

The use of Choices has been a pillar of my practice for years now and has enabled me to help my clients bring about transformations in their lives, not just symptom alleviation (–> Luthke). It has helped to make permanent some magnificent insights that have appeared in the course of therapy. I estimate that about 75% of my sessions with clients at the present time end up with us formulating some personal Choices which the client then takes home and uses. This procedure facilitates our therapy work by a multiple I can only guess at.

Another advantage of this approach is that making a Choice puts the person in the driver's seat in their life. The person making a Choice is exercising their will, deciding on and committing to a course of action. I have found that this freely entered into commitment can have a powerful influence on the desired result, often making it more likely to be obtained. It doesn't by-pass the ego of the person in the manner that the traditional affirmation does, but instead it engages the ego (or self) in the process. Since it also accepts the reality of the present state of affairs, this makes for a healthy juxtaposition of present reality and desired outcome – creating a strong pull toward the latter.

One way of using Choices – it's a way that can also be used with traditional affirmations, although I've seldom seen this done – is that the conflicting self-statements ("tail-enders") which almost always exist can often be handled by the wording of the Choice itself – built into it so to speak.

A client of mine, Judy (name changed) provides an example of this. She wanted to move into a "beautiful, sunny, spacious apartment" but had not been able to get herself to do the things required to bring about such a move. Clearly there were hidden issues blocking her, and as we tapped on "Even though I'm afraid I'll never find that great apartment", her thoughts tuned to her older sister who was resentful about having to live in her own dingy walk-up. This sister had been jealous of Judy all their lives. Judy had been prettier and more popular from day one, but had always tried to please her sister whom she had looked up to greatly as a child.

As she tapped, Judy realized that her need for her sister's love was an important factor blocking her from going all out to obtain a new apartment, and so we turned to working on this aspect:

"Even though (sister's name) will be jealous of me if I get a great apartment...."
"Even though she won't love me if I get a great apartment..."
"Even though she'll be mad at me if I get a great apartment..." etc.,

We continued until Judy's SUD rating level (her emotional intensity rating on a 0-10 scale) had come down to zero. She was now able to visualize herself going out and actively seeking the apartment, and finding it.

When we came to the end of this session we formulated a Choice for her to take home and work with. Since the need for a family member's love is likely to have many aspects to it, some of which we had not handled as yet, I wanted to facilitate her dealing with this issue outside of therapy and so suggested that she build into her Choice a phrase that would address the potential tail-ender. The wording we settled on for her Choice was:

"I choose to feel loved while living in a beautiful, spacious, sunny apartment.".

Notice that I didn't suggest she say, "I choose to have my sister love me while ... etc.". We can't choose for another person how they should feel or act or be – only for ourselves. So instead I suggested she formulate the Choice so that she would have a subjective feeling of being loved as she lived in that apartment. We can choose to have any feeling that we want.

This simultaneously addressed her wish for a lovely apartment and her reservations (tail-enders) at the same time. While we had to do some more tapping on other aspects of this issue in the next therapy session, Judy was actively looking for apartments and getting the word out among friends by the time she arrived for her session. Within three weeks she had found a "beautiful, sunny, spacious apartment" which she moved into confidently.

Of course, people sometimes find a choice such as "feeling loved" very difficult to make. If so, then we can use an energy therapy to deal with that issue. After removing some of the blocks, we can then help them formulate some additional all-encompassing choices such as: "I choose to feel lovable." or "I choose to feel loved.", or address deservedness issues through a Choice.

An occasional person may experience the Choice phraseology as setting the goal off in the future and therefore as less compelling than a direct traditional form of affirmation. I have rarely found this to be the case, however. My experience has been that the subconscious mind does not interpret the wording of a Choice in this manner, but because making the Choice is an act in the present time it readily accepts the current validity of this process and acts upon the Choice rapidly. I can't count the number of times a Choice made by a client, or one of my friends, or me, has been realized – whether two hours from the moment they conceived of the choice, or three weeks from the date it was first used daily, or a year, or whenever.

Much of what I've been saying about the use of Choices with energy therapy applies in most cases to all affirmations, be they couched as Choices or as direct reframes of present reality as in traditional affirmations. I find that the traditional forms of affirmation can be superbly effective in certain therapeutic contexts and the preferred method for them. For example, when I use Gary Craig's Advanced EFT intuiting technique (where he suggests progressive changes in phrasing to deal with core issues while the client taps the karate chop point) I have found that by using direct statements and affirmations, with no "frills" or anything else to impede the process, I can go right to the heart of the matter and join with the client in a deep and complete sense. It would be inappropriate to water down these powerful statements in any way.

Also, there are some global issues that seem to cry out for a direct statement – they seem to be beyond choice. For example, a client of mine had been struggling with an issue of individuation – she constantly saw herself through her mother's eyes ("What would Mom think about this?"). After she had dealt in her therapy with some of the issues around her mother, she made this choice to help her progress – it followed from an insight that had come to her during tapping:

"The real me is known only to me and God."

It would have been inappropriate to have formulated this as a Choice as in, "I choose to have the real me known only to me and God." This client's belief system fully supported the affirmation she had made and to artificially introduce an act of choice here could have watered down the impact of the affirmation. In fact, her affirmation turned out to be extremely helpful for this young woman, reminding her repeatedly as she worked with it at home, of her existence apart from her mother, in a very positive way.

It is a clinical judgment whether or not to suggest a Choice or a traditional affirmation in a given instance. While I've found that Choices are preferred most of the time, the direct reframe used in a traditional affirmation, where appropriate, can have a powerful impact often not obtainable by a Choice.

An important factor in the use of affirmations with an energy therapy is that the regular use of affirmations following successful removal of blocks during the therapy, accents the positive aspects of this form of treatment and this can bring even more profound change into the client's life. It can serve to move an energy therapy beyond mere symptom control or the alleviation of distress, and place it in the service of the client's self-actualization. I see this process as a next and obvious step in the development of the energy therapies, one that can be deeply gratifying for both clients and therapists alike (–> Handelsman). I would therefore encourage you to use affirmations (either the conventional form or the Choice form) freely and creatively in your energy psychology work.

20

Freedom from Fear Forever
The Acu-Power Way[1]

Jim Durlacher

Introduction

Many people know more about the moon, which is 250,000 miles from earth than they do about themselves. This lack of knowledge is the result of the fact that most people seem to try to find out about themselves by looking around rather than at and within themselves.

There is a story about God and three angels in which God says to the angels, "Where shall we hide the secret of life?" "One angel replies by proposing that it should be buried in the depths of the ocean but God said, "No, with modern technology it would be found fairly fast." The next angel proposed that it should be hidden on the highest mountain, to which God replies, "No, where there is a mountain, it will be climbed and explored and the secret will be found." The third angel said, "I know, let's hide the secret of life inside each individual." And God replied, "I think you've got it, no one will think of looking there!"

In this book you will be able to look into your own body, your body's nervous system, where all things that have happened to you from the time of conception are recorded. Through the use of the procedures that you will learn, you will be able to literally ask if the body has any phobias, fears, anxieties, addictions, compulsive behaviors, negative life beliefs, unresolved issues or evidence of post traumatic stress syndrome. In addition, it will teach you to treat and in most cases abolish these things without the use of drugs or long drawn out counseling sessions so you will be free at last. The new method is done by stimulating certain acupuncture points on the body – tapping on them with your fingers. This has the same effect as inserting an acupuncture needle without being invasive. The tapping procedure can take as little as five minutes in very simple cases or hours over the course of a number of sessions if there is a very complex problem. Usually, however, most problems are overcome in less than fifteen minutes.

Free yourself, your loved ones, your friends, or your patients of the self-defeating behaviors that have kept you or them prisoners with the use of Acu-POWER. Whether lay person or professional, you can use the Acu-POWER procedures so that:

- phobias
- anxieties
- addictions
- love pain
- rejection
- post traumatic stress disorder
- compulsive behavior
- self-limiting and
- self-destructive negative life beliefs

will no longer rule your life or the lives of your loved ones and or individuals you treat. You can learn step-by-step how to conquer and eliminate even life long phobias with a rapid, effective method which was originally pioneered by clinical psychologist, Roger J. Callahan, Ph.D. I call it Acu-POWER Emotional Technique. This method does not require any 'talk-out' sessions or getting 'deep insight' into the origins of the problem. In fact, it is not necessary to reveal the phobia or any painful or embarrassing events. Your body knows exactly what is bothering it and how to correct it.

One in nine people have a significant phobia, which affects how they live their lives. Almost everyone has a phobia of some kind. Many of these individuals do not realize they have a phobia, but will say, "I just don't like to be in crowds" or "I feel nervous when meeting new people" or "I'd rather drive because I enjoy the scenery". Acu-POWER will enable you to be free at last.

Your Body Knows

Fortunately, your body has a screening or filter system that neutralizes many of the adverse effects of these events, so that you are not overwhelmed with non life-threatening information. This system, when functioning normally, sorts the important information (that affecting survival) from the not-so-important information. When this system is not functioning normally, stimuli that ordinarily would not bother us are allowed to create a state of fear or anxiety because we begin to view the stimuli as life threatening, rather than just a mild disturbance. This system also acts on the life-threatening information and records survival procedures, which will help us if we encounter the same or similar events in the future. It also neutralizes the fight or flight mechanism for that event, so we are prepared to act on a new-life threatening event if necessary (–> Sise, Weil).

We have all known individuals who have been affected by horrendous and/or tragic events suffered by themselves or by their loved ones, and who have grown from the experiences. Conversely, we all know individuals who crumble when facing the most minor problems like spilling a cup of water or being criticized. Others are afraid of common things that would not even bother most people. Those in the latter group have a malfunction in their screening system, which predisposes them to "make mountains out of mole hills".

Most of what is recorded is not in your conscious memory but rather in your sub-conscious where it can affect you physically, chemically, or emotionally throughout your life. Dr. George J. Goodheart, Jr., a chiropractic physician and lecturer, always starts his seminars with quotations from the great humanitarian and physician, Dr. Albert Schweitzer and the renowned researcher Dr. Hans Selye. The first said, "Happiness is good health and a bad memory." The words of Selye are, "God will forgive you but your nervous system will not." Goodheart explains that if you do not correct the disturbance in the nervous system, there will be adverse effects in the physical, chemical and emotional sides of the health triangle.

There are two basic fundamentals of life – happiness and misery (unhappiness). The dictionary defines happiness as "the state of well-being and contentment or pleasurable satisfaction." It defines misery as "a condition of great suffering, a state of emotional distress."

It would then follow that the state of real or imagined fear which makes up a phobia, produces anxieties, addictions, love pain, rejection, post traumatic stress syndrome, compulsive behavior, self-limiting and self-destructive negative life beliefs. Fear causes misery.

Fear, real or imagined, produces pain. This can be physical and/or mental. We've all heard the expression, "I just can't think (or talk) about that, it's too painful", or "thinking (or talking) about that gives me a headache".

In his book *Quantum Healing*, Deepak Chopra discussed the fact that the brain produces internal painkillers, endorphins and enkephalins, which every neuron in the body has the ability to produce. These natural narcotics made by the body are up to two hundred times stronger than any man made painkillers and are non-addictive. He goes on to suggest the possibility of doctors anesthetizing their patients by stimulating some regions of the brain through the use of Chinese acupuncture.

This book is not about covering up pain with natural internal painkillers, but rather balancing the subtle energies of the acupuncture system so the individual can deal with his/her fears. If the body, in the process, eliminates physical pain as well, so be it.

Cousens, in his introduction to Gerber's book *Vibrational Medicine*, says, "...we, as human organisms, are a series of interacting multidimensional subtle-energy systems, and that if these energy systems become imbalanced there may be resulting pathological symptoms which manifest on the physical/emotional/mental/spiritual planes."

Fortunately, there is a way to diagnose and treat the fear causing these adverse states. Your body knows what is causing this misery. Remember, everything has been recorded in the nervous system. Because your body knows exactly what the problem is and will share this secret if asked, there is a way to handle all fears. The key to understanding and treating phobias is balancing the energies in the body with a very simple stimulation of specific acupuncture points. I call this Acu-POWER Emotional Technique. The process is simple. By manually tapping on these points for about fifteen seconds and monitoring the body's responses, you can put an end to your misery and be free at last.

Applied Kinesiology – Its Discovery and Development

Whenever a new discovery is reported to the scientific world, they say first, 'It is probably not true.' Thereafter, when the truth of the new proposition has been demonstrated beyond question, they say, 'Yes, it may be true, but it is not important.' Finally, when sufficient time has elapsed to fully evidence its importance, they say, 'Yes, surely it is important, but it is no longer new.'
– Michel de Montaigne in the 16th century

A breakthrough in diagnoses occurred in 1964 when a Detroit chiropractic physician, Dr. George J. Goodheart, Jr., made an observation so profound that it will forever be a landmark in the history of all health care – whether provided by medical, osteopathic, chiropractic, dental, podiatric, naturopathic, homeopathic or psychologic doctors. He noted that although a patient had a significant weakness of his right serratus anticus muscle (which is attached to the underside of the shoulder blade on one end and goes around to the side of the rib cage to insert on the ribs in front, holding the shoulder blade flat against the ribs), which prevented him from pushing his arm forward, there was no atrophy of muscle size. However, on palpation (touching and feeling a part of the body with the fingers) of the origin and insertion of the muscle, there were nodules that were quite painful.

After rubbing the nodules at the origin and insertion and re-testing the muscle, Dr. Goodheart was surprised to notice an immediate strengthening. After re-testing for several weeks, the muscle remained strong! His first thought was, 'why is that'? He then began testing the muscles of other patients and noted that with certain deviations of posture that certain muscles would be weak—not able to "lock" into a resistance state. He also observed that when a muscle was in an obvious contracture state or spasm, there was a weak antagonist. He hypothesized that the spasm occurred because the muscle had no opposition from its antagonist (the opposing muscle). The good muscle simply did its job and contracted, causing the spasm. Goodheart then reasoned that rather than treating the spasmed muscle, if the weak one were to be made strong again using the origin and insertion method, the body's normal physiology should, in theory, relax the spasmed muscle. And it did!

Being an insatiable researcher, Goodheart regularly read many medical, osteopathic and chiropractic journals and books. Chapman, an osteopath, wrote of the organ reflexes he discovered on the abdomen and back, which when stimulated by a rubbing action, released toxins from the organ through the lymphatic system. Bennett, a chiropractor, discovered reflexes on the head that when stimulated by a very light steady tugging touch, restored normal blood circulation to their respective organs. Goodheart observed that when certain reflexes were stimulated, certain muscles would regain their strength consistently. The same reflexes strengthened the same muscles every time. In addition to the normal diagnostic procedures, he then had another way of diagnosing the function of particular organs, at least on an empirical basis.

Goodheart read the discoveries of another osteopath, W.G. Sutherland, who measured the rhythmic movements of the skull bones, Sutherland found that if certain skull bones did not move normally, there would be symptoms of disease or abnormal function in the body and corresponding weak muscles. Goodheart also found that restoring normal motion to the skull would abolish the symptoms or abnormal function. He observed that it also strengthened the corresponding weak muscle.

Goodheart next studied acupuncture and its relationship to the nervous system. He found that Asians used the word Qi (pronounced, chee) meaning "life force" to describe energy they said flowed through the various meridians of the body. Again, Goodheart found that the same muscles associated with the organs were also associated with the corresponding energy organ meridians.

Goodheart shared the discoveries of his continuing research with others through lectures and seminars. He was in great demand by various state and national chiropractic associations and colleges. Very soon after his initial discovery he was invited to speak to the Wayne State Medical School. Upon arriving at the lecture hall, he noticed that an unidentified medical student, having learned that Goodheart was a chiropractor, had added "????" after the title of "Dr." on the poster announcing his appearance that day. After the lecture Dr. Goodheart noted the poster again and found that the "????" had been crossed out, and "!!!!" took its place.

Soon, Goodheart found that he alone was not going to be able to keep up with the demand to learn this new science, which he has named Applied Kinesiology. He began conferring the title of "Study Group Leader" to doctors who had demonstrated proficiency and ability to teach the science to others. As more and more doctors learned the techniques, they too added new discoveries. In 1974 one of Goodheart's Study Group Leaders, John Thie, D.C., suggested that rather than remaining a loose group of doctors, they band together and form an organization to perpetuate Goodheart's teachings and standardize the curriculum and establish criteria for new teaching doctors. There were 39 original Study Group Leaders who were named as Diplomates of the newly formed International College of Applied Kinesiology (ICAK). This author was one of them.

At first, only chiropractic physicians were allowed to join the study groups; many felt that it should stay that way. Dr. Goodheart was instrumental in convincing members of the ICAK to change the by-laws to allow any type of doctor licensed to diagnose, the opportunity to attend the college. Dr. Goodheart felt that bridges, as opposed to barriers, would lead to better understanding.

Attracted by this policy, psychiatrist John Diamond, M.D. studied applied kinesiology and became a member of ICAK. He learned that Goodheart had discovered that if a patient thought of something that made him/her anxious, a previously strong muscle would "weaken". He used this phenomenon in working with patients and found that he could reach the core of emotional problems far faster than by using orthodox counseling. It changed his entire practice.

Diamond was an officer of the International Academy of Preventive Medicine, which at that time refused to admit chiropractic physicians as full members. Because he felt that this was discriminatory, Diamond educated members of the board of directors, who subsequently changed their by-laws to allow chiropractic physicians to become full members. Dr. Goodheart, and many other members of the ICAK, including this author, subsequently applied and were admitted as full members of the IAPM.

Goodheart was a featured speaker at one of the IAPM annual conventions and introduced applied kinesiology to the attending doctors. Among them was nationally renowned psychiatrist Harvey Ross, M. D., who was very impressed with applied kinesiology – particularly the diagnostic phenomenon of a muscle weakening when a person experienced anxiety or when he/she made a statement that was false.

On returning to Los Angeles, Ross shared what he had learned with his good friend, Roger Callahan, Ph.D. Ross demonstrated the technique, and Callahan, who was very impressed, wanted to learn more of the procedure. He contacted Goodheart and found that there was a 100 hour course beginning in Los Angeles.

In 1985 Callahan wrote a book, *Five Minute Phobia Cure*, for both laymen and professionals. He states in the book, "The idea that mental attitude could so directly affect body reactions intrigued me. I investigated further and subsequently attended a course in applied kinesiology, taught by David S. Walther, D.C. and Robert Blaich, D.C., at which I was the only psychologist present. Gradually, I began to see connections that permitted me to take what I had learned and adapt it to psychological problems."

A revised edition of the book was published in 1986 and renamed, *How Executives Overcome Their Fear of Public Speaking and Other Phobias*. Two papers Callahan wrote in 1981, after he became a member of the ICAK, entitled *A Rapid Treatment of Phobias* and *Psychological Reversal* intrigued me. After using the procedures with much success I soon found that they had potential for treating difficult cases. After meeting Callahan for the first time in l985, I phoned him and found him to be very generous in sharing new information and treatments.

Since the beginning of Callahan's discovery, which he first called The Callahan Techniques, he has subsequently called it Thought Field Therapy. There have been many derivatives of TFT and there are now hundreds of psychologists, psychiatrists, social workers and chiropractic physicians who have joined together to form the Association for Comprehensive Energy Psychology (–> Grudermeyer). This author is proud to be a member of ACEP, its Advisory Board and humbled to be the recipient of its Pioneer Award 2000.

The Basic Acu-POWER Treatment

To begin, have the person think about his/her fear, anxiety or urge. Quantify the degree which he/she suffers from the problem by using the SUD scale of one to ten – ten being the worst (highest) and one being totally relaxed.

As soon as the person states e.g,. "I am at 9", test the strong arm to determine if the statement is correct. This is the person's degree of fear or discomfort; now you have a measuring point with which to gage the person's progress or lack of it. Write it down. People will forget how high it was!

Next, have the individual think about the fear, anxiety or urge. Test the person's strong arm, and it should weaken. Ask him/her to continue to think of their fear or anxiety and have him/her touch treatment point located on the cheek bone just below the eyes, with their free hand, and then test the previously weakened arm. If it becomes strong, you have found the correct energy meridian.

If touching treatment point while he/she was thinking of the fear, anxiety or urge did not make the arm strong, then progress to the treatment point five inches below the arm pit on the side of the chest. If this does not strengthen the weak muscle and continue through the following treatment points until you find the meridian treatment point that makes the test arm becomes strong:

- inside corner of the eye on the side of the nose.
- outside corner of the eye.
- 2/3rds out on the eyebrow.
- directly in front of the ear.
- on the side of the nostrils.
- between upper lip and nose.
- just below the lower lip
- under the collar bone.
- on the front of the shoulder.
- three inches below the shoulder on the chest.
- just below the breast on the ribs.
- inside end of the little finger.

Instruct the person to tap the treatment points (bilaterally) with the index or middle finger of each hand for ten to fifteen seconds while thinking of their fear, anxiety or urge. After the allotted time, instruct the person to stop and quantify the degree of fear, anxiety or urge. It usually will have gone down at least one to two points, If a person comes down from a 9 to a 7, for instance, and stops progress after two additional tapping segments, it means that he/she may have suffered a mini-reversal on the subject. These occur when individuals are so afraid of the subject that they cannot even imagine not being afraid, and do not want to be exposed to the subject, even on a trial basis. It is a form, albeit irrational, of the fear of fear.

Test the person by having him/her say, "I want to get below 7 on my fear of (urge for, etc.)...". If the arm weakens, it confirms that he/she does indeed have a mini-psychological reversal.

Treat this by having the person tap on the psychological reversal point on the side of the hand between the wrist and the beginning of the little finger while re-peating three times, "I deeply accept myself even though I can't get below a 7 on my fear of (urge for)...". Retest by having the person say, "I want to get below 7 on this fear (urge)". If he/she still tests weak, repeat the mini-psychological reversal treatment until the arm stays strong on testing for the reversal.

Have the person continue to tap on the original treatment points. The degree of fear, anxiety or urge should decrease progressively to 1. If it does not, and there is no mini psychological reversal, and he/she still tests strong while touching the original treatment point while thinking of their fear, anxiety or urge, it is time to balance the right and left side of the brain. I call it the Brain Balance Treatment (*Editor's comment: 9 Gamut in EFT and TFT*). Its purpose is to balance the front and back brain and the left and right brain to create an unimpeded communication through the corpus callosum (the nerve fibers that connect the brain hemispheres).

The treatment consists of nine steps, which can be completed in just thirty seconds. While the person is thinking of his/her fear, anxiety or urge, he/she proceeds as follows: With each step, the person taps on the interspace half an inch behind the fourth and fifth knuckles of the left or right hand (this is the Brain Balance Point) for approximately three seconds. In acupuncture this point is known as Triple Warmer 3.

Brain Balance Treatment Steps
1. with eyes open.
2. with eyes closed.
3. with eyes open, point eyes down and to the left without moving the head.
4. with eyes open, point eyes down and to the right without moving the head.

5. with eyes open, roll eyes in large circles in a clock-wise rotation.
6. with eyes open, roll eyes in large circles in a counter-clockwise rotation
7. with eyes open, hum any tune such as Happy Birthday, Yankee Doodle, or make up a tune.
8. with eyes open, count to ten.
9. with eyes open, hum again as in step 7.

This procedure allows the imagination (right) side of the brain to communicate with the logical (left) side of the brain and allows the memory (front) portion of the brain to com-municate with the present time (back) portion of the brain, bringing all portions of the brain into balance so logic and imagination can be in tune with present and past memory.

On completion of the Brain Balance treatment, the individuals will usually experience one to two point drops in their fears, anxieties or addictive urges. If the fear, anxiety or addictive urge has not completely dropped to a 1, instruct the person to continue thinking of the fear, anxiety or urge and tap on the original treatment points.

If continued tapping does not bring the fear, anxiety or urge down to a SUD rating of 1, and he/she is not reversed and you have had them perform the Brain Balance treatment with no addi-tional progress, the person has switched to a different facet of the fear, anxiety or urge. Instruct the person to think of the fear, anxiety or urge and have him/her touch the original treatment point. You will note that this will no longer make the arm strong. In-struct the person to touch the treatment point 5 inches below the armpit and retest the indicator arm. If this makes it strong, tap these treat-ment points on both sides of the chest and instruct the person to think of the fear, anxiety or urge while tapping these new treatment points.

If touching this treatment point did not strengthen the indicator arm, have the person progressively touch each of the other treatment points in sequence (while thinking of their fear, anxiety or urge) while you test the indicator arm. As soon as the indicator arm strengthens, instruct the person to continue tapping the new treatment points until he/she gets down to a SUD rating of 1.

The person may suffer another mini-reversal, and on rare occasions may switch to still another facet of the fear, anxiety or urge, in which case you would repeat the testing procedure as described previously.

Recurring psychological reversals may occur despite the continued tapping of the psychological reversal point and giving Bach Rescue Remedy (five drops under the tongue). In this case, have the person rub the recurring reversal points on either side of the sternum between the second and third rib vigorously for twenty seconds while saying, "I deeply accept myself even though…". It is also useful to recommend Bach Rescue Remedy at this time (five drops under the tongue). Immediately after treating the recurring psychological reversal point(s), continue with tapping the previous treatment point.

The basic Acu-POWER treatment can be used for all types of phobias, anxieties, addictions, compulsive behaviors and post-traumatic stress disorders. Its skillful use can, in many cases, be the only type of treatment needed. However, in some cases traditional counseling may be necessary as well. Many psychologists and counselors use the treatment in combi-nation with traditional therapy and find that it reduces treat-ment time and improves the end results. They also find that the muscle testing gives them a direct line to their patient's real problem. Your body knows!

Notes

1. This chapter is excerpted from *Freedom From Fear Forever* by the author.

References

Callahan, R. (1985). *The Five Minute Phobia Cure.* Wilmington, DE: Enterprise Publishing.
Deepak Chopra (1989). *Quantum Healing.* New York: Bantam Books.
Goodheart, Jr., G.J.(1984). *You'll Be Better.* Privately Published, Grosse Point, MI 1984.
Gerber, R. (1988). *Vibrational Medicine,* Santa Fe, NM: Bear & Co.
Durlacher, J.V. (1985). *Freedom From Fear Forever.* Mesa, AZ: Van Ness Publishing.

21

Conscious Healing and Repatterning Therapy (CHART): Free the Adult by Healing Childhood Pain and Patterns

Paula Shaw

Conscious Healing and Repatterning Therapy (CHART) is an energy-based system that incorporates traditional therapeutic models as well as components of the most prominent energy psychology methods. It's a therapy for a new millennium, a synthesis of many systems with the unique aspect of focusing the energy treatment on the specific part of the personality that holds a given emotional issue. The CHART system utilizes intention, diagnostic muscle testing, keywords, visualization, and chakra and meridian contact, to energetically clear emotional issues being held by the Inner Child, the Inner Adolescent, and the Adult Self. These critical components of the psyche each carry their own energetic patterns that must be individually treated and healed. Another unique and critical component of CHART work is the Repatterning piece. Once an issue has been cleared, we plug into that energetic space, the optimal positive belief or condition that is desired.

CHART is an outgrowth of many years of my personal and professional experience. I began as a teacher of children and I guess my heart has always been with them. Even though I left teaching and entered the adult worlds of resort marketing and motion picture location management, I was destined to return to school to do post-graduate specialty study to earn certification to counsel in the area of addictive disorders. In addition, I attended a Loyola Marymount University Program and earned certification as a Grief

Specialist. Unreconciled grief became the central focus of the work in my private practice because I believe it is so critical an issue in the evolution of addictive dysfunctional behavior, as well as so many other mental/emotional disorders.

While developing CHART, I became acutely aware of a universal grief that we all carry inside, the unhealed grief whose origin is in childhood trauma. This grief is still felt and held onto by our Inner Children who carry the energetic patterns of our past pain and trauma. It keeps them stuck and imprisoned in fear and darkness. Implementation of the CHART process frees those Inner Children from having to sit and wait in the dark painful silence. It gives them the opportunity to speak up, express their pain and get the attention they have needed for years. Once that happens, in my experience, both the Child and the Adolescent are able and willing to let go of the pain and fear, heal, and move on. I have seen this time and time again. We aren't blocked because they are stubborn and won't budge, we're blocked because we refuse to acknowledge them and listen to their pain. In the face of that reality, they simply hold onto the dysfunction that has helped them survive (–> Sise, Weil). It's all they know. Once they've been heard and freed, however, they happily let go and open the way for the Adult to heal and grow.

If we as Adults are to function optimally we have to first clear the "damaged undergrowth" existing in the psyches of both the Inner Child and the Inner Adolescent. This outgrowth of the pain and trauma of the early years blocks energy in the present and prevents us from living successfully. We become stuck, dysfunctional, vulnerable to mental disorders, addictive self-defeating behaviors, and unhealthy relationships. However, if we clear this negative patterning from the past, we open up a space in which we can create the future we really desire (–> Feinstein).

The CHART approach is based on the belief that severe unresolved trauma and attachment conflicts interrupt the normal human developmental process of integration of the personality. The result is fragmentation of the personality manifested as personality disorders and other unproductive beliefs and behavior patterns. The goal of CHART work is integration of the personality and healing of the psyche, brought about by clearing and eliminating unproductive beliefs and behavior patterns where they began and still reside, within the Inner Child. In most cases this is where the initial trauma and the resulting attachment conflicts were first experienced. However, CHART also addresses emotional issues held by the Inner Adolescent and the Inner Adult whose psychological makeup was built on the damaged foundation of the Child's psyche.

This paradigm can best be illustrated with the example of childhood sexual abuse. A child who is sexually abused and has no opportunity to process and clear the emotional scarring, will often develop a negative set of beliefs that initially helps him/her to cope. Beliefs like "I'm bad and I deserved what happened to me." or "I'm only lovable when I'm sexual," place "badness" on the child and in a perverse way aide the child in coping through creating the illusion of power and control. The thinking that follows is something like: "I'm the one who's bad so if I change, the abuse will stop." Even though this never materializes as truth, the hope attained by holding on to this belief helps the child to survive the abuse.

In addition to this damaging delusion, probability is high that the Inner Child is experiencing attachment conflicts because the natural biological urge of the child is to attach to the care taking adult for protection and love. After being violated in what's supposed to be a place of sanctuary, the understandable desire of the child would be to withdraw. However, the need to attach is so strong that it drives the child to maintain a bond with the perpetrator. Imagine how damaging this is to the child's psyche. If no opportunity to process this damage occurs during childhood, the Inner Child will hold on to the core of this trauma and the negative outcomes it produced. Adolescent beliefs and behaviors will be built on the damaged psychological foundation created in childhood, resulting in the perpetuation of unproductive behavior patterns in the Adolescent and eventually the Adult.

In my opinion, energy psychology systems that only clear issues on the Adult level have limited effectiveness because they may not be impacting the core of the pain and shame held by the Child and/or the Adolescent. Consequently, the problematic beliefs and behaviors may persist or recur. The client continues to think, "I'm bad." "Men are bad." "I only have value when I'm pleasing someone." etc. and behaviors like the inability to commit or be intimate, persist as well. Even if the Adult self is anxious to clear negative energy patterns in order to create a more effective life, the Child and Adolescent parts of the psyche may be immobilized in dysfunctional behavior, old pain and trauma. Until those hurts are healed, the Adult cannot go forward in a productive pain free manner. The Child and the Adolescent will create the physical or emotional upheaval necessary to draw attention to what they need. A kind of psychic "tantrum" can even occur, manifesting itself in physical pain, illness, or psychological disorders.

Our vulnerable Children experience most of the initial trauma that occurs in a given life. Rarely do they get the opportunity to process and release the impact of the trauma, so it gets locked into their energetic circuitry. A matrix of unproductive beliefs and behaviors forms around it, and after a time it is almost impossible to separate the child's personality from the traumas that initially formed it. Before they are damaged or traumatized, children are open, loving, happy, inquisitive, full of awe and vitally alive. Then the pain comes and the trust and aliveness become deadened with fear. Without help from a trusted adult, the child is doomed to remain this way.

Sadly, it's upon this damaged foundation that the psyche of the adolescent is built. That psyche then becomes further decompensated by the unresolved traumas experienced in adolescence. This is the legacy that will then be passed on to the adult person. Is it any wonder that by the time we are adults we are fearful, neurotic, frustrated, anxiety-ridden isolated beings, with no sense of wonder or awe and little ability to live creatively? Way too many of us are walking around numb, afraid, and emotionally dead. It doesn't have to be this way (–> Eden & Feinstein, Hover-Kramer).

When childhood is a happy, secure experience, grounded in open, honest communication, adolescence will progress normally. The adolescent feels safe to devalue authority figures, individuate, and learn through trial and error who s/he is and what s/he believes. The growth and independence attained during adolescence will contribute positively to the formation of a healthy adult. However, when the client as a child has been frightened and damaged the normal developmental tasks can't progress smoothly. The courage, independence, safety, and security necessary for the adolescent to rebel and become his/her own person won't be there.

If we as adults take no action to heal the wounds of the Child and the Adolescent, how can we realistically expect success with moving beyond the pain and deadness that weigh us down? Who we are is built on who the child and adolescent were. We can't build a strong house on a faulty foundation. We have to go back and begin the healing where the wounds were incurred. Caroline Myss describes this beautifully in *Anatomy of the Spirit*.

> The "wounded child" in each of us contains the damaged or stunted emotional patterns of our youth, patterns of painful memories, of negative attitudes and of dysfunctional self-images. Unknowingly, we may continue to operate within these patterns as adults, albeit in a new form. Fear of abandonment, for example, becomes jealousy. Sexual abuse becomes dysfunctional sexuality, often causing a repetition of the same violations with our own children. A child's negative self-image can later become the source of dysfunctions such as anorexia, obesity, alcoholism, and other addictions as well as obsessive fear of

failure. These patterns can damage our emotional relationships, our personal and professional lives, and our health. Loving oneself begins with confronting this archetypal force within the psyche and unseating the wounded child's authority over us. If unhealed, wounds keep us living in the past."

With these ideas as my guiding thoughts, I began to work with clearing the issues of the Inner Child, Adolescent and Adult with all my clients. I had been working with several clients on the Matrix Key Core Traumatic Patterns, so I decided to go back and recheck the issues we'd already cleared. This time I checked the Child, Adolescent and Adult. In every case, the Adult was still clear, but the Child and the Adolescent were not. Low and behold, as we began clearing the traumas of all three of these aspects of the psyche, the back pain in one client disappeared completely, as did the life-long depression issues of another. These successes were soon followed by a host of other physical and emotional issues getting cleared and staying cleared.

My belief is that when we heal the pain of the Inner Child and the Inner Adolescent as well as that of the Adult, we get a deep clearing that lasts because we have eliminated the issue on the level where the pain was first experienced and on the levels that were later impacted. I feel this is an important piece of the puzzle that may add to our understanding of why people sometimes "take an issue back" or why it may take several treatments to get it cleared in the first place. What may be going on is that the Inner Child or the Inner Adolescent hasn't yet had his/her "day in the sun," and therefore isn't ready to let go of the issue.

The goal of this system is to help you CHART a different course. A course back to happiness, joy and freedom.

First, you must gain the trust of the Inner Child, but that's easy to do because they are so ready for some attention. Begin by saying goodnight and good morning to them and thinking of them when you are enjoying things you enjoyed as a child, or when you are afraid of things you feared as a child. Put your arms around them and tell them, "It's ok, I'm aware of your pain and I'll always be there." That kind of acknowledgment is like a banquet to this child who is starving for attention.

Before you know it, you will be clearing issues you've carried for years. In my experience these Inner Kids don't want to stay in pain nor should they. They're ready to let go once they trust us to show them how. Don't keep walking by your Inner Child ignoring its tears! It takes so little effort to achieve so much.

Everyone can do this. Just have the desire to take your life to a better place. Set the course and invite them to join you. Have no fear; the Inner Child and the Inner Adolescent will be happy to accompany you on the journey.

Chart Protocol Script

Step 1. Initial Discussion with Client to Gather Information and Determine Treatment Goal

Get a clear picture of the present issues and their impact on the client's life. A thorough intake is the most desirable procedure, gathering as much information about childhood and adolescence as possible.

Step 2. Target the Issue to be Worked On.

Write the issue down in the form of a statement, i.e.; "I suffer severe anxiety whenever I have to speak in public." This is similar to highlighting what you want to delete on your computer.

Briefly explain to the client: The rationale for energy psychology work is that negative emotions, beliefs, and behaviors are a result of disruptions in the energy system. These disruptions often occur as a result of childhood trauma. They get locked into our energetic circuitry and continue to cause problems until they are shifted or cleared. The goal of this process will be to clear and eliminate the energy disruptions that exist in the consciousness of the Inner Child, the Inner Adolescent and the Inner Adult. If the client is now comfortable with doing the work, go to Step 3.

Step 3. Intention Statement

Intention is the most powerful force for creation in the universe. It determines the destination you desire to reach at the end of any given journey. Without intention a clear goal has not been designated. Therefore, events are random and the ultimate creation unpredictable. Its importance is immeasurable.

Have the client begin by stating his/her intention for the session. I usually lead with this statement then have the client add to it anything specific they want to say: "My Intention for this session is to clear and eliminate the unproductive beliefs, behaviors, attitudes, patterns and emotions that exist in my life today. I wish to let go of the pain and trauma from which they originated, and create myself anew. I give permission for my life, my soul, and my body to be healed now." Any additional statements of the client's will go here.

Conscious Healing and Repatterning Therapy: Chart

Step 4A. Muscle Test Client to Get a Baseline

Explain to the client that muscle checking is a way of finding out what his/her energy system and subconscious mind resonates with. Whatever the system resonates with will produce a strong response (locked muscle) and what the system doesn't resonate with will produce a weak response (flaccid muscle). Then muscle check the client to get a baseline of their strong/positive test and their weak/negative test. Then go on to

Step 4B. Muscle Test to See if a Client is Properly Polarized Using Three Tests

- Hand over head: Palm down about 1 inch above head – should produce a strong muscle response.
  Hand over head: Palm up about 1 inch above head—should produce a weak muscle check.
- Stating real name: strong muscle test.
  Stating fictitious name—weak muscle test.
- Collarbone test – (Muscle test each point, all tests should be strong.)
  First, finger pads on left collarbone point (just under collarbone in the indentation toward midline of body). Then test right collarbone point. Repeat using knuckles on both points.

If client fails any of these tests do one of the usual correction procedures and retest. When all tests are passed go to Step 4C. If this is the first session, go on to Step 4C and install the client's keyword. If this is not the first session go on to Step 4D.

Step 4C. Install the Client's Keyword (first session only)

Have the client select a word s/he likes and wants to use as the keyword, which will initiate the clearing of targeted issues and problems. After the keyword has been installed have client say "My subconscious mind and all its aspects have heard the instructions given and agree to do this for me from now on." Muscle test this statement – it should be strong.

Now proceed with the steps below. If the client is a child or an adolescent some obvious alterations in the protocol will need to be made.

Step 4D. Muscle Test for Any Global Psychoenergetic Reversals, Using Statements

Muscle test after each statement:
1. "I deserve to live."/"I deserve to die."
2. "I want to be happy."/"I want to be miserable."
3. "I deserve love, help and healing."/"I don't deserve love, help and healing."

Correction Procedure: If there is a positive response to one of the negative statements: Have the client rub the NLR (Pledge of Allegiance) spot located on right side of upper chest above breast. Rub in a clockwise direction and say three times: "I deeply and profoundly love and accept myself with all my faults, problems and limitations." Then retest. If this doesn't work try the Grudermeyer version: "I deeply and profoundly accept myself with all my strengths, gifts and ability to love." Then retest. When tests are passed, go on to Step 4E.

Step 4E. Check Client for Any Psychoenergetic Reversals

Ask, "Are there currently any psychoenergetic reversals affecting this issue?" If yes, use the psychoenergetic reversal test statements and clearing procedures below. If test is strong on a negative statement, do correction procedure and retest. When any necessary corrections have been completed or if the client tests that there are no reversals, go on to Step 5.

Test Statements:
- "I want to get over this issue."/"I don't want to get over this issue." (NLR point)
- "It's safe for me to get over this issue."/"It's not safe for me to get over this issue." (Side of Hand, Karate Chop point.)
- "I deserve to get over this issue."/"I don't deserve to get over this issue."(UL point)
- "I give myself permission to get over this issue."/"I don't give myself permission to get over this issue." (NLR point)
- "It will benefit me to get over this issue."/"It will not benefit me to get over this issue." (NLR point)
- "It's possible for me to get over this issue."/"It's not possible for me to get over this issue." (UC, kidney 27 Point)
- "I will get over this issue."/"I will not get over this issue." (UN point)
- "I will do whatever is necessary to get over this issue."/"I will not do whatever is necessary to get over this issue. (NLR point)

Correction Procedure: In most cases the reversals will be those in the above list. If this is the case, have the client tap the meridian point indicated or rub the NLR spot and repeat after you the appropriate clearing statement three times. For example, while tapping the side of the hand: "Even though it's not safe for me to get over my grief, I deeply and profoundly love and accept myself." Or if there is more than one reversal, use the NLR spot and say for example: "Even though I will not give myself permission and don't deserve to get over this problem, I deeply and profoundly love and accept myself." Now retest the original reversal statement. It should be "off" or weak; if not, repeat clearing procedure or muscle test to see if there is another meridian spot or chakra that would be better to tap. When reversals are clear or if there are none, go to Step 5A.

Step 5A. Permission from Protective Consciousness

Permission: Ask the Protective Consciousness (the protector and controler of the subconscious mind) if you have permission to go forward with the work. Say "Do we have permission from the Protective Consciousness to go forward with the work?" (muscle test the client - should be strong.) If you do not get a strong response, dialogue with the Protective Consciousness and explain why you're doing the work and how it will ultimately improve the quality of life for the person you are working with, then retest. Repeat dialoguing process if necessary, expanding on your initial explanation until test is strong. Rarely is permission withheld but if it is, do not do the work.

Step 5B. Permission from Inner Child

Ask the Inner Child if you have his/her permission to go froward with the work. Say, "Do we have permission from the Inner Child to go forward with the work?" Muscle test the Client – should be strong. If you do not get a strong muscle test, dialogue with the part and explain why you're doing the work and how it will ultimately improve the quality of life for the person you are working with, then retest. Repeat this dialoguing process if necessary expanding on your initial explanation until test is strong. Rarely is permission withheld but if it is, do not do the work.

If this were the first session, this would be the time to ask the Inner Child if it feels comfortable using the word that the Adult has chosen to be the keyword. If you don't get a strong test then ask the client what other word they feel might be more appealing to the Inner Child. Test that word. Repeat this process if necessary until you get a strong affirmative muscle test. Then make a statement to the subconscious mind that the keyword for the Child will be this new word.

Step 5C. Permission from the Inner Adolescent

Ask the Inner Adolescent if you have his/her permission to go froward with the work. Say, "Do we have permission from the Inner Adolescent to go forward with the work?" Muscle test the client – should be strong. If you do not get a strong muscle test, dialogue with the part and explain why you're doing the work and how it will ultimately improve the quality of life for the person you are working with, then retest. Repeat dialoguing process if necessary, expanding on your initial explanation, until test is strong. Rarely is permission withheld but if it is, do not do the work. If this is the first session go through the same steps as with the Child making sure that the Adolescent is comfortable with the keyword chosen.

Step 5D. Permission from the Inner Adult

Ask the Inner Adult if you have his/her permission to go froward with the work. Say, "Do we have permission from the Inner Adult to go forward with the work?" Muscle test the client - should be strong. If you do not get a strong muscle test, dialogue with the client present and discuss why you're doing the work and how it will ultimately improve the quality of life for the person you are working with, then retest. Repeat if necessary until test is strong. Rarely is permission withheld but if it is, do not do the work. The conscious mind of the client present might be desirous of doing the work, but if the subconscious mind has objections it might sabotage the work you try to do.

Step 6. Optimize the Energy System

Using a brief visualization and deep rhythmic breathing, have the client visualize him/herself standing in a "power place" (wherever that might be for them) surrounded by white light that comes in and energizes each chakra in turn. This should only take a minute or two. This step is not always necessary. If client is calm and ready to do the work just proceed with step 7.

Step 7A. Present the Issue Statement to the Inner Child

In the form of a statement that you have written down, present the issue to this aspect of the subconscious mind (i.e., "My Child suffers severe anxiety whenever she has to speak in public."). Have client either repeat this statement or say "true" after you say the statement. Muscle test the client to see if he/she is holding an emotional charge on the issue or a belief that the statement is true. This will be indicated by a strong muscle test. If the test is weak, there is no issue with the Inner Child, go on to the Adolescent.

Step 7B. If the Test is Strong

Note it, then have the client close his/her eyes. This isn't mandatory but I find that when eyes are closed often images of past pain or the instance when this belief was created tend to come up almost like a movie. This is powerful. Encourage the client to be with those images as long as they need to in order to enhance detail and clarity regarding the emotions experienced, the people and places involved, and the physical sensations felt. If the client wants to dialogue about the experience, encourage them to do so. All this information just gives the subconscious a more precise understanding of what it is that needs to be cleared and eliminated from the client's life experience (again, this is similar to highlighting what you want to delete when working on the computer). When the client feels ready, have them say their keyword.

Step 7C. Retest the Exact Same Statement as Before
Repeat the exact same statement you began with and muscle test to see if it is still being "held." This would be indicated by another strong muscle test. What you want to see is a weak muscle test indicating that there is no longer an emotional charge on the issue or a strong belief being held. If the test is still strong, have the client focus on the same statement again and then use the keyword.

Step 7D. Retest the Same Statement
When you get a weak test, you have cleared the issue. Note it and you are ready to go on to the next step. If the test grows weaker each time and you can see that progress is being made, then proceed with the same process. However, if the test remains very strong and no progress is being made after two or three trials, test to see if there is a "completely-level" psychoenergetic reversal afoot. Ask, "Is there a reversal?" If the muscle test is strong, go to the list of test statements we started with when checking for psychoenergetic reversals at the beginning of the session. Find the reversal. This time, however, the treatment statement would be adjusted in the following way, "Even though I don't deserve to be completely over this issue, I deeply and profoundly love and accept myself." Say this while tapping the appropriate meridian point. After this procedure has been followed, retest the reversal statement, it should be clear (weak test). If not repeat the treatment and retest. It is also possible to skip the above and simply say "Subconscious mind, clear this reversal." Then retest.

When it is clear, return to the presenting statement, again using the keyword, and attempt to clear the issue. If the issue won't clear, try encouraging the client to visualize the Child as s/he looks in pain when the issue is present, then see the Child's eyes light up as we remind him/her that s/he doesn't have to stay in pain any longer. S/he has a tool now, a magical tool, a keyword that can unlock the door that imprisons the Child and allow him/her to be free. All s/he needs to do is take a nice deep empowering breath and say the keyword. After the word is said, retest. It is possible that there might not be enough safety or trust for the Child to let go at this time. I usually ask them and muscle test for the answer. You may have to leave the issue and try another time. When the issue tests clear or when you determine that the Child won't let go at this time, note it and go on to Step 7 E.

Step 7E. Have the Client Repeat the Same Statement Focusing on the Adolescent
"My Inner Adolescent suffers severe anxiety whenever she has to speak in public." Then follow the preceding steps until the issue is cleared.

Step 7F. Have the Client Repeat the Same Statement Focusing on the Adult.
"My Adult suffers severe anxiety whenever she has to speak in public." Follow the preceding steps until the issue is cleared.

Step 8. Repatterning.
Now that the energetic space has been cleared, you can align the client's energy with a positive belief or goal (i.e., "I speak calmly and clearly in public and really enjoy the experience." or "Every opportunity to speak in public offers me a chance to realize how much I'm capable of handling.") You can also use a statement that is the opposite of the one that was just cleared but in my experience the client is already "on" for the positive opposite once the negative has been cleared. Therefore, I think it's optimal to create a statement that represents the ideal condition that you want to exist. When all the issues that are to be worked on in that session are cleared and repatterned, proceed to Step 9.

Step 9. Fear/Hurt/Judgment/Anger and Forgiveness/Clearing (with thanks to Larry Nims).
Muscle test whether you need to clear fear, hurt, judgment or anger. Ask, "Do we need to clear *fear*?" Muscle test and repeat this with each emotion. If *fear* tests strong: While tapping the point under the eye (St-1), say three times, "I'm eliminating all of the fear I have of myself, others (specific name if appropriate) and God". Retest.

If *hurt* tests strong: While tapping the gamut spot, say three times, "I'm eliminating all of the hurt I have towards myself, others (specific name if appropriate) and God". Retest.

If *judgment* tests strong: While tapping the insides of the thumbs together (Lu-1) say three times, "I'm eliminating all of the judgment I have toward myself, others (specific name if appropriate) and God". Retest.

If *anger* tests strong: While tapping the insides of the little fingers near the nail (Ht-1) say three times, "I'm eliminating all of the anger I have toward myself, others (specific name if appropriate) and God. Retest.

e) Always do the *forgiveness* procedure: While tapping the side of the index finger have client say "I forgive myself, I know I'm doing the best that I can. I forgive others (specific name if appropriate). I know they are doing the best that they can. I forgive God. I know he/she is doing what's best for me."

Step 10. Anchor the Work

Close the session with an anchoring visualization. Have the client take about seven deep slow continuous breaths with eyes closed while the left hand covers the heart chakra and the right hand touches a meridian point. Muscle test prior to this what point it should be out of the 14 EFT points. Then open the eyes, look up and blink slowly, then look down and do the same. Then client should close the eyes and visualize themselves standing in their "power place" (i.e. a high plateau, a mountaintop, the beach etc.) with their Child and Adolescent. They are surrounded by sparkles of glowing light (whatever color comes to them). Atoms of newly freed energy dart all around them (–> Eden & Feinstein). A feeling of exuberance and unlimited possibilities fills the air. Allow that to integrate for a couple of minutes and open eyes.

References
Myss, C. *Anatomy of the Spirit.*

A more extended version of this procedure is described in the CHART manual. The manual also contains directions for trouble shooting with each of the steps.

22

Energy Psychology Treatment of Allergy-like Reactions

Sandi Radomski

Allergy Antidotes Overview

Allergy Antidotes™ is a comprehensive system for assessing, identifying, and treating substance sensitivities with the goal of eliminating undesirable physical and emotional symptoms. The Allergy Antidotes system has been highly successful in reducing symptoms from substance sensitivities, the incidence of which continue to rise at an alarming rate. For example, asthma, especially in children, has increased dramatically. More patients than ever before with environmental illnesses or multiple chemical sensitivities, appear at my office with masks and oxygen tanks. Many churches and office buildings have become perfume and scent- free in an effort to accommodate people with allergies. More and more buildings are labeled "sick" due to chemical toxicity. It is becoming apparent that it is difficult for many people to cope with the numerous chemicals of our modern world.

I first became aware of the importance of food and environmental sensitivities through the work of Dr. Roger Callahan, the founder of Thought Field Therapy (TFT). Despite the success of TFT in most cases, Callahan sought to understand the minority of cases when TFT failed to eliminate symptoms and those instances when negative symptoms reoccurred. Dr. Callahan discovered that certain people undergo psychological reversal and a subsequent return of symptoms when exposed to a substance to which they are particularly sensitive. He calls these substances energy toxins since they are toxic to or weaken the body's energy system. I call this weakening of the body's energy system an allergy. When I refer to allergies, it is, therefore, not in the strict medical definition of allergy involving a histamine reaction. A discussion of the Allergy Antidotes™ system involves the interchangeable terms allergy, allergy-like reaction, sensitivity, and energy toxins.

There are several reasons for the astonishing increase in food and environmental sensitivities. The most obvious is that we are exposed to a greater quantity and diversity of chemicals and substances today than at any other time in human evolution. We inhale and ingest chemicals on a daily basis whose names we can't even pronounce. As a result, our natural immune defenses, which constantly process information to determine the safety of substances and simultaneously adjust our internal environment to maintain homeostasis in relationship to those substances, have become overloaded and are forced to succumb to allergy-like reactions. The result can be likened to the "rain barrel effect," where the rain barrel represents the immune system, which gives up trying to adjust to the substances to which it is confronted and simply overflows. The affected person then experiences reactions to those substances.

In addition to an overworked immune system, allergy-like reactions are known to increase after a trauma. Sensitivities to particular substances can arise when a person is traumatized while being exposed to that substance. Association of reactive substances to trauma follows the findings of Dr. Robert Ader, who coined the term psychoneuroimmunology. Dr. Ader conducted the first study of how our body is conditioned to associate external events with foods ingested during those events. He did this by first lowering the effectiveness of the immune system of mice by giving them an immune suppressant drug in a saccharine solution, and then by observing that saccharine alone produced a similar decrease in immune system function. The mice quickly began to associate the taste of saccharine to simultaneous immune suppression, just as the human body may associate a trauma to foods or smells linked in time to the trauma (–> Eden & Feinstein).

Any Symptom Can be From Substance Sensitivities

Reactions to various substances can produce a myriad of symptoms including ADD (–> Tenpenny), anxiety, depression, arthritis, respiratory problems, menstrual difficulties, digestive problems, chronic fatigue, brain fog, panic attacks, headaches, weight gain, learning disabilities, hyperactivity and aches and pains. The severity of the symptom runs the gamut from nasal congestion to psychosis.

Assessing Symptoms

As clinicians, we must assess whether a patient's symptoms may be an allergic response to a substance. It is important to ask if allergies tend to run in the family. Note whether the symptoms are better or worse at particular times of the day, week, month or year, and dependent on what a person is doing or eating. For example, is it better or worse before or after meals? Inside or outdoors? In the morning, afternoon or evening? Do you see 180° shifts in behavior?

When evaluating food sensitivities, it is also important to note what types of foods someone craves. We tend to be reactive to those foods we crave. If a person has a main food that they "have to have," they are probably sensitive to it.

Any Substance can Cause a Sensitivity Reaction

As discussed, any symptom can be from a substance sensitivity. In turn, any substance can trigger a reaction. The possible culprits range from toxic chemicals such as petrochemicals to non-toxic substances such as eggs and vitamin C, which would be harmless to most people.

One of the goals of the Allergy Antidotes system is to open our minds to the possible contribution of sensitivity reactions to a client's behavior and health. To this end, we must become aware of those substances that have been clinically found most often to promote allergy-like reactions. We must also have a way to assess whether a particular substance is weakening a person's energy system.

Identification of Substance Sensitivities

Sensitive substances can be easily identified using non-invasive muscle testing. This variety of muscle testing, adapted from Applied Kinesiology, involves the patient holding or thinking about different substances while consistent pressure is applied to the patient's outstretched arm. If the arm weakens or "gives way," it is an indication that the held substance is weakening the muscle energy system.

What to Test First?

Once you have determined that substance sensitivities may be a contributing factor in your patient's health, you need to begin testing various substances. Since we are imbalanced by so many influences, the question is always, "What to test first?"

First Test Allergy Antidotes Core Collection

It is important to initially test and treat the substances contained in Allergy Antidotes Core Collection. The Core Collection is composed of essential nutrients as well as toxic chemicals to which we are exposed. A patient who is weak on a nutrient is unable to absorb and utilize that nutrient properly. For example, if you are sensitive to calcium, you would not absorb the calcium in your foods or supplements. Toxic chemicals and heavy metals tend to set the body up for further problems with bacteria, viruses, yeast, molds and parasites. Research findings increasingly link childhood vaccinations with impaired functioning.

<u>Allergy Antidotes Core Collection</u>
- Egg/Chicken
- Calcium/Milk
- Vitamin C
- B Complex Vitamins
- Sugar
- Minerals Heavy Metals
- Toxic Chemicals
- Petrochemicals
- Pesticides
- Vaccines.

<u>Other Substances to Check for Sensitivity Reactions</u>
The identification process proceeds with questioning and then testing those items that patients ingest, inhale, contact or inject. Patients are asked to bring in samples from home and we also assess and test past exposures to problem substances.

Allergy Antidotes techniques check foods eaten, medications, supplements, personal care products, school and office products, toxic metals and chemicals, animals, outdoor environment, body fluids, hormones, neurotransmitters, digestive enzymes, organs, and infectants such as mold, virus, bacteria and parasites. People can also be reactive to persons and places. Severely sensitive people have even been reactive to basic elements such as oxygen and hydrogen.

Allergy Antidotes Energy Frequency Tubes

Allergy Antidotes Energy Frequency Tubes facilitate muscle testing to uncover reactive substances. These tubes contain the electromagnetic frequency of various substances. Holding the tube creates the same reaction in the body as holding the actual substance. Since the electromagnetic energy of the tubes is magnified 10 times, Energy Frequency Tubes are often more efficient than the actual substance in identifying reactions.

Currently, there are five Allergy Antidotes Collections:

- Expanded Core Collection
- Basic Body Collection
- Foods Collection
- Emotions Collection
- Neurotransmitters and Digestive Enzymes Collection

Smaller, mini-packets of Vaccines, Heavy Metals, Additional Emotions, and Elements are also available, along with a 48-tube set of Immune System components.

Once a Reactive Substance is Identified

By merely identifying the substance sensitivities, a higher quality of life is afforded to a sensitive person who can now avoid the reactive substance. However, it is often difficult, impossible or merely undesirable to avoid the substance. For example, it is difficult to avoid dust, perfumes or formaldehyde. It is impossible to avoid implants in one's body or one's hormones and it is dangerous to avoid vitamins or minerals. In these cases it is necessary to alter the body's reaction to the substance.

Treatment of Substance Sensitivities
Energy psychology treatments for substance sensitivities help to reprogram the body so that it no longer reacts negatively to the substance. Once reprogrammed the body essentially no longer views the substance as a poison. All of the treatments are done with the patient focused on the reactive substance. The focus can be while holding the substance, holding a tube with the energetic signature of the substance, holding a piece of paper with the name of the substance, or saying and thinking of the substance. The body's energy system is then balanced in relation to the offending substance. The treatment of stimulating acupuncture points eliminates the energy imbalance in relation to that substance and thereby ends the body's negative reaction. The treatment is complete when the body has been reprogrammed to accept the substance.

It is clear that the energy psychology treatments for allergies are analogous to the TFT and EFT treatments for negative emotions. The reactive substance causes changes in the body's energy system similar to the disturbance caused by a negative emotion, thought or scene. The energy system is then balanced in relation to the substance by stimulating specific acupuncture points as is done in TFT and EFT for negative thoughts or scenes. Other treatment modalities utilize reflex points or other points of the body to regain balance of the body in relation to the offending substance.

Basic Treatments for Substance Sensitivities
The Allergy Antidotes system uses five basic treatment modalities:

1. Spinal Release
2. Laser Spray
3. Emotional Freedom Technique (EFT)
4. Body Talk
5. Holloway Technique

Spinal Release stimulates acupuncture points on the back on either side of the spine, to balance the meridians in relation to the offending substance. These points on the bladder meridian correspond to all of the other meridians in the body. Laser Spray stimulates ear acupuncture points to balance the reflex points that refer to all parts of the body. Laser Spray is also used to stimulate reflex points on the hands and feet. Emotional Freedom Technique (EFT) uses meridian endpoints to clear the negative reaction. Body Talk uses tapping on the head and sternum and the Holloway Technique uses points along the sides of the body on the spleen meridian.

In conjunction with the basic treatments the Allergy Antidotes system also uses four specialized protocols:

1. Emotional Sensitivity Treatment
2. Body Sensitivity Treatment
3. Trauma Sensitivity Treatment
4. Body Wisdom Treatment

The Emotional Sensitivity Treatment identifies events and emotions that may be blocking a treatment. The Body Sensitivity Treatment is used when a problem with a body organ, system, hormone or fluid has influenced a sensitivity reaction. Trauma Sensitivity Treatment combines the allergy treatment with clearing the emotional trauma associated with onset of the reaction or contact with the substance. The Body Wisdom Technique determines whether a specific infectant (bacteria, virus, parasite, mold) is the cause of the problem.

Research Findings
Dr. Penny Montgomery and Dr. Margaret Ayers have conducted two landmark studies with great relevance to the treatment of allergy-like reactions to substances (–>

Tenpenny). Using real time EEG findings, Drs. Montgomery and Ayers have discovered specific brain wave patterns that denote sensitivity to a particular substance. In the first study, they have successfully proven that brain waves return to normal after using N.A.E.T. (Nambudripad's Allergy Elimination Technique) – a similar procedure to Spinal Release – to clear the reaction. The importance of this research is in documenting not only the presence of the sensitivity but the effectiveness of the treatment as well. The second study documents changes in brain waves when the subject merely holds an energy frequency tube containing a substance to which he or she is reactive, illustrating the effectiveness of Energy Frequency Tubes to detect and treat sensitivity reactions.

References

Craig, G. *Emotional Freedom Techniques.*
Craig, G. (1998). *The Ultimate Therapist – A Transcript.*
Cutler, E. (1998). *Winning the War Against Asthma and Allergies.* Delmar Publishers.
Cutler, E. (1998). *Winning the War Against Auto-immune Disorders and Allergies.* Delmar Publishers.
Haas, E. (2000). *The False Fat Diet.* Ballantine Publishing Group.
Jaeckie, R. G. Yeast-Related Mental Disturbances. *Mastering Food Allergies,* Vol. X, No. 1, #83, Jan-Feb 1995.
Monti, D. et al. Muscle Test Comparisons of Congruent and Incongruent Self-Referential Statements. *Perceptual and Motor Skills.* 1999, 88, pp. 1019-1028.
Nambudripad, D. (1999). *Say Goodbye to ADD and ADHD.* Delta Publishing.
Nambudripad, D. (1999). *Say Goodbye to Autism.* Delta Publishing Co.
Nambudripad, D. (1999). *Say Goodbye to Illnes.* Delta Publishing Co., 2nd Edition.
Oleson, T. (1996). *Auricular Therapy Manual: Chinese and Western Systems of Ear Acupuncture.* Health Care Alternatives. Los Angeles.
Radomski, S. (2000). *Allergy Antidotes – Energy Psychology Treatment of Allergy-Like Reactions.*
Rapp, D. (1989). *Allergies and Your Family.* Practical Allergy Research Foundation. Buffalo.
Rapp, D. (1989). *The Impossible Child.* Published by Practical Allergy Research Foundation, Buffalo, NY.
Thie, D.C., John F., *Touch for Health: A New Approach to Restoring Our Natural Energies.* Touch for Health Foundation.
Veltheim, J. (1999). *The Body Talk System.* PaRama, Inc.
Walther, D.S. (1988). *Applied Kinesiology, Vol. I.* Basic Procedures and Muscle Testing, Systems DC, Pueblo, CO.
Walther, D.S. (1988). *Applied Kinesiology - Synopsis.* Systems DC, Pueblo, CO.

23

Treating ADD/ADHD Through Allergy Elimination[1]

Sherry Tenpenny

The single biggest health care fraud in US history is the representation of ADHD to be an actual disease, and the drugging of millions of entirely normal American children, as "treatment".
– Janet Reno, US Attorney General, April 15, 1998.

Introduction

Attention Deficit Disorder (ADD) and Attention Deficit Hyperactivity Disorder (ADHD) are a loose assemblage of symptoms used to define behavioral abnormalities frequently seen in childhood. First reported in 1902 in the British medical journal, *The Lancet*, Dr. G.F. Still's assessment of 49 children with aggressive behavior, defiance and limited attention span concluded that the problem was a defect in "conformity to moral conduct."(Still, 1902). Over the years, these behaviors have been variously described as a "hyperkinetic impulse disorder," "minimal brain dysfunction" and "neurosocial disorders." None of the literature suggests or identifies an underlying cause for the abnormal behavior.

Since 1948, the combined specialty of "neuropsychiatry" has been divided into neurology and psychiatry. A neurologist treats organic, physical diseases of the brain. A psychiatrist deals with emotional and behavioral problems, almost exclusively with prescription medications. Patients without identifiable organic disease are referred to the psychiatrist for "evaluation and treatment." Since no organic, objective cause for the hyperactivity seen can be found, children are labeled as having "poor impulse control" and are considered to have a psychiatric disorder.

The pharmaceutical industry joined ranks with the psychiatrists in the 1950s, proclaiming that behavioral disorders were caused by "chemical imbalances" within the brain. External, pharmaceutical intervention was deemed the "treatment of choice," and the drugging of American children began.

By 1980, the American Psychiatric Association had officially listed the term "hyperactive child syndrome" in the DSM-III, the Diagnostic and Statistical Manual of Mental Disorders, and called this disorder ADD. Revised in 1987, the DSM-IV listed official creation of the term Attention Deficit/Hyperactivity Disorder, or ADHD. It is interesting to note that the number of "disorders" and "diseases" currently listed in the DSM-IV grew from 112 to 374 between 1952 and 1994.

Difficulty continues in determining the actual diagnosis of ADHD. It was reported to the ADHD consensus development panel conference of the National Institutes of Health held November 16-18, 1998 that "we do not have an independent, valid test of ADHD and there are no data to indicated that ADHD is due to a brain malfunction. Further research to establish the validity of the disorder continues to be a problem." (Carey, 1998).

Clinically, professionals reserve the term ADD for children with inattention and distractibility, and ADHD for children who also exhibit hyperactivity. However, there are no x-rays, laboratory tests, neurological tests or even signs identifiable through a physical examination that clearly and reproducibly establishes the diagnosis of ADHD.

The Official Diagnosis

Without specific biological markers, the diagnosis is based on observations from parents and teachers, behavioral assessment tests and clinical evaluations from health care providers. From the following list of symptoms, 8 or more must be present for at least six months for the diagnosis of ADHD to be given:

- Symptoms appear before the age of 7;
- frequent mistakes or failure to pay close attention to details;
- often does not listen when spoken to directly;
- fails to finish work and does not follow instructions;
- lacks organizational skills;
- avoids sustained mental effort;
- misplaces items;
- easily distracted and forgetful;

- frequently fidgets or squirms;
- frequently leaves expected sitting area;
- frequently acts inappropriately;
- has difficulty being quiet while in leisure activities;
- talks excessively;
- shouts answers out of turn;
- impatient;
- interrupts or intrudes on others.

Additional features must also be taken into consideration. The symptoms must occur both at home and in school, and clearly interfere with social and academic functioning. ADHD must be diagnosed as an entity separate from any other mental disorder, such as schizophrenia or mania (APA, DSM-IV).

This loosely defined group of symptoms includes the typical behaviors of a normal child less than 7 years of age and can be widely interpreted...or misinterpreted. A recent study performed by researchers at the Center for Pediatric Research at Eastern Virginia medical School in Norfolk evaluated the nurse medication records of students in grades two to five in two separate schools. The number of students enrolled in city A was 5,767 and the number in city B were 23,967. The prevalence of ADHD was found to be 12% in city A and 63% in city B. The researchers concluded that the criteria for ADHD diagnosis can vary substantially across U.S. populations, with the potential for over diagnosis and over treatments in some groups (LeFerver, 1999).

In fact, psychosocial problems are the most common chronic condition precipitating pediatric office visits, surpassing visits for asthma and heart disease, and ADHD is the most commonly diagnosed behavioral disorder in children. Approximately 13% of the nation's school-aged children, or 6 million kids, are now "labeled" as having ADHD. Up to 90% of these children are also taking Ritalin, making Ritalin almost synonymous with ADHD.

The production of Ritalin increased by nearly 700% between 1990 and 1997 and more than 85% of the world's supply of Ritalin is consumed in the U.S. and Canada (Day, 2001). In fact, Ritalin use is at an all-time high, making the financial windfall from Ritalin sales surpass that of Valium, Viagra or Prozac (Walker, 2001). Even worse, nearly 1% of children between the age of 2 and 4 are on Ritalin, even though the drug has never been approved for use in children under the age of five and the PDR is very clear in warning that Ritalin and similar drugs are not recommended for children in this young group. Furthermore, in an eight-year longitudinal study published in 1990 in the Journal of the American

Academy of Child and Adolescent Psychiatry, there was no difference between those that had been treated with medications and those who had not. In fact, nearly 60% of the children had advanced to Oppositional Defiant Disorder, and Conduct Disorder, both of which are considered worse than ADHD (Barkley et. al. July 1990).

If Not Drugs, Then What?

Since there are no reproducible biological markers, the diagnosis of ADHD is hardly more than an assemblage of symptoms. And given that the potential complications with conventional medications are serious, alternatives for addressing the behavioral problems associated with the ADHD criteria must be sought.

There are many etiological factors that can generate symptomatologies that closely resemble ADHD. Chronic sleep deprivation, hypothyroidism, nutritional deficiencies, environmental exposures to lead and other heavy metals, and a diet with large quantities of refined carbohydrates – white table sugar, white flour and white rice – are all considerations that need to be completely investigated before labeling a child with the diagnosis of ADHD.

In my experience, the most important and most overlooked causes of mental and emotional disturbances are food sensitivities and intolerances. Dr. Ben Feingold first discussed the concept of an underlying food cause for behavioral disorders in his book *Why Your Child is Hyperactive*. Feingold's original research included 1,200 children. He claimed that nearly 50% of all hyperactive children were sensitive to food additives and artificial food colorings. His research demonstrated that when children consumed food dyes and additives, their behavior mimicked that of those seen with the diagnosis of ADHD. In addition, when these substances were removed from the diet, they symptomatically improved.

There are more than 5,000 different food additives now in widespread use. On average, the per capita consumption of food additives is 13-15 grams or approximately one heaping tablespoonful, each day. Food additives include BHA, BHT, nitrites, and sulfites, all of which are found in the wide variety of processed foods that are in a typical Western diet. In addition to food additives, the worldwide population is reported to consume a staggering 100 million pounds of just food colorings each year (Murray, Pizzarno, 1998).

Another leading researcher in this area is Dr. Doris Rapp, a pediatrician that has documented her research findings in books, professional articles and videotapes. Her data confirms that 67% of children diagnosed with ADHD are reacting to unrecognized food and environmental allergies. Data from two double-blind studies indicated that 73-76% of ADHD children responded favorably to food elimination diets (Rapp, 1978 and 1979).

Allergies and the Brain

The basis behind why food additives, food colorings and a myriad of food and environmental allergies result in behaviors that are identical to ADHD is that these substances cause a reaction in the brain that disrupts appropriate functioning (–> Radomski). In 1990, Staudenmayer and Seiner published a report in the Journal of Psychosomantic Research indicating that beta activity in the brain is increased in individuals who present with allergies to environmental chemicals. Many studies have reported the relationship between food allergies and increased beta activity in the brain.

The neurochemical interferences with ADHD are believed to occur in the frontal cortex of the brain, the area that is the command center for attention, concentration, shifting attention, regulation of emotions, moral decision-making and strategic planning. Real-time EEG technology has documented changes in the beta waves that occur when a child comes in contact with an allergen. Beta waves are those that are generated when a person concentrates or controls impulsivity. Normally, the graph will record a cyclical pattern of approximately 16-20 Hz (cycles per second). When children come in contact with an allergen, the recording can accelerate to greater than 40 cycles/second. The faster the pattern, the more disrupted the function. Children with fast patterns will have difficulty concentrating, focusing, following commands and paying attention: all part of the ADHD criteria.

Eliminating Allergies Instead of Avoiding Them

Following the suggestions of Feingold and Rapp to eliminate the offending allergen will result in great improvement in the hyperactive symptoms demonstrated with the diagnosis of ADHD. However, avoidance can be difficult, and in some cases, nearly impossible, especially when a number of substances are causing the difficulties.

A better way to neutralize the effects of food additives, food colorings, environmental irritants and foods (–> Radomski) is through a method developed by Dr. Ellen Cutler called BioSET allergy elimination. Not only can the effects all types of allergens and hypersensitivities be neutralized, the effect is nearly 100% permanent.

In 1997, Ellen Cutler published her first book *Winning the War Against Asthma and Allergies*. Even though the title of this book suggests that the technique is designed for only the treatment of asthma, the principles also apply to "allergic irritation" within the brain associated with ADHD and nearly any other health symptom imaginable.

The conventional medical model of an allergic response involves a particular type of cellular memory. When an allergen invades the blood stream, it is recognized as a foreign particle. A specialized type of white blood cell, called a B-lymphocyte, creates an antibody that will work to eliminate it. The next time the allergen is present, the antibody combines with the allergen, and the antibody-allergen complex attaches to another type of specialized white blood cell called a mast cell. When these three components unite, histamine is released from the mast cell, causing the generally recognized symptoms of an "allergic reaction": watery eyes, sneezing, itchy nose, cough, etc. This is the body's attempt to rid itself of the allergen. Sometimes a severe reaction occurs, involving hives and life-threatening anaphylaxis due to the extreme amount of histamine suddenly released into the blood stream. Anti-histamine tablets are designed to inhibit these reactions. Allergy shots are designed to override this response by making the body less sensitive to the allergen.

A Different Kind of Allergy

The BioSET definition of an allergic reaction goes beyond the commonly understood mechanism of histamine release. In order to understand how and why the BioSET treatment works, some basic principles of acupuncture must be explained.

Within the body there are energy-carrying channels called meridians. These tracts carry the life force energy, called Qi, throughout the body in much the same way that arteries and veins transport the blood. Within the meridian system, another type of "memory" occurs. When offending allergens are present, it is the electromagnetic charge from the allergen—not its chemical structure—that is "remembered" and stored within the meridians. As more and more of these charges accumulate, a blockage is created that leads to stagnation within the energy flow through the meridians. Acupuncture theory states it is the stagnation of the flow of Qi that eventually results in symptoms (–> Stoler).

The brain and the acupuncture meridians are all part of the same energy system. Blockages in the peripheral energy circulation are monitored by the central nervous system. Therefore, when a person comes in contact with the electromagnetic charge of an allergen, such as wheat, it creates a signal that can be thought of as "static" in the circulating meridians. The "static" signal is picked up by the brain and is manifested on a larger scale as accentuated beta wave activity, contributing to the symptoms often thought of as hyperactivity. The most extensive disruptions, commonly caused by gluten in wheat and casein in dairy, can contribute to problems associated with the full spectrum of behavioral disorders, including autism.

Instead of using drugs to treat the symptoms of ADHD, BioSET allergy elimination is directed toward eliminating the cause. The method uses acupressure, an energy treatment, to release the blockages from the meridian systems. Allergens can be identified through the use of muscle testing or kinesiology.

While a patient holds a homeopathic vial of a suspected allergen, the physician applies pressure to the arm to see if the muscle is weakened by the presence of the allergen. If the muscle response is weak, that is a sign that the substance is impairing the patient's energy pathways. Babies and children can be tested through the use of a surrogate.

Once the allergies have been identified, specific acupuncture points along the spine, the arms and the legs are stimulated, releasing the blockages within the meridians. No needles are involved; therefore the treatment is painless. Immediately following the treatments, the patient rests quietly for fifteen minutes. The person may be instructed to avoid contact with the allergen for a predetermined period of time – up to 24 hours. As each allergen is neutralized, the brain "calms down" and normal functioning returns.

Although each patient's treatment response varies, the BioSET protocol eliminates many symptoms within the first 5-6 treatments. Children are observed to be more alert, calmer and more focused. The best part is that once the series of treatments is complete, the results are long lasting...and no drugs are needed and the allergen no longer needs to be avoided.

It is essential to have a thorough medical evaluation done, looking for other underlying medical problems, prior to initiating BioSET. In addition, BioSET is not a stand-alone treatment. All cellular detoxification and drainage pathways must be functioning to achieve the best results. In addition, adequate sleep and wholesome dietary habits are essential for a full recovery. For example, just because a child is no longer reacting violently to refined sugar it does *not* mean that he should be consuming unrestricted amounts of the substance.

The best option for long-term resolution of ADHD symptoms can be accomplished by incorporating BioSET allergy elimination into a full spectrum of therapeutics. There are no side effects, no complications and a very high success rate: more than 85% of patients get positive results.

Note

1. This chapter is an excerpt from *Ritalin: More Harm than Good* by the author.

References

American Psychiatric Association, Diagnostic and Statistical Manual of Mental Disorders DMS-V, Washington, DC.
Barkley, R., Fischer, M. et. al. (1990). The adolescent outcome of hyperactive children diagnosed by research criteria. J. Am. Acad. *Child Adoles Psychiatry*, 29(4)4546-556.
Carey, W.B (1998). Presentation entitled *Is ADHD a valid disorder?*, NIH. Consensus Conference on ADHD, November 16-18.
Cutler, E. (1997). *Winning the war against Asthma and allergies.* Delmar.
Day, L. (2001). at www.drday.com/attentiondeficit.htm
LeFerver, G.B. et. al. (1999). *The extent of drug therapy for attention deficit-hyperactivity disorder among children in public schools.* Am J. Public Health; 89(9).
Murray M.T., & Pizzarno J.T. (1998). *Encyclopedia of Natural Medicine.* Rocklin, DA: Prima Publishing.
Rapp, D.J. (1978). Does diet affect hyperactivity? *J Learn Disabil*;11:56-62
 – (1979). Food allergy treatment for hyperkinesis. *J Learn Disabil*;12:42-50.
Still, G.F. (1902). *Some abnormal psychical conditions in children.* Lancet I:1008-1012.
Walker, S. (2001). *Drug evasion is now a crime – Swallow this!* The Detroit News, January 11, Detroit, MI.

24

Evaluating the Effects of Energy Psychology on Acupuncture Meridians Using Prognos Analysis

Tom Narvaez, Peter Rohsmann, Jim Stegenga

Energy psychology techniques are now being used throughout the world with great effectiveness. Therapists of every description and training consider them useful and powerful. Some of the techniques boast a success rate in excess of 80%. In spite of the reported unprecedented success rate, these techniques have been under scrutiny and attack by professional organizations and the media alike. The biggest criticism is that most of the data available are not scientifically valid. This criticism has been leveled at virtually all techniques outside the framework of traditional academic science.

A need exists to validate energy psychology techniques using a device with extensive scientific validation in its own right and demonstrates the results of energy psychology interventions in a scientific way. The validation of any one protocol could open the door to scientific acceptance of other techniques. This paper will address a method of validation using a machine called Prognos, developed and successfully used for Russian space exploration. The protocol under scrutiny will be Emotional Freedom Techniques as developed by Gary Craig.

EFT (Emotional Freedom Techniques) is an exceptional tool to help clear out many energetic imbalances that contribute to negative emotions, addictive cravings, and limiting negative beliefs. Once the energy system is cleared, subjects have major opportunities to become more whole and self-actualized. EFT, like many meridian therapies, originated as a derivative of Thought Field Therapy. The technique is simple, easy to learn and faster than many similar meridian interventions. There are numerous testimonials available concerning its effectiveness. Practitioners of EFT and other parallel techniques are found throughout the world, especially in the United States, Canada, Switzerland, Germany, England, New Zealand and Australia, but actual acceptance of these meridian therapies has been limited due to academic skepticism and the lack of any scientific proof that the therapies actually work.

The Basis for Measurement: The Meridian System

According to Traditional Chinese Medicine, a form of bodily energy called *Qi* is generated in internal organs and circulates throughout the body, forming pathways called acupuncture meridians. This whole-body network is called the meridian system, which indirectly relates to body organs. Acupuncture points are points on the skin, located on meridians where the circulation of Qi can be manipulated. Stimulating a skin acupuncture point through needle insertion, pressure, tapping, or touching affects the circulation of Qi. This in turn seems to affect related internal organs. The meridian energy flow also carries information about internal organs that can be used in comparative measurement or for diagnosis.

The use of the meridian system for healing purposes has a tradition of more than 5000 years. In 1991 the corpse of "Oetzi", the Ice Man, was found in a Tyrolean glacier, covered with strange tattoos made from burnt wood and located on each of the traditional acupuncture points. This seems to parallel the ancient Tibetan acupuncture practice, which used burnt wooden needles to enter the skin. Oetzi was carbon-dated to be 5,200 years old. Historically, very few changes seem to have been made in the acupuncture system until modern times, where electro-acupuncture, acupressure, lasers, and now energy psychology methods enter the picture.

Evaluation of Acupuncture-related Techniques

In the late 1940's, Reinholt Voll, M.D. began an investigation of the effects of electricity on the human physiology. These studies were not unlike earlier procedures developed and used by Nikola Tesla in the 19th century. In his studies, Voll used an ohmmeter to measure impedance, i.e. resistance to an electrical current, through physical material. An ohmmeter measuring electrical resistance (impedance) also measures conductance through a simple mathematical formula.

Voll found that if he tested the conductance in any general area of the human body, there was a fairly high level of electrical resistance. The body has a large volume of electrically conductive fluids within it, but the skin is very resistant to electrical current. Voll also found that at certain specific locations on the anatomy, the electrical flow is much higher, and these points generally corresponded to the Chinese acupuncture points. This became the basis for Electro-Acupuncture according to Voll (EAV) and Electro-Dermal Screening (EDS).

In the routine course of EAV Testing a subject, Voll noticed that remedies that were placed into the energy field significantly altered readings of subjects. He had found a way to measure the balancing of energy meridians with a variety of reagents in the energy field. A single measurement was taken without the reagent and a second reading taken with it. The change informed the practitioner of the potential use or harm of the reagent.

Over the course of two decades, Voll and his associates perfected EAV Testing, basing all of their findings on clinically proven cases in hospitals in Germany. EAV has been accepted as the standard for investigative work with Western acupuncture. Another energy protocol, Reiki, has had at least one study accepted in the scientific community by the use of EAV measurements. Many of these machines have been accepted for experimentation by the Food and Drug Administration, and have been used to verify results.

These devices, however, often need trained acupuncturists to operate them. Also, their criteria for measurement is small, conceptual and nebulous, based on a scale of 1–100 with 45–55 being acceptable. Finally, results are based on only one measurement, which has been challenged as being unscientific. Therefore, a number of measurements must be made to assure scientific validity.

Developing the Prognos Device for Meridian Measurement and Meridian Stimulation

The renowned Russian scientist Vladimir Zagriadskii was commissioned by the Russian government to solve difficulties with the cosmonauts' health in outer space on a proposed mission to planet Mars. After studying medical techniques from all over the world, he was most impressed by the effects of Chinese acupuncture. He searched for scientific proof for its curing effects.

Attempting to find an explanation for the specificity of acupuncture points, Zagriadskii examined anatomical characteristics in the tissue and found an acupuncture point hole in the muscle fascia where traditional acupuncture points were supposed to be located. These holes allowed arteries and veins to get through to the skin. He concluded that inserting an acupuncture needle enlarges the hole and thus relieves pain. He had found an anatomical-mechanical basis for acupuncture, but rejected the existence of meridians, because they did not follow the complete nerve path all the time.

Next he decided to try using soft laser light to see how a specific signal, when applied to different parts of the skin, was distributed within the body. To his surprise, he found that if the laser was put at one end of the Lung Meridian, his detector could only find the signal at the points along a pathway that corresponded to the Chinese description of the Lung Meridian localization. Other places he checked did not show that frequency.

Zagriadskii was convinced that meridians did carry information and that they were actually superconductors. If they conducted light, he concluded they would also conduct electricity. The current he determined to be the best for this conduction was 0.4 micro Amps. (The electrical current used in EAV devices is 50 micro amps, over 100 times stronger. This level of electro-stimulation can better be described as a treatment rather than a measurement.) With the 0.4 micro Amps, he was able to measure the whole meridian, even in places of scars where the laser light was not conducted. The principle of measurement is that the more resistance is put up against the current, the more the meridian is impaired in performing its function, i.e. the flow of Qi or energy.

Prognos was then built with these specifications, including a piezo-electric stimulation device to stimulate meridians to regain health. (It should be noted that some energy therapists believe that tapping is piezo-electric). To meet scientific standards for testing, Prognos was equipped with a tip that would only give a reading when there was exactly twenty grams of pressure. Also the tip had to be flat and measure an area that was comparatively large (as compared to the pinpoint needed for EAV) so that anyone could easily find the acupuncture point. Since only one analogue reading is not scientific, his device would give four hundred readings in two hundred milliseconds with a distinctive beep when the readings were correct and complete – as compared to a single reading by EAV.

Initial testing was done on a sample of over 3,000,000 Russian citizens. It was field-tested when the Russians sent Dr. Polyakov up to the Mir Space Station with it. Polyakov measured himself three times a day on the acupoints of the classical meridian endings. If a meridian was imbalanced, he stimulated the "tonification point" of that meridian with a simple piezo-electric stimulation device. He did this three times a day until all the meridians were in perfect balance. Polyakov stayed in perfect health for 430 days in space without harmful after-effects.

Evaluating the Effects of EFT using Prognos

Prognos Analysis, EAV, and Emotional Freedom Techniques presume the existence of a meridian system within the human body. The authors asked the question: "Will a single EFT session result in a change of energy meridian readings of subjects as measured by the Prognos device?" Since a major tenet in EFT (as in virtually all meridian therapies) is that the cause of all negative emotions is a disruption in the body's energy system, treatment effects will be measurable at the level of meridian energy flow. A traditional EAV machine (Aquatron 2000) was rejected because of the need to conduct more than one measurement. The Prognos, which conducts 400 measurements in 0.2 seconds, was used instead. Also, the EAV required a licensed acupuncturist to perform the measurements, whereas an assistant with a short instruction could operate the Prognos.

Ten subjects were exposed to the complete sequence, one of which was with the Aquatron 2000. Of the nine remaining subjects, only one did not have an immediate positive reaction to a single round of the modified EFT sequence. In all other cases, the SUD level went from the presenting level (3 to 10) to a SUD rating of zero or one. Two cases uncovered secondary and tertiary issues that were reduced or disappeared.

One of the Prognos sub-programs deals with affirmations, which could easily be used for EFT affirmations. Several deal with tonification and tranquilization points, which provide more specific acupuncture points, similar to Thought Field Therapy and other energy psychology methods. Still others deal with Bach Remedies and Color Therapy, which are far beyond the scope of this chapter.

A complete traditional experimental setup was designed to answer the question. Parameters included an experimental set-up, with measurements of the hypothesis group, the null hypothesis group, and control group. A major obstacle was discovered developing the "affirmation setup" for EFT. Clients often recognized only minimal symptoms while Prognos seemed to uncover the results of the symptoms. The EFT sequence was modified as follows:

1. Determine the presenting issue and SUDS level;
2. Locate the most imbalanced meridian using Prognos Analysis;
3. Develop an affirmation using the imbalanced meridian instead of the presenting problem, e.g. "Even though I have this imbalanced left kidney meridian, I totally and completely..."
4. Complete a round of EFT;
5. Remeasure the meridian system with Prognos;
6. Determine any change in the SUDS level of the presenting issue.

The use of Prognos required only one full measurement consisting of an average of 400 readings within 0.2 seconds. In several cases, an intake interview was performed uncovering any possibly fruitful areas for discussion or intervention. It was found that equal or better results could be obtained by having the client use the specific meridian imbalance as part of the affirmation process. Prognos Analysis showed the pre-test condition (prior to any exposure to EFT). The first measurement for the control group was made prior to a casual conversation about specific meridian imbalances with a length of time similar to a session of EFT.

Only one round of Emotional Freedom Techniques was used when the meridian imbalance was used in the affirmation. The second Prognos Analysis showed the differences of any change caused by the use of EFT.

Preliminary results demonstrated positive changes in meridians based on EFT, conducted by a trained acupuncturist on three subjects using the Aquatron 2000 Voll machine. Prognos Testing (under the supervision of a physician, November 1999) of three subjects demonstrated positive changes in meridians based on EFT. In addition, all subjects reported physical improvements.

Conclusions

1. Measurable changes in acupuncture meridian measurements were found in subjects tested as a result of using Emotional Freedom Techniques. The Prognos device not only proved scientifically the existence of acupuncture meridians, but also demonstrated the body's reactions to stressful or harmful foods, medicines, and even thoughts. It clearly demonstrated meridian reactions to tested protocols of energy psychology.
2. Prognos updates EAV and overcomes most of its shortcomings. Although virtually anyone can be the operator of the machine, training in oriental medicine is needed to fully take advantage of all the analyses and treatment.
3. While the cost of Prognos could easily be absorbed by consortium of therapists, a hospital or clinic, it would be financially impractical for the average therapist to acquire. Future plans of the parent company are to have smaller units available to be interpreted by a central facility.

Recommendations

Ongoing programs for research and analysis should be pursued using this device because of its scientific capabilities. Additional studies are needed to correlate and verify the results of this initial study. Prognos clearly demonstrates a major breakthrough in energy psychology analysis and treatment. Numerous additional studies are needed to fully exploit its potential. These include, but are not limited to, the following:

- What other energy psychology interventions could be verified by Prognos Analysis?
- What will be the response of the traditional academic scientific environment to this work?
- What are the results of tapping individual tonification or tranquilization points shown in the program rather than doing a complete "round" of EFT tapping?
- What are the objective effects of the therapist on the treatment of the client? How do we know when to change therapists?
- What are the objective effects of theoretical and subtle field interventions (Intrinsic Data Field and radionic broadcasts) on the meridians of the body?
- What are the immediate and long-term effects of use of certain therapeutic interventions, such as the Australian Bio-Electric Field Enhancer Hydrotherapy device?

References

Callahan, R. (1998). *Callahan Techniques' TFT Diagnosis technique (manual)*.
Hartmann-Kent, S. (2000). *Adventures in EFT*. Eastbourne, UKDragon Rising Press.
Rohsmann, P., M.D. (2000). *Audiotape of talk delivered to World Water Resources*. Yelm, WA.
Zagriadskii, V. (1966). *Scientific basis of the Elektroakupunktur diagnostics and therapy*. Academy of the Sciences of Russia, Russian Space Travel Technology, 1966.

Internet ressources

Bio-Electric Field Enhancer – www.Q2.com.au.
Email forum on BEFE use and research: To subscribe send email to BEFE-subscribe@yahoogroups.com
Polyakov – www.rocketry.com/mwade/astros/polyakov.htm
Prognos device information – www.germanmedtec.com.
Email forum on Prognos:
To subscribe send email to Prognos-subscribe@yahoogroups.com.
Zagriadskii – www.beckerbernd.de/Sagriadskii.html.

η
Home

Homer

"If the gods make your old age a happier time," the sagacious Penelope replied, "there is a hope of an end to your troubles."

While they were talking, Eurynome and the nurse, by the light of torches, were putting soft bedclothes on their bed. When the work was done and the bed comfortably made, the old woman went back to her own quarters for the night, and the housekeeper Eurynome, with a torch in her hands, lit them on their way to bed, taking her leave when she had brought them to their room. And blissfully they lay down on their own familiar bed.

A
About the Authors

Pati Beaudoin, Ed.D., is a licensed psychologist in Georgia, U.S., where she is in private practice. She co-chairs the Ethics Task Force (ETF) of the Association of Comprehensive Energy Psychology. Dr. Beaudoin is a Past President of the Georgia Hypnosis Society and currently chairs their Ethics and Legal Issues Committee.Contact: drpati@mindspring.com.

Daniel J. Benor, M.D. is a psychiatrist who includes wholistic, bodymind approaches, spiritual awareness and healing in his practice. Dr. Benor has taught this spectrum of methods internationally for 15 years to people involved in wholistic, intuitive, and spiritual approaches to caring, health and personal development. He founded The Doctor-Healer Network in England and America. After 10 years in England he has returned to work in Philadelphia and in Medford, New Jersey. He founded Helios: Network for Whole Person Healing, a group of health carers and alternative/ complementary therapists who seminar regularly on how to develop integrated care. Dr. Benor is the author of *Healing Research, Volumes I-IV* and many articles on wholistic, spiritual healing. He is a Founding Diplomate of the American Board of Holistic Medicine. Contact: www.WholisticHealingResearch.com DB@WholisticHealingResearch.com.

Dr. Marla Brucker, received her Doctorate in Clinical Hypnotherapy and her M.S. degree in Rehabilitation Counseling with a specialty in Deafness. She is a Registered Hypnotic Anesthesiologist, and is certified in Neuro-Linguistic Programming and is a Certified National Seminar Leader. Dr. Brucker has been practicing in the area of performance enhancement, counseling and pain management since 1978, working in hospitals, mental health clinics, educational institutes and social service agencies. She conducts seminars and leadership training programs nationally in Energy Therapies, Psychokinesis and peak performance. Dr. Brucker is a Certified Instructor for Hypno-Anesthesiology, Hypnotherapy, and Energy Therapies. She has the first state approved and certified 50-hour training program in Energy Therapies, along with a training manual that she co-wrote. Marla offers this course twice a year. Marla Brucker is in private practice in San Diego, Ca. working with individuals and groups. Contact: Hpnotik2U@aol.com.

Patricia Carrington, Ph.D. is a Clinical Professor of Psychiatry at the University of Medicine & Dentistry - Robert Wood Johnson Medical School in Piscataway, NJ. and for 11 years previous to that was a member of the psychology faculty of Princeton University. She is the author of over 35 articles in professional journals and four books in stress management methods. With 16 years of experience using meridian-based therapies in clinical practice, she is currently Chairperson of the ACEP Research Committee. Contact: email@pcarrington.com.

Sharon Cass Toole, MTC, Ph.D. is a psychotherapist in private practice in Toronto, Canada, and international workshop leader. Masters in Counselling and a Doctorate in Alternative Medicine. Organizes and coordinates the annual Energy Psychology Conference in Toronto. Professional Associations: Clinical Member, OSP (Membership Chair), ACEP (Reg.Dir., Eastern Canada), EMDRIA, GPPA (affiliate), IRPH, Spirituality in Healthcare Network, founder of Meridian Psychotherapy Services. Contact: sharont@iprimus.ca or www.iprimus.ca/~sharont.

John Diepold, Ph.D. is a New Jersey licensed psychologist who has been in practice for 20 years. Dr. Diepold integrates TFT with traditional clinical psychology in the treatment of PTSD, anxiety, dissociative disorders, pain & stress management and peak performance issues. He is the originator of TAB and the concept of Elaters and the Emotional Signaling Mechanism. Dr. Diepold is a member of the APA, the NJPA and a Diplomate of the American Academy of Pain Management. He is in private practice in Moorestown, NJ. Contact: jdiepold@uscom.com.

James V. Durlacher, D.C., DIBAK has practiced holistic alternative health care for 38 years caring for the physical, nutritional and emotional sides of the health triangle. He is a licensed chiropractic physician, member of the Arizona Association of Chiropractors, a Diplomate of the International College of Applied Kinesiology and a member of the Advisory Board of the Association for Comprehensive Energy Psychology which awarded him their Pioneer Award, May 2000. He is the author of *Freedom From Fear Forever,* teaching his Acu-POWER Emotional Technique and a contributor to Fred Gallo's new book, *Energy Psychology in Psychology*. Contact: freedom1@extremezone.com.

Donna Eden: A pioneer in the field of Energy Medicine for more than two decades, Donna Eden has taught people worldwide how to understand the body as an energy system.

About the Authors

Donna is widely recognized for her in-born ability to clairvoyantly see the body's energies, to accurately determine the causes of physical and psychological problems based on the state of those energies, and to devise highly effective treatments. Her classes teach people to understand the body as an energy system, to recognize their aches and pains as signals of energy imbalance, and to reclaim their natural healing and self-healing capacities. A deeply loving and joyful personality, Donna has treated over 10,000 clients individually and has taught hundreds of classes, speaking to packed houses throughout the United States, Europe, Australia, New Zealand, and South America. Contact through David Feinstein. Contact: david@innersource.net.

David Feinstein, Ph.D., is a clinical psychologist and Director of the non-profit Energy Medicine Institute. He has taught at The John Hopkins University School of Medicine, Antioch College, and the California School of Professional Psychology. He has lectured and consulted internationally on the application of a mythological perspective to personal, organizational, and social change. He is co-author of *The Mythic Path, Mortal Acts* and *Rituals for Living and Dying*, and is the *with* author of *Energy Medicine* by Donna Eden, his wife. Contact: david@innersource.net.

Philip Friedman, Ph.D., is a licensed clinical psychologist and energy and spiritual coach in Philadelphia & Plymouth Meeting, Pa., USA. He is director of the Foundation for Well-Being and the author of "Creating Well-Being: The Healing Path to Love, Peace, Self-Esteem and Happiness"; the "Integrative Healing Manual: an Energy, Spiritual and Positive Psychology Approach" and the Friedman Assessment Scales on Well-Being, Affect, Beliefs, Quality of Life and Personal/Spiritual Growth". Dr. Friedman is a founder of "Integrative Therapy" (IT) and "Integrative Energy and Spiritual Therapy" (IEST). He is an Assistant Professor at Hahnemahn University & Medical School and an approved supervisor for the Association of Marital and Family Therapy. Dr. Friedman moderates 3 email Lists on energy & spiritual healing. Contact: energyspirit1@aol.com or www. integrativeenergyspiritualtherapy .com.

David Grudermeyer, Ph.D., co-founded the Association for Comprehensive Energy Psychology, authored the Energy Psychology Desktop Companion and developed the first Energy Psychology training program ever awarded Continuing Education credit for California licensed psychologists. Co-director of Willingness Works in Del Mar, California, he is a licensed psychologist, relationship therapist, and accomplished speaker and trainer. In addition to Energy Psychology, and relationship intelligence training, he also specializes in financial literacy training and marketing consulting.
Contact: drgrudermeyer@willingness.com or http://www.willingness.com.

APPENDIX A

Alan Handelsman, CHT, has been a One Brain Facilitator since 1994. He has taken over 600 hours of training (TFT, EFT, One Brain, Reiki, Source Integration Therapy), including classes with Dr. Roger Callahan (TFTdx), Gary Craig, Gordon Stokes, and Daniel Whiteside. He now works with individuals and groups worldwide with training, and performance and personal issues. Alan began developing the Resonance Tuner in 1996 and the Tuner is now being used in at least 45 of the United States and 11 other countries. He is known for his relaxed, humorous style. Contact: AlanHand@aol.com.

Joan Hitlin, MFA, CCHT is a hypnotherapist with a private practice in Northern California, near San Francisco. Joan is also a working artist and writer, with an MFA in sculpture. She has studied energy therapies, hypnotherapy, Neuro-Linguistic Programming, process work, gestalt and spiritual psychology with many contemporary masters. She is now a member of Don Elium's iSt (Integrative States) research group. Contact: joan@besler.org or www.joanhitlin.org

Dorothea Hover-Kramer, Ed.D., CNS (Clincal Nurse Specialist) is a psychologist is private practice in Poway (near San Diego), CA who specializes in Mind/Body, or health, psychology and is co-founder of ACEP. She has been involved in energy-oriented healing for twenty years and is the author of *Healing Touch* (1996, 2001) and *Energetic Approaches to emotional healing* (1997) as well as contributing articles and chapters to many professional publications. She is also a graduate of WW II, having been born in Berlin and living there the first decade of her life before moving to the States. In addition she is a pianist, a poet, a grandmother, and mountain climber. Contact: DorotheaH@aol.com.

Beate Kircher, Mag.phil, is a licensed physical therapist in the Principality of Liechtenstein, with additional training in many wholistic approaches, especially shiatsu, Healing Tao, and cranio-sacral therapy. She also has a Master's degree in English and American Studies and Dramatic Sciences. Loving to deal with language and meaning, she has been involved in translation work in the field of energy medicine and spiritual awareness over the last ten years. She trained in meridian-based psychotherapy and counseling methods at IAS, where she also translates workshops. Contact: beatekircher@supra.net.

Willem Lammers, drs., TSTA, CTS, is a licensed psychologist, a psychotherapist and a consultant to organizations. He is founding director of IAS, the Institute for the Application of the Social Science in Maienfeld, Switzerland. As a psychotherapist and supervisor, he is an ATSS Certified Trauma Specialist, and a Certified Trainer and Supervisor of EATA, EAIP and EAS. He also trained in NLP and EMDR. After extensive training in the USA he founded with Thomas Weil the Institute for Meridian-based Psychotherapy and Counselling (IMPC). He developed many new techniques and applications, like ICIPR and SPP. He initiated and directed the First European Conference on Energy Psychology, and teaches in many different countries. Contact: willem.lammers@iasag.ch or www.iasag.ch.

James R. Lane, Ph.D. is an Arizona Licensed Psychologist with thirty years of clinical experience. He is a member in good standing of: the AmericanPsychological Association (APA); the Arizona Psychological Association(AZPA); the Association for Comprehensive Energy Psychology (ACEP), EMDR International Association (EMDRIA) and is a certified by the National Board of Certified Clinical Hypnotherapists (NBCCH) . He has supervised and trained other clinicians in advanced counseling skills, marital counseling, hypnosis, and substance abuse counseling. He specializes in trauma resolution and relationship counseling. Contact: 110373.3074@compuserve.com.

Martin F. Luthke, Ph.D. is a clinical psychologist licensed in Ohio. He is the founder and director of the Institute of Psychoenergetic Healing near Cleveland, Ohio. Originally from Germany, Dr. Luthke received his Ph.D. from the University of Hamburg and a Certificate of Respecialization in Clinical Psychology from the University of Cincinnati. After working with children and adolescents at a child guidance center he established a private practice specializing in Psychoenergetic Healing, an advanced energy-based therapy that he developed together with his wife Linda Stein-Luthke. He is the (co-) author of six books and a dozen scholarly publications. Dr. Luthke is also the chair of the Humanitarian Committee of ACEP. Contact: expansion@u-r-light.com or www.u-r-light.com.

Tom Narvaez, Ph.D., retired Army Officer, Hypnotherapist, NLP Trainer, and now Energy Psychotherapist, has studied Intrinsic Data Field Analysis (SE-5) for over twelve years. He integrates his SE-5 work with PROGNOS (Russian scientific space program device) and the Australian Bio-Electric Field Enhancer (quantum mechanical hydrotherapy detoxifier) for both healing and research. His current study uses PROGNOS to prove the effects of energy psychology tapping protocols (EFT et al) on acupuncture meridians. This work will eventually extend to documenting the effects of the balancing activities of the SE-5 on these same meridians.. Contact mindsusrgeo@aol.com.

Gregory Nicosia, Ph.D., BCFE, is a licensed psychologist with extensive academic and clinical experience who has helped to explore and elaborate the newest psychotherapies in the last 25 years including: biofeedback, EMDR, and most recently Thought Field Therapies. He is the founder and President of Advanced Diagnostics, P.C., Pittsburgh's premiere center for the thought energy based psychotherapeutic treatment of trauma and remediation of cognitive dysfunction. He was nominated as Pittsburgh's Man of the Year in Science and Medicine for 1997. Dr. Nicosia has trained thousands of healthcare professionals throughout the U.S. in the use of TFT and in his more recently developed Thought Energy Synchronization Therapy® (TEST©) diagnostic and treatment procedures. Contact: No1HedDoc@aol.com.

Sandra Radomski, ND, LCSW, MSSW is a psychotherapist and a naturopathic doctor. Her background includes teaching in the medical school at University of Wisconsin for 8 years, doing biofeedback with pain patients for 10 years and conducting research in psychoneuroimmunology with children with cancer. Her experience in energy work includes Energy Psychology techniques such as TFT (diagnostically trained), EFT, TAT, and BSFF, and chiropractic techniques such as NAET, TBM, Biokinetics, NET and JMT. Currently specializing in allergy work, Sandi has written the manual, Allergy AntidoesTM – The Energy Psychology Treatment of Allergy-Like Reactions. Contact: sandiradom@aol.com.

Paula Shaw, CADC counsels within a private practice, lectures, writes and teaches workshops for professionals within her fields of expertise, Addictive Disorders, Co-Dependency, and Grief. She is a graduate of Long Beach State University with post graduate specialty training at Loyola Marymount University. She initially brought Energy work into her practice through a system called Holographic Repatterning. After using this system for three years, she attended the First International Energy Psychology Conference in 1999. In the following year after doing training in several of the Energy Psychology Systems, she developed a system of her own. CHART (Conscious Healing And Repatterning Therapy) was introduced at the second International Energy Psychology Conference in Las Vegas in 2000. She continues to evolve this system and has experienced very exciting results with the clients who use it. Contact: CHARTTEC2000@aol.com.

Linda Stein-Luthke is a writer, medical intuitive, metaphysical teacher and healer, as well as a professional astrologer. She has received training in various spiritual disciplines and has worked with several masters in the USA, India, Nepal and Cyprus. Linda is a Senior Student at the Cleveland Buddhist Temple, where she received the dharma name "Unhindered Light". In collaboration with her husband, psychologist Dr. Martin Luthke, she has developed *Psychoenergetic Healing*, an advanced energy-based method for growth and healing. She is the co-author of four books, of which three contain channeled material from the Ascended Master St. Germain.

Mary T. Sise, CSW-R, TFTdx is a Certified Social Worker working in private practice in the Albany, New York area who specializes in the treatment of trauma and dissociative disorders. An adjunct professor at Siena College, she is trained in TFT, BSFF, WHH, Matrix Work,

About the Authors

TAT, EMDR and Reiki. In addition to integrating all of these therapies in her work with trauma survivors, she has trained hundreds of therapists over the past two and a half years and has presented both nationally and internationally on using the Energy therapies for trauma. Contact: MSISE3@aol.com.

Larry Stoler, Ph.D. has been practicing Energy Psychotherapy for 4 years and is a Certified Chilel Qigong™ instructor. He specializes in integrative healing methods. His practice is at one of the leading Integrative Medical Centers in the US, WholeHealth Chicago. Contact:LStoler@aol.com

Sherri J. Tenpenny, D.O. is the Director and Founder of OsteoMed II, a clinic integrating traditional, complementary, and preventative medicine in Strongsville, Ohio (a suburb of Cleveland). In addition to her conventional medical education and 9 years as Director of a hospital Emergency Department, Dr. Tenpenny has undertaken advanced courses in alternative medicine including acupuncture and complex homeopathy. She lectures at Cleveland State University and Case Western Reserve Medical School, and speaks, both nationally and internationally, on topics related to alternative health. Contact: osteomed2@aol.com.

Thomas Weil is founding director of the Institut für Transaktionsanalyse und Integrative Tiefenpsychologie in Kassel, Germany. He trained in Transactional Analysis, Gestalt, Hypnotherapy, Body Work and meridian-based psychotherapy. He is a Teaching Member of the International Transactional Analysis Association (ITAA), a Trainer and Supervisor of the European Association for Integrative Psychotherapy (EAIP), a Trainer and Supervisor of the European Association for Supervision (EAS), and a director of the Institute for Meridian-based Psychotherapy and Counselling (IMPC). Thomas worked for a long time as a lutheran pastor in areas as hospital, prison, crisis line services. He offers psychotherapeutic services in his private practice. He runs different training programs in TA, MPC, supervision and leadership. Contact: info@ttta.de.

B

Abbreviations Used in Energy Psychology & Psychotherapy

1B	– One Brain
ACIM	– A Course in Miracles
AT	– AcuPower
BBSH	– Barbara Brennan School of Healing
BK	– Behavioral Kinesiology
BSFF	– Be Set Free Fast
CHART	– Conscious Healing And Repatterning Therapy
Edu-K	– Educational Kinesiology
EDxTM	– Energy Diagnostic Treatment Method
EFT	– Emotional Freedom Techniques
EF	– Energy Flow
EH	– Esoteric Healing
ER	– Floor-to-ceiling eye roll
EMF	– electromagnetic fields
ESM	– Emotional Self-Management
EMDR	– Eye Movement Desensitization and Reprocessing
FACT	– Friedman Acupressure Chakra Technique
HBLU	– Healing from the Body Level Up
HR	– Holographic Repatterning
HT	– Healing Touch
ICIPR	– Willem Lammers' Inner Child, Inner Parent Resolution
IEP	– Individualized Energy Psychotherapy
IEST	– Integrative Energy and Spiritual Therapy
IHES	– Integrative Healing from an Energy and Spiritual perspective
MATT	– Miracle Acupressure Technique
MPT	– Meridian-based Psychotherapy
MPC	– Meridian-based Psychotherapy and Counseling
NAEM	– Negative Affect Erasing Method

NAET	– Nambudripad Allergy Elimination Technique
NET	– Neuroemotional Technique
PEAT	– Psycho-Energetic Auro Technology
PR	– Psychological reversal
PT	– Pranic healing
RITT	– Rapidly Integrated Transformation Technique
SPP	– Willem Lammers' Successive Point Process
SUD	– Subjective Unit of Distress
SUDS	– Subjective Unit of Distress Scale
TAT	– Tapas Acupressure Technique
TBM	– Total Body Modification
TCM	– Traditional Chinese Medicine
TEST	– Thought Energy Synchronization Therapy
TFH	– Touch for Health
TFT	– Thought Field Therapy
TIR	– Traumatic Incident Reduction
TEST	– Thought Energy Synchronization Techniques
TAB	– Touch And Breathe
UH	– Ultimate Healer
V/KD	– Visual Kinesthetic Dissociation
VoC	– Validity of Cognition

C

Resources

Books

Brennan, B. (1987). *Hands of Light*. Bantam Books.
Brennan, B. (1993). *Light Emerging*. Bantam Books.
Brennan, B. Seeds of the Spirit, available through www.barbarabrennan.com.
Brugh, J.W. (1979). *Joy's Way: A Map for the Transormational Journey*. An Introduction to the Potentials for Healing with Body Energies, Tarcher/Putnam.
Callahan, R. J. (1981). Psychological reversal. Collected Papers of the International College of Applied Kinesiology.
Callahan, R. J. (1985). *Five Minute Phobia Cure*. Wilmington, DE: Enterprise.
Callahan, R. J. (1990). *The Rapid Treatment of Panic, Agoraphobia, and Anxiety*. Indian Wells, CA: Author.
Callahan, R. J. (1991). *Why Do I Eat When I'm Not Hungry?* New York: Doubleday.
Callahan, R. J., and Callahan, J. (1996). *Thought Field Therapy and Trauma: Treatment and Theory*. Indian Wells, CA: Author.
Callahan, R., with Turbo, R. (2001). *Tapping the Healer Within*. Chicago: Contemporary.
Craig, G., and Fowlie, A. (1995). *Emotional Freedom Techniques: The Manual*. The Sea Ranch, CA: Author.
Craig, G., and Fowlie, A. (1995). *Emotional Freedom Techniques: The Course*. The Sea Ranch, CA: Author.
Craig, G. H. (1998). *Steps Toward Becoming the Ultimate Therapist: Building on EFT*. (Video program/course.)
Dennison, P. E., and Dennison, G. (1989). *Brain Gym Handbook*. Ventura, CA: Educational Kinesiology Foundation.
Diamond, J. (1978). *Behavioral Kinesiology and the Autonomic Nervous System*. New York: The Institute of Behavioral Kinesiology.
Diamond, J. (1979). *Behavioural Kinesiology*. New York: Harper and Row.
Diamond, J. (1980a). *The Collected Papers of John Diamond, MD, Volume II*. New York: Archaeus.
Diamond, J. (1980b). *Your Body Doesn't Lie*. New York: Warner Books.

Diamond, J. (1985). *Life Energy.* New York: Dodd, Mead and Co.
Durlacher, J. V. (1994). *Freedom From Fear Forever.* Tempe, AZ: Van Ness.
Eden, D. (1998). *Energy Medicine.* Tarcher/Putnam.
"EFT and........" a range of handbooks linked to other therapies. Available through www.meridiantherapies.org.uk
Fleming, T. (1996b). *Reduce Traumatic Stress in Minutes: The Tapas Acupressure Technique (TAT) Workbook.* Torrance, CA: Author.
Flint, G. A. (1999). *Emotional Freedom: Techniques for Dealing with Psychological, Emotional and Physical Distress.*
Furman, M. E., and Gallo, F. P. (2000). *The Neurophysics of Human Behavior: Explorations at the Interface of the Brain, Mind and Behavior.* Boca Raton: CRC Press.
Gallo, F. P. (1996). Reflections on active ingredients in efficient treatments of PTSD, Part 1. *Electronic Journal of Traumatology,* 2(1). Available at < http://www.fsu.edu/~trauma/>.
Gallo, F. P. (1996). Reflections on active ingredients in efficient treatments of PTSD, Part 2. *Electronic Journal of Traumatology,* 2(2). Available at <http://www.fsu.edu/~trauma/>.
Gallo, F. P. (1996). Therapy by energy. *Anchor Point,* June, 46-51.
Gallo, F. P. (1997). A no-talk cure for trauma: thought field therapy violates all the rules. *The Family Therapy Networker,* 21 (2), 65-75.
Gallo, F. P. (1997). *Energy Diagnostic and Treatment Methods (EDxTM): Basic Training Manual.* Hermitage, PA: Author.
Gallo, F. P. (1998). *Energy Psychology: Explorations at the Interface of Energy, Cognition, Behavior, and Health.* Boca Raton: CRC Press.
Gallo, F. P. (2000). *Energy Diagnostic and Treatment Methods.* New York: W. W. Norton & Company.
Gallo, F. P., & Vincenzi, H. (2000). *Energy Tapping: How to Rapidly Eliminate Anxiety, Depression, Cravings, and More Using Energy Psychology.* Oakland, CA: New Harbinger Publications.
Gallo, F. P. (Ed.) (2001). *Energy Psychology in Psychotherapy: A Comprehensive Source Book.* New York: W. W. Norton & Company.
Gerber, R. (1996). *Vibrational Medicine.* Bear & Company.
Gordon, M. (1998). *Energy Therapy: Tapping The Next Dimension in Healing.* WiseWord Publishing. Available through www.hypnotherapycenter.com or (800) 398-0034.
Gordon, M. (2000). *Extraordinary Healing.* WiseWord Publishing. Available through www.hypnotherapycenter.com or (800) 398-0034.
Gordon, M. (1999). *The New Manual for Transformational Healing with Hypnotherapy and Energy Therap.* WiseWord Publishing. Available through www.hypnotherapycenter.com or (800) 398-0034.
Hartmann-Kent, S. (1999). *Adventures in EF.* DH Publications. Available through

www.meridiantherapies.org.uk.
Johnson, R. (1998). *Reclaim Your Light through the Miracle of Rapid Eye Technology.* Raintree Press. Available from www.Amazon.com. Further info available at www.rapideyetechnology.com.
Lake, D. and Wells St. (1999). *New Energy Therapies: Rapid Change Techniques for Emotional Healing.* Available through wells@iinet.net.au.
Lambrou, P. and Pratt G. (2000). *Instant Emotional Healing: Acupressure for the Emotions.* Broadway Books/Random House.
Mountrose and Mountrose J. (2000). *Getting Through to Your Emotions with EFT.* Holistic Communications.
Mountrose and Mountrose J. (2000). *Getting Through to Your Soul.* Holistic Communications.
Phillips, M. (2000). Finding the Energy to Heal: *How EMDR, Hypnosis, TFT, Imagery, and Body-Focused Therapy Can Help Restore Mindbody Health.* Norton.
Rothman, St., *3-in-1 Positive Solutions in Energy Therapy.* Available through www.lets-talk.com.
Sutherland, Ch. (2000). *Welcome to EFT.* Available from www.lifeworks-group.com.au.
Tiller, W. (1997). *Science and Human Transformation.* Pavior.
Zimmerman, K. (1999). *Breakthrough: The Emotional Freedom Techniques.* available through www.trancetime.com.

Websites

Altaffer, Tom – www.net-energy.com/ is an online interactive tutorial which teaches EFT over the computer. Also, www.home.att.net/~tom.altaffer/ provides information about and links to many different energy therapies and how to use them with different populations.
Association for Comprehensive Energy Psychology (ACEP) – www.energypsych.org.
Attractor Field Therapy (ATF) – www.the-tree-of-life.com.
Barbara Brennan – www.barbarabrennan.com.
Be Set Free Fast (BSFF) – www.besetfreefast.com – offers instructional manual.
Body Talk – www.parama.com.
Callahan, Roger – www.tftrx.com – offers books and instructional videotapes.
Durlacher, James – www.freedomfromfearforever.com.
EFT – www.emofree.com – a fantastic site with lots of applications and free downloadable handbooks.
eTox – http://members.aol.com/donelium/etox.html – re energy toxin elimination. Also, through the Machine Shop, has links to technological ressources.

Appendix C

European Conference on Energy Pychology – www.impc.ch.
Gallo, Fred – www.energypsych.com – offers trainings.
Healing Touch – www.HealingtouchofGWA.com and www.healingtouch.net.
Heart Math – www.heartmath.com.
Holographic Memory Resolution – www.healingdimensions.com.
Holographic Repatterning – www.holographic.org and www.hrsalesusa.com.
Integrative States Therapy (iSt) – http://members.aol.com/eliums/ist.html.
JMT – Jaffee-Mellor Techniques – www.jmt-jafmeltechnique.com.
Lammers, Willem – www.impc.ch, www.iasag.ch.
Lasers for sale, for use with meridian-based methods – www.iasag.ch/store.html.
Matrix Work – www.MatrixWork.org.
NAET – www.naet.com.
Narvaez, Tom – Experimental Energy Field Training – www.wel.net/mindsurgeon.
Nicosia, Greg – www.ThoughtEnergy.com – offers instructional videotapes.
Rapid Eye Technology – www.rapideyetechnology.com.
Reiki – www.reikilinks.com and www.reiki.net/GRMA.
Resonance Tuner – www.hometown.aol.com/alanhand/myhomepage/index.html.
Sedona Method – www.sedona.com.
Tapas Acupressure Technique (TAT) – www.tat-intl.com or by calling toll free 1-877-TAT-INTL (828-4685) – offers instructional audio and videotapes.
Therapeutic Touch – www.therapeutictouchnetwk.com and www.therapeutic-touch.org.
This book for sale – www.iasag.ch/books.html.
Transformation Training Network carries books, manuals, videotapes and Energy Psychology Conference audiotapes – www.ttn.org or 624 N. Humphreys St., Flagstaff AZ 86001.
United Kingdom Association for Meridian Therapies (UK AMT) – www.meridiantherapies.org.uk .
Whole Life Healing – www.wel.net/wlh.html – offers training manual.
Whole Life Healing's protocol combines the essentials of BSFF with hypnosis.
Whole Hearted Healing – www.PeakStates.com.
Young-Sowers, Meredith – www.stillpoint.org.

Thanks for preparing earlier versions of this resource list go to Debby Vajda, LCSW-C, Gaithersburg, Maryland, USA, debby@the4dgroup.com, and to Fred Gallo, Ph.D. fgallo@energypsychcom.